HORSEMEN'S

VETERINARY

ADVISOR

Joseph B. Davidson, D.V.M.

New York

First Arco Edition, 1973

Published by Arco Publishing Company, Inc.
219 Park Avenue South, New York, N.Y. 10003

Copyright © 1971 by Dr. J. B. Davidson

Library of Congress Catalog Card Number 70-169096
ISBN 0-668-03333-9

Printed in United States of America

FOREWORD

A sincere effort has been made throughout this book to present useful material in as concise a manner as possible so it will be of actual value to horsemen. Hopefully, it will be read by everyone connected with horses and better care will be the results.

Every effort has been made to present accurate information. Obviously many of the recommendations must be of a general nature because we have not seen the patient in question. Nowhere are we suggesting a substitute for professional diagnosis and treatment by competent veterinarians. The purpose of remedies included in the contents of this book are presented for better understanding of modern and past accepted treatments. Some are simple and effective when applied to properly diagnosed cases. Any failure to respond should be viewed with proper respect for complicating factors and referred to a veterinarian who has spent years of study in the basic sciences that enable him to understand the many interrelated and complicated systems that make up a horse.

J. B. Davidson, D.V.M.

Contents

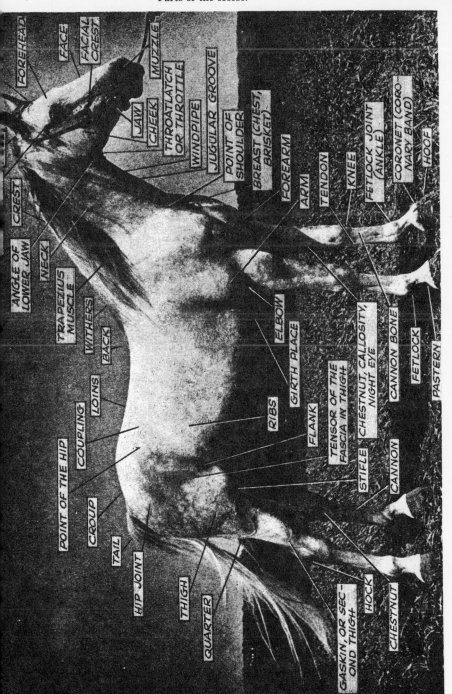

Plate I

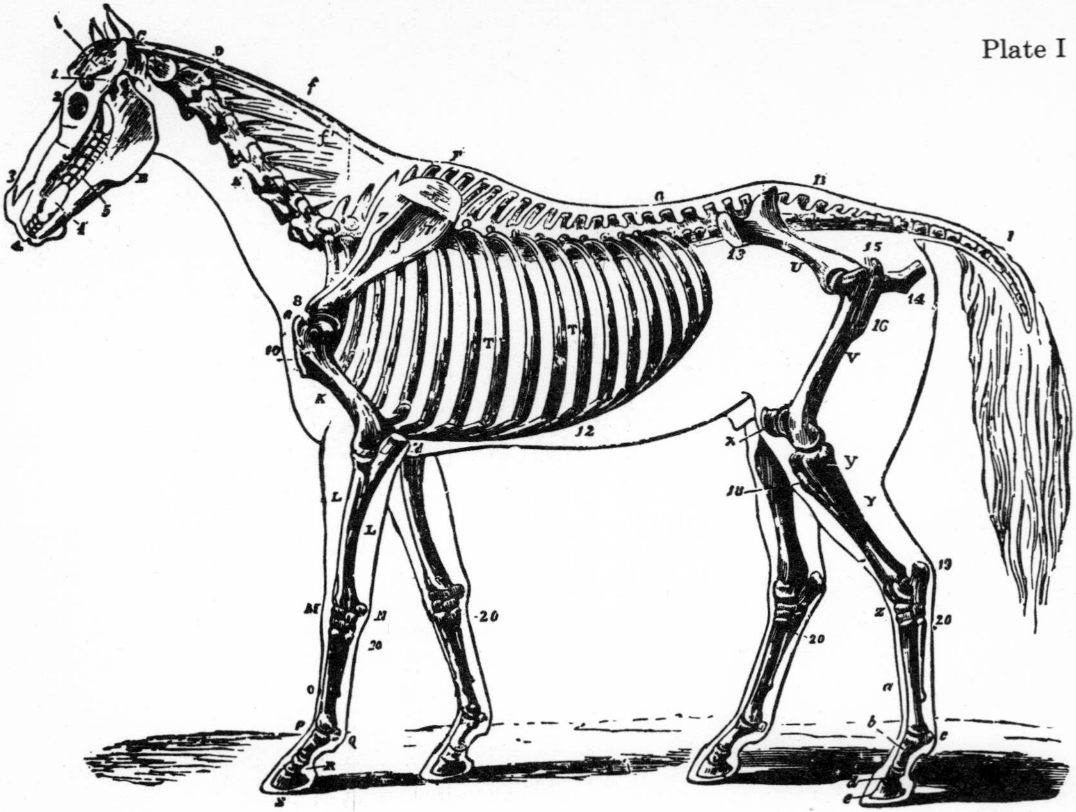

SKELETON OF HORSE—*after Megnin.*

EXPLANATION OF PLATE I.

Skeleton of the Horse,

Showing its relation to the contour of the animal, viewed laterally.

A. Temporal fossa.
B. Inferior maxilla.
C. Atlas.
D. Destata.
E. Cervical vertebrae.
F.   Dorsal   do.
G. Lumbar   do.
H. Sacral   do.
I. Coccygead do'.
J. Scapula.
K. Humerus.
L. Radius.
L.' Ulna.
M. Carpus.
N. Trapezium.
O. Metacarpus.
P. *b.* Os suffraginis.
Q. *c.* Sesamoids.
R. *d.* Os coronae.
S. *e.* Os pedis.
T T. Ribs.
U. Ilium.
V. Femur.
X. Patella.
Y. Tibia.
y. Fibula.
Z. Tarsus.

a. Metatarsus.
f. Ligamentum nuchae,
    funicular portion. *f'.*
    lamellar portion.
1. Zygoma.
2. Orbital fossa.
3. Nasal peak.
4. Incisor teeth.
4'. Canine teeth.
5. Molar teeth.
6. External humeral trochanter.
7. Scapular fosse.
8. Coracoid apophysis.
9. Cartilage of prolongation.
10. Deltoid ridge, and external tuberosity.
11. Olecranon.
12. Costal cartilages.
13. Anterior iliac spine.
14. Ischium.
15. Trochanter major.
16. Trochanter minor.
18. Anterior tibial tuberosity.
19. Calcaneum.
20. Small metacrapal and metatarsal, or splint bones.

Plate II

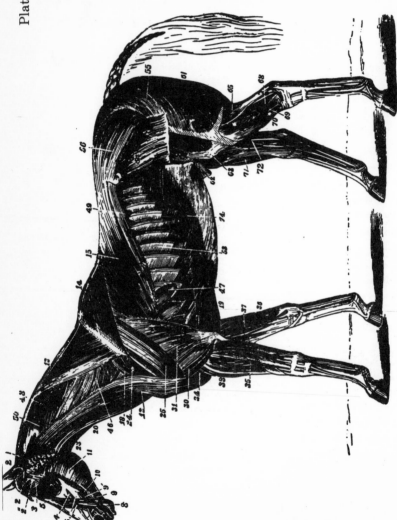

MUSCLES OF THE HORSE—SUPERFICIAL LAYER—*after Megnin.*

EXPLANATION OF PLATE II.

Muscles of the Horse

Superficial Layer.

The panniculus and tunica abdominalis are removed

1. Abducens.
2. Retrahentes muscles.
2'. Attollens maximus.
2.'' Attollens anticus.
3. Temporalis.
4. Nasalis longus.
5. Orbicularis palpebrarum.
6. Levator labii superioris alaeque nasi.
7. Dilatator naris lateralis.
8. Orbicularis oris.
9. Zygomaticus.
9'. Buccinator.
10. Depressor labii inferioris.
11. Masseter.
12. Levator humeri.
13. Trapezius cervicalis.
14. Trapezius dorsalis.
15. Latissimus dorsi.
18. Pectoralis parvns.
19. Pectoralis magnus.
20. Sterno-maxillaris.
23. Subscapulo-hyoideus.
24. Antea-spinatus.
25. Teres externus.
26. Postea-spinatus.
30. Caput medium ⎫ of the triceps
31. Caput magnum ⎭ extensor brachii

33. Extensor metacarpi maguus.
34. Humeralis obliquus.
35. Extensor pedis.
36. Flexor metacarpi externus and medius.
37. Flexor metacarpi internus.
46. Cervical ⎱ serratus magnus.
47. Dorsal ⎰
48. Rhomboideus longus.
49. Superficialis costarum.
50. Splenius.
52. Intercostales.
54. Tensor fasciae latae.
55. Triceps abductor femoris.
56. Gluteus externus.
61. Biceps rotator tibialis.
62. Rectus femoris.
63. Vastus externus.
65. Gastrocnemius.
68. Flexor pedis perforans.
69. Peroneus.
70. Extensor pedns.
71. Flexor metatarsi.
72. Flexor pedis accessorius.
74. Obliquus abdominis externus.

Plate III

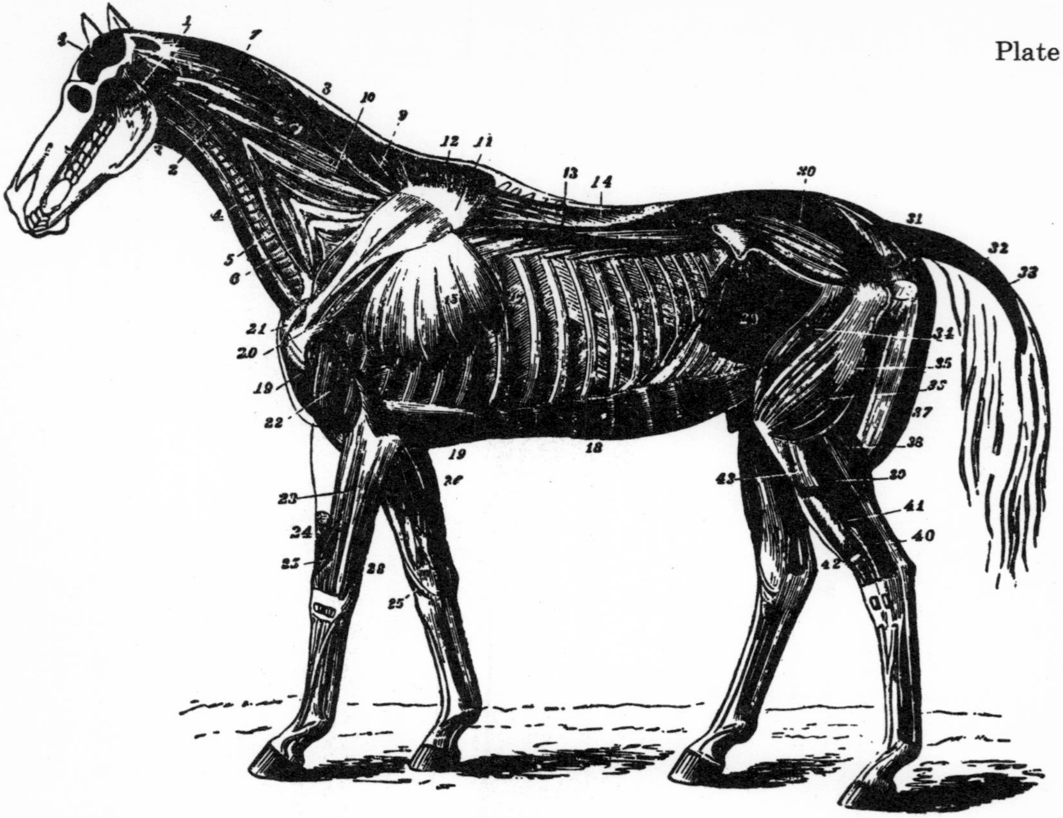

MUSCLES OF THE HORSE—DEEP LAYER—*after Megnin.*

EXPLANATION OF PLATE III.

Muscles of the Horse

Deep Layer.

1. Temporalis.

1ʹ Stylo-maxillaris.

2. Rectus capitis anticus major.

3. Sterno-thyro-hyoideus.

4. Sterno-maxillaris.

5. The Trachea.

6. Scalenus.

7. Splenius.

8. Funicular part of ligamentum nuchae.

9. Rhomboideus longus.

10. Cervical serratus magnus.
15. Costal

11. Cartilage of prolongation.

12. Rhomboideus brevis.

13. Transversalis costarum.

14. Longissimus dorsi.

15. Serratus Magnus.

16. External intercostals.

17. Internal intercostals.

18. Rectus abdominis.

19. Pectoralis magnus.

20. Postea-spinatus minor.

21. Flexor brachii.

22. Humeralis obliquus.

22ʹ Caput parvum (of triceps extensor brachii).

23. Extensor suffraginis.

24. Extensormetacarpimagnusdivided.

25. Extensor metacarpi obliquus.

25ʹ Its tendon.

26, 28. Flexor pedis perforans and perforatus.

29. Obliquus abdominis internus.

30. Gluteus maximus.

31. Erector coccygis.

32. Curvator coccygis.

33. Depressor coccygis.

34. Rectus femoris.

35. Vastus externus.

36. Part covered by triceps abductor.

37. Biceps rotator tibialis.

38. Gastrocnemius externus.

39. Plantaris.

40. Flexor pedis perforans.

41. Peroneus.

42. Flexor metatarsi.

43. Extensor pedis (cut accross).

Plate IV

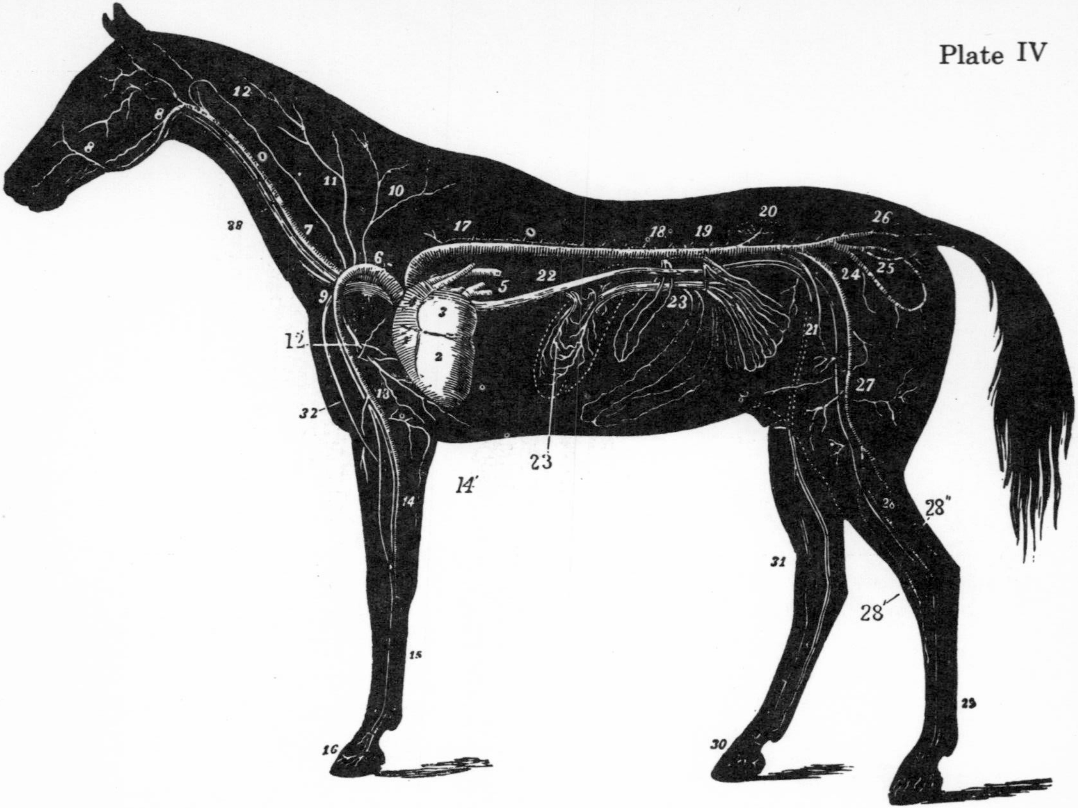

THE HEART AND CHIEF BLOOD VESSELS OF THE HORSE—*after Megnin.*

EXPLANATION OF PLATE IV.

Blood-Vascular System of the Horse.

1. Heart, right ventricle
2. Heart, left ventricle.
3. Heart, left auricle.
4. Pulmonary artery.
5. Pulmonary veins.
6. Anterior aorta.
7. Carotid artery.
8. Glosso-facial artery.
9. Left brachial artery.
10. Dorsal artery.
11. Superior cervical artery.
12. Vertebral artery.
12'. Internal thoracic artery.
13. Humeral artery.
14. Radial artery.
14'. Cubital artery.
15. Great metacarpal artery.
16. Ungual branches.
17. Posterior aorta.

18. Coeliac axis.
19. Mesenteric arteries.
20. Renal artery (left).
21. Small testicular artery.
22. Posterior vena cave.
23. Portal vein.
23'. Hepatic circulation.
24. External iliac artery.
25. Internal iliac artery.
26. Lateral sacral artery.
27. Femoral artery.
28. Posterior tibial artery.
28'. Anterior tibial artery.
28''. Femoro-popliteal artery.
29. Metatarsal vessels.
30. Venous plexus of the foot.
31. Internal saphenic vein.
32. Cephalic vein.
33. Jugular vein.

Plate V

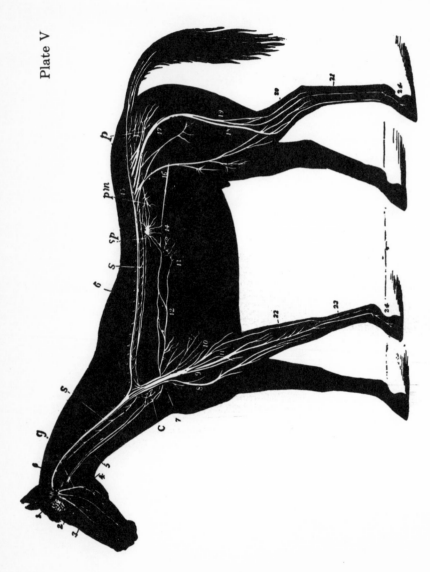

NERVOUS SYSTEM OF A HORSE—*after Megnin.*

EXPLANATION OF PLATE V.

Nervous System of the Horse.

1. Brain.
2. Optic nerve.
3. Superior maxillary nerve (5th).
4. Inferior maxillary nerve (5th).
5. Pneumo-gastric nerve.
6. Medulla oblongata.
7. Right brachial plexus.
8. Musculo-cutaneous nerve.
9. Median nerve.
10. Radial nerve.
11. Cubital nerve.
12. Pneumogastric nerve.
13. Solar plexus.
14. Semilunar ganglion.
15. Lumbo-sacral plexus.
16. Anterior crural nerve.
17. Great sciatic nerve.
18. External popliteal nerve.
19. External saphenic nerve.
20. Tibial nerve.
21. Metatarsal nerve.
22. Radial portion of median nerve.
23. Metacarpal nerves.
24. Digital branches.

s.s. Sympathetic chain.
c. Inferior cervical plexus.
g. Gutteral ganglion.
Sp. Great splanchnic nerve.
p.m. Posterior mesenteric plexus.
p. Pelvic plexus.

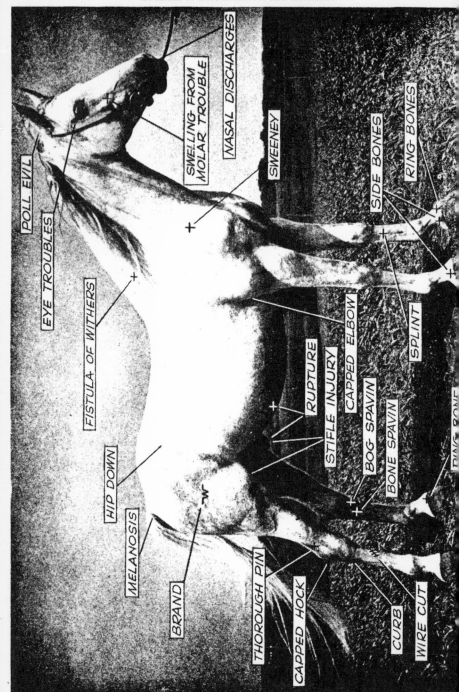

EXAMINATION OF A SICK HORSE

In the examination of a sick horse it is important to have a method or system. If a definite plan of examination is followed one may feel reasonably sure when the examination is finished that no important point has been overlooked and that the examiner is in a position to arrive at an opinion that is as accurate as is possible for him. Of course, an experienced eye can see, and a trained hand can feel, slight alterations or variations from the normal that are not perceptible to the unskilled observer. A thorough knowledge of the conditions that exist in health is of the highest importance, because it is only by knowledge of what is right that one can surely detect a condition that is wrong. A knowledge of anatomy, or of the structure of the body, and of physiology, or the functions and activities of the body, lie at the bottom of accuracy of diagnosis. It is important to recognize animals of different races or families may react differently under the influence of the same disease process. In other words, in sickness as in health, Thoroughbreds, Standardbreds, Quarterhorses, or any others will show individual symptoms and responses to treatment.

The following order of examination is easy to follow and will be sufficiently thorough for most practical situations.

History

It is important to know, first of all, something of the origin and development of the disease, therefore the cause should be looked for. The cause of a disease is important, not only

1

in connection with diagnosis, but also in connection with treatment. The character of food that the horse has had, the use to which he has been put, and the kind of care he has received should all be inquired into closely. It is important to know whether the particular horse that is under examination is the only one in the stable or on the premises that is similarly afflicted. It is most important to know any previous treatment.

Before beginning the special examination, attention should be paid to the attitude and general condition of the animal. Sometimes horses assume positions that are characteristic of a certain disease. For example, in tetanus, or lockjaw, the muscles of the face, neck, and shoulders are stiff and rigid, as well as the muscles of the jaw. This condition produces a peculiar attitude, that once seen is subsequently recognized as rather characteristic of this disease. A horse with tetanus stands with his muscles tense and his legs in a somewhat bracing position, as though he were gathered to repel a shock. The neck is stiff and hard, the head is slightly extended upon it, the face is drawn, and the nostrils are dilated. The tail is usually held up a little and when pressed down against the thighs it springs back to its previous position. In inflammation of the throat, as in pharyngolaryngitis, the head is extended upon the neck, and the angle between the jaw and the lower border of the neck is opened as far as possible to relieve the pressure that otherwise would fall upon the throat. In dumminess, or immobility, the hanging position of the head and the stupid expression are rather characteristic. In pleurisy, peritonitis, and some other painful diseases of the internal organs, the rigid position of the body denotes an effort of the animal to avoid pressures upon and to protect the inflamed sensitive region.

The horse may be down in the stall and unable to rise. This condition may result from paraplegia, from azoturia, from forage poisoning, from tetanus, or from painful conditions of the bones or feet, such as osteoporosis or founder. Lying down at unusual times or in unusual positions may indicate disease. The first symptom of colic may be a desire on the part of the horse to lie down at a time or place that is unusual or inappropriate. Sometimes disinclination to lie down is an indication of disease. Where there is difficulty in breathing, the horse knows that he can manage himself better upon his feet than upon his breast or side. It happens, therefore, that in nearly all serious disease of the respiratory tract, the horse stands persistently, day and night, until recovery has commenced and breathing is easier, or until the animal falls from sheer exhaustion. Where there is stiffness and soreness of the muscles, as in rheumatism, inflammation of the muscles from overwork, or of the bones in osteoporosis, or of the feet in founder, or where the muscles are stiff and beyond control of the animal, as in tetanus, a standing positio is maintained, because the horse seems to realize that when he lies down he will be unable to rise.

Abnormal attitudes are assumed in painful diseases of the digestive organs (colic). A horse with colic may sit upon his haunches, like a dog, or may stand upon his hind feet and rest upon his knees in front or may endeavor to balance himself upon his back, with all four feet in the air. These positions are assumed because they give relief from pain by lessening pressure, or tension upon the sensitive structures.

Under the general condition of the animal it may be necessary to observe the condition, or state, of nutrition; the conformation, so far as it may indicate the constitution and the temperament. By observing the condition of nutrition one may be able to determine to a great extent the effect that the disease has already had upon the animal and to estimate the amount of strength that remains and that will be available for the repair of the diseased tissues. A good condition of nutrition is shown by the rotundity of the body, the pliability and softness of the skin, and the tone of the hair. If the subcutaneous fat has disappeared and the muscles are wasted, allowing the bony prominences to stand out; if the skin is tight and inelastic and the coat dry and harsh, we have evidence of a low state of nutrition. This may have resulted from a severe and long-continued disease or from lack of proper food and care. Where an animal is emaciated—that is, becomes thin—there is first a loss of fat and later the muscles shrink. By observing the amount of shrinkage in the muscles one has some indication as to the duration of the unfavorable conditions that the animal has lived under.

By constitution we understand the innate ability of the animal to withstand disease or unfavorable conditions of life. The constitution depends largely upon the conformation. The type of construction that usually accompanies the best constitution is a deep, broad chest, allowing plenty of room for the lungs and heart, indicating that these vital organs are well developed; capacious abdomen, allowing sufficient space for well-developed organs of digestion; the loins should be short—that is, the space should be short between the last rib and the point of the hip; the head and neck should be well molded, without superfluous or useless tissues; this gives a clear-cut throat. The ears, eyes, and face should have an expression of alertness and good breeding. The muscular development should be good; the shoulders, forearms, croup, and thighs must have the appearance of strength. The withers are sharp, which means that they are not loaded with useless, superfluous tissue; the legs are straight and their axes are parallel; the knees and hock are low, which means that the forearms and thighs are long and cannons relatively short. The cannons are broad from in front to behind, and relatively thin from side to side. This means that the bony and tendinous structures of the legs are well developed and well placed. The hoofs are compact, tense, firm structures, and their soles are concave and frogs large. Such a horse is likely to have a good constitution and to be able to resist hard work, fatigue, and disease to a maximum degree. On the other hand, a poor constitution is indicated by a shallow, narrow chest, small bones, long loins, coarse neck and head, with a thick throat, small bony, and muscular developments, short thighs and forearms, small joints, long round cannons, and hoofs of open texture with flat soles.

The temperament is indicated by the manner in which the horse responds to external stimuli. When the horse is spoken to, or when he sees or feels anything that stimulates or gives alarm, if he responds actively, quickly, and intelligently, he is said to be of lively, or nervous, temperament. On the other hand, if he responds in a slow, sluggish manner, he is said to

4

have a sluggish, or lymphatic, temperament. The temperament is indicated by the gait, by the expression of the face, and by carriage of the head and ears. The nature of the temperament should be taken into consideration in an endeavor to ascertain the severity of a given case of illness, because the general expression of an animal in disease as well as in health depends to a large extent on the temperament.

The Skin and the Visible Mucous Membranes

The condition of the skin is a fair index to the condition of the animal. The effect of disease and emaciation upon the pliability of the skin have been referred to above. There is no part of the body that loses its elasticity and tone as a result of disease sooner than the skin. The practical herdsman or flockmaster can gain a great deal of information as to the condition of an animal merely by grasping the coat and looking at and feeling the skin. Similarly, the condition of the animal is shown to a certain extent by the appearance of the mucous membranes. For example, when the horse is anemic as a result of disease or of inappropriate food the mucous membranes become pale. This change in the mucous membranes can be seen most readily in the lining of the eyelids and in the lining of the nostril. For convenience of examination the eyelids can readily be everted. Paleness means weak circulation or poor blood. Increased redness occurs physiologically in painful conditions, excitement, and following severe exertion. Under such conditions the increase of circulation is transitory. In fevers there is an increased redness in the mucous membrane, and this continues so long as the fever lasts. In some diseases red spots or streaks form in the mucous membrane. This usually indicates an infectious disease of considerable severity, and occurs in blood poisoning, purpura hemorrhagica, hemorrhagic septicemia, and in urticaria. When the liver is deranged and does not operate, or when the red-blood corpuscles are broken down, as in serious cases of influenza, there is a yellowish discoloration of the mucous membrane. The mucous membranes become bluish or blue when the blood is imperfectly oxidized and contains an excess of carbon dioxide. This condition exists in any serious disease of the respiratory tract, as pneumonia, and in heart failure.

The temperature of the skin varies with the temperature of the body. If there is fever the temperature of the skin is likely to be increased. Sometimes, however, as a result of poor circulation and irregular distribution of the blood, the body may be warmer than normal, while the extremities (the legs and ears) may be cold. Where the general surface of the body becomes cold it is evident that the small blood vessels in the skin have contracted and are keeping the blood away, as during a chill, or that the heart is weak and is unable to pump the blood to the surface, and that the animal is on the verge of collapse.

The skin is moist, to a certain degree, at all times in a healthy horse. This moisture is not in the form of a perceptible sweat, but it is enough to keep the skin pliable and to cause the hair to have a soft, healthy feel. In some chronic disease conditions and in fever, the skin becomes dry. In this case the hair has a harsh feel that is quite different from the condition observed in health, and from the fact of its being so dry the individual hairs do not adhere to one another, they stand apart, and the animal has what is known as "a staring coat." When, during a fever, sweating occurs, it is usually an indication that the crisis is passed. Sometimes sweating is an indication of pain. A horse with tetanus or azoturia sweats profusely. Horses sweat freely when there is a serious impediment to respiration; they sweat under excitement, and, of course, from the well-known physiological causes of heat and work. Local sweating, or sweating of a restricted area of the body, denotes some kind of nerve interference.

Swellings of the skin usually come from wounds or other external causes and have no special connection with the diagnosis of internal diseases. There are, however, a number of conditions in which the swelling of the skin is a symptom of a derangement of some other part of the body. For example,

6

there is the well-known "stocking," or swelling of the legs about the fetlock joints, in influenza. There is the soft swelling of the hind legs that occurs so often in draft horses when standing still and that comes from previous inflammation (lymphangitis) or from insufficient heart power. Dropsy, or edema of the skin, may occur beneath the chest or abdomen from heart insufficiency or from chronic collection of fluid in the chest or abdomen (hydrothorax, ascites, or anemia). In anasarca or purpura hemorrhagica large soft swellings appear on any part of the skin, but usually on the legs, side of the body, and about the head.

Gas collects under the skin in some instances. This comes from a local inoculation with an organism which produces a fermentation beneath the skin and causes the liberation of gas which inflates the skin, or the gas may be air that enters through a wound penetrating some air-containing organ, as the lungs. The condition here described is known as emphysema. Emphysema may follow the fracture of a rib when the end of a bone is forced inward and caused to penetrate the lung, or it may occur, when, as a result of an ulcerating process, an organ containing air is perforated. This accident is more common in cattle than it is in horses. Emphysema is recognized by the fact that the swelling that it causes is not hot or sensitive on pressure. It emits a peculiar crackling sound when it is stroked or pressed upon.

Wounds of the skin may be of importance in the diagnosis of internal disease. Wounds over the bony prominence, as the point of the hip, the point of the shoulder, and the greatest convexity of the ribs, occurs when a horse is unable to stand for a long time and, through continually lying upon his side, has shut off the circulation to the portion of the skin that covers parts of the body that carry the greatest weight, and in this way has caused them to mortify. Little, round, soft, dough-like swellings occur on the skin and may be scattered freely over the surface of the body when the horse is afflicted with urticaria. Similar eruptions, but distributed less generally, about the size of a silver dollar, may occur as a symptom of dourine, or colt distemper. Hard lumps, from which radiate welt-like swellings of the lymphatics, occur in gland-

7

ers, and blisterlike eruptions occur around the mouth and pasterns in horsepox.

Temperature

The temperature of the horse is determined roughly by placing the fingers in the mouth or between the thighs or by allowing the horse to exhale against the cheek or back of the hand. In accurate examination, however, these means of determining temperature are not relied upon, but recourse is made to the use of thermometer. The thermometer used for taking the temperature of a horse is a self-registering clinical thermometer, similar to that used by physicians, but larger, being from 5 to 6 inches long. The temperature of the animal is measured in the rectum.

The normal temperature of the horse varies somewhat under different conditions. It is higher in the young animal than in the old, and is higher in hot weather than in cold. The weather and exercise decidedly influence the temperature physiologically. The normal temperature varies from 99.5° to 101°F. If the temperature rises to 102.5° the horse is said to have a low fever; if the temperature reaches 104° the fever is moderate; if it reaches 106° it is high, and above this point it is regarded as very high. In some diseases, such as tetanus or sunstroke, the temperature goes as high as 108° or 110°. In the ordinary infectious diseases it does not often exceed 106°. A temperature of 107.5° and above is very dangerous and must be reduced promptly if the horse is to be saved.

The Organs of Circulation

The first item in this portion of the examination consists of taking the pulse. The pulse may be counted and its character may be determined at any point where a large artery occupies a situation close to the skin and above a hard tissue, such as a bone, cartilage, or tendon. The most convenient place for taking the pulse of the horse is at the jaw. The external maxillary artery runs from between the jaws, around the lower border of the jawbone and up on the outside of the jawbone to the face. It is located immediately in front of the heavy muscles of the cheek. Its throb can be felt most distinctly just before it turns around the lower border of the jawbone. The balls of the first and second or of the second and third fingers should be pressed lightly on the skin over this artery when its pulsations are to be studied.

The normal pulse of the healthy horse varies in frequency as follows:

Stallion . . . . 28 to 32 beats per minute.
Gelding . . . . 33 to 38 beats per minute.
Mare . . . . 34 to 40 beats per minute.
Foal 2 to 3 years old . . . . 40 to 50 beats per minute.
Foal 6 to 12 months old . . 45 to 60 beats per minute.
Foal 2 to 4 weeks old . . . . 70 to 90 beats per minute.

The pulse is accelerated by the digestion of rich food, by hot weather, exercise, excitement, and alarm. It is slightly more rapid in the evening than it is in the morning. Well-bred horses have a slightly more rapid pulse than sluggish, cold-blooded horses. The pulse should be regular; that is, the separate beats should follow each other after intervals of equal length, and the beats should be of equal fullness, or volume.

In disease, the pulse may become slower or more rapid than in health. Slowing of the pulse may be caused by old age, great exhaustion, or excessive cold. It may be due to depression of the central nervous system, as in dumminess, or be the result of the administration of drugs, such as digitalis or strophantus. A rapid pulse is almost always found in fever, and the more severe the infection and the weaker the heart, the more rapid is the pulse. Under these conditions, the beats may rise to 80, 90, or even 120 per minute. When the pulse is above 100 per minute the outlook for recovery is not promising, and especially if this symptom accompanies high temperature or occurs late in an infectious disease. In nearly all of the diseases of the heart and in anemia the pulse becomes rapid.

The pulse is irregular in diseases of the heart, and especially where the valves are affected. The irregularity may consist of varying intervals between the beats or the dropping of one or more beats at regular or irregular intervals. The latter condition sometimes occurs in chronic diseases of the brain. The pulse is said to be weak, or soft, when the beats are indistinct, because little blood is forced through the artery by each contraction of the heart. This condition occurs when there is a constriction of the vessels leading from the heart and it occurs in certain infectious and febrile diseases, and is an indication of heart weakness.

In examining the heart itself it is necessary to recall that it lies in the anterior portion of the chest slightly to the left of the median line and that it extends from the third to the sixth rib. It extends almost to the breastbone, and a little more than half of the distance between the breastbone and the backbone. In contracting, it rotates slightly on its axis, so that the point of the heart, which lies below, is pressed against the left chest wall at a place immediately above the point of the elbow. The heart has in it four chambers—two in the left and two in the right side. The upper chamber of the left side (left auricle) receives the blood as it comes from the lungs, passes it to the lower chamber of the left side (left ventricle), and from here it is sent with great force (for this chamber has very strong, thick walls) through the aorta and its branches (the arteries) to all parts of the body. The blood returns through the veins to the upper chamber of the right side (right auricle), passes then to the lower chamber of the right side (right ventricle), and from this chamber is forced into the lungs to be oxidized. The openings between the chambers of each side and into the aorta are guarded by valves.

If the horse is not too fat, one may feel the impact of the apex of the heart against the chest wall with each contraction of the heart, by placing the hand on the left side back of the fifth rib and above the point of the elbow. The thinner and the better bred the horse is the more distinctly this impact is felt. If the animal is excited, or if he has just been exercised, the impact is stronger than when the horse is at rest. If the horse is weak, the impact is reduced in force.

The examination of the heart with the ear is an important matter in this connection. Certain sounds are produced by each contraction of the normal heart. It is customary to divide these into two, and to call them the first and second sounds. These two sounds are heard during each pulsation and any deviation of the normal indicates some alteration in the structure or the functions of the heart. In making this examination, one may apply the left ear over the heavy muscles of the shoulder back of the shoulder joint, and just above the point of the elbow, or, if the sounds are not heard distinctly, the left foreleg may be drawn forward by an assistant and the right ear placed against the lower portion of the chest wall that is exposed in this manner.

The first sound of the heart occurs while the heart muscle is contracting and while the blood is being forced from the heart and the valves are rendered taut to prevent the return of the blood from the lower to the upper chambers. The second sound follows quickly after the first and occurs during rebound of blood in the arteries, causing pressure in the aorta and tensions of the valves guarding its opening into the left ventricle. The first sound is of a high pitch and is longer and more distinct than the second. Under the influence of disease these sounds may be altered in various ways. It is not profitable, in a work such as this, to describe the details of these alterations. Those who are interested will find this subject fully discussed in the veterinary textbooks.

The Organs of Respiration

In examining this system of organs and their functions it is customary to begin by noticing the frequency of the respiratory movements. This point can be determined by observing the motions of the nostrils or of the flanks; on a cold day one can see the condensation of the moisture of the warm air as it comes from the lungs. The normal rate of respiration for a healthy horse at rest is from 8 to 16 per minute. The rate is faster in young animals than in old, and is increased by work,

11

hot weather, overfilling of the stomach, pregnancy, lying upon the side, etc. Acceleration of the respiratory rate where no physiological cause operates is due to a variety of conditions. Among these is fever; restricted area of active lung tissue, from filling of portions of the lungs with inflammatory exudate, as in pneumonia; compression of the lungs or loss of elasticity; pain in the muscles controlling the respiratory movements; excess of carbon-dioxide in the blood; and constriction of the air passages leading to the lungs.

Difficult or labored respiration is known as dyspnea. It occurs when it is difficult, for any reason, for the animal to obtain the amount of oxygen that it requires. This may be due to filling of the lungs, as in pneumonia; to painful movements of the chest, as in rheumatism or pleurisy; to tumors of the nose and paralysis of the throat, swellings of the throat, foreign bodies, or weakness of the respiratory passages, fluid in the chest cavity, adhesions between the lungs and chest walls, loss of elasticity of the lungs, etc. Where the difficulty is great the accessory muscles of respiration are brought into play. In great dyspnea the horse stands with his front feet apart, with his neck straight out, and his head extended upon his neck. The nostrils are widely dilated, the face has an anxious expression, the eyeballs protrude, the up-and-down motion of the larynx is aggravated, the amplitude of the movement of the chest walls increased, and the flanks heave.

The expired air is of about the temperature of the body. It contains considerable moisture, and it should come with equal force from each nostril and should not have an unpleasant odor. If the stream of air from one nostril is stronger than from the other, there is an indication of an obstruction in a nasal chamber. If the air possesses a bad odor, it is usually an indication of putrefaction of a tissue or secretion in some part of the respiratory tract. A bad odor is found where there is necrosis of the bone in the nasal passages or in chronic catarrh. An ulcerating tumor of the nose or throat may cause the breath to have an offensive odor. The most offensive breath occurs where there is necrosis, or gangrene, of the lungs.

In some diseases there is a discharge from the nose. In order to determine the significance of the discharge it should be examined closely. One should ascertain whether it comes from one or both nostrils. If but from one nostril, it probably originates in the head. The color should be noted. A thin, watery discharge may be composed of serum, and it occurs in the earlier stages of coryza or nasal catarrh. An opalescent, slightly tinted discharge is composed of mucous and indicates a little more severe irritation. If the discharge is sticky and pus-like, a deeper difficulty or more advanced irritation is indicated. If the discharge contains flakes and clumps of more or less dried, agglutinated particles, it is probable that it originates within a cavity of the head, as the sinuses or guttural pouches. The discharge of glanders is of a peculiar sticky nature and adheres tenaciously to the wings of the nostrils. The discharge of pneumonia is of a somewhat red or reddish brown color, and, on this account, has been described as a prune-juice discharge. The discharge may contain blood. If the blood appears as clots or as streaks in the discharge, it probably originates at some point in the upper part of the respiratory tract. If the blood is in the form of a fine froth, it comes from the lungs.

In examining the interior of the nasal pasage one should remember that the normal color of the mucous membrane is a rosy pink and that its surface is smooth. If ulcers, nodules, swellings, or tumors are found, these indicate disease. The ulcer that is characteristic of glanders is described fully in connection with the discussion of that disease.

Between the lower jaws there are several clusters of lymphatic glands. These glands are so small and so soft that it is difficult to find them by feeling through the skin, but when a suppurative disease exists in the upper part of the respiratory tract these glands become swollen and easy to feel. They may become soft and break down and discharge as abscesses; this is seen constantly in strangles. On the other hand, they may become indurated and hard from the proliferation of connective tissue and attach themselves to the jawbone, to the tongue, or to the skin. This is seen in chronic glanders. If the glands are swollen and tender to pressure, it indicates that the disease causing the enlargement is acute; if they are hard and insensitive, the disease causing the enlargement is chronic.

The manner in which the horse coughs is of importance in diagnosis. The cough is a forced expiration, following immediately upon a forcible separation of the vocal cords. The purpose of the cough is to remove some irritant substance from the respiratory passages, and it occurs when irritant gases, such as smoke, ammonia, sulphur vapor, or dust, have been inhaled. It occurs from inhalation of cold air if the respiratory passages are sensitive from disease. In laryngitis, bronchitis, and pneumonia, cough is very easily excited, and occurs merely from accumulation of mucus and inflammatory product upon the irritated respiratory mucous membrane. If one wishes to determine the character of the cough, it can easily be excited by pressing upon the larynx with the thumb and finger. The larynx should be pressed from side to side and the pressure removed the moment the horse commences to cough. A painful cough occurs in pleurisy, also in laryngitis, bronchitis, and bronchial pneumonia. Pain is shown by the effort the animal exerts to repress the cough. The cough is not painful, as a rule, in the chronic diseases of the respiratory tract. The force of the cough is considerable when it is not especially painful and when the lungs are not seriously involved. When the lungs are so diseased that they cannot be filled with a large volume of air, and in heaves, the cough is weak, as it is also in weak, debilitated animals. If mucous or pus is coughed out, or if the cough is accompanied by a gurgling sound, it is said to be moist; it is dry when these characteristics are not present—that is, when the air in passing out passes over surface not loaded with secretion.

In the examination of the chest we resort to percussion and auscultation. When a cask or other structure containing air is tapped upon, or percussed, a hollow sound is given forth. If the cask contains fluid, the sound is of a dull and of quite a differnt character. Similarly, the amount of air contained in the lungs can be estimated by tapping upon, or percussing, the walls of the chest. Percussion is practiced with the fingers alone or with the aid of a special percussion hammer and an object to strike upon known as a pleximeter. If the fingers are used, the middle finger of the left hand should be pressed firmly against the side of the horse and should be struck with the ends of the fingers of the right hand bent at a right angle so as to form a hammer. The percussion hammer sold by instrument makers is made of rubber or has a rubber tip, so that when the pleximeter, which is placed against the side, is struck the impact will not be accompanied by a noise. After experience in this method of examination one can determine with a considerable degree of accuracy whether the lung contains a normal amount of air or not. If, as in pneumonia, air has been displaced by inflammatory product occupying the air space, or if fluid collects in the lower part of the chest, the percussion sound becomes dull. If, as in emphysema or in pneumothorax, there is an excess of air in the chest cavity, the percussion sound becomes abnormally loud and clear.

Auscultation consists of the examination of the lungs with the ear applied closely to the chest wall. As the air goes in and out of the lungs a certain soft sound is made which can be heard distinctly, especially upon inspiration. This sound is intensified by anything that accelerates the rate of respiration, such as exercise. This soft, rustling sound is known as vesicular murmur, and wherever it is heard it signifies that the lung contains air and is functionally active. The vesicular murmur is weakened when there is an inflammatory infiltration of the lung tissue or when the lungs are compressed by fluid in the chest cavity. The vesicular murmur disappears when air is excluded by the accumulation of inflammatory product, as in pneumonia, and when the lungs are compressed by fluid in the chest cavity. The vesicular murmur becomes rough and harsh in the early stages of inflammation of the lungs, and this is often the first sign of the beginning of pneumonia.

By applying the ear over the lower part of the windpipe in front of the breastbone a somewhat harsh, blowing sound may be heard. This is known as the bronchial murmur and is heard in normal conditions near the lower part of the trachea and to a limited extent in the anterior portions of the lungs after sharp exercise. When the bronchial murmur is heard over other portions of the lungs, it may signify that the lungs are more or less solidified by disease and the blowing, bronchial murmur is transmitted through this solid lung to the ear from a distant part of the chest. The bronchial murmur in an abnormal place signifies that there exists pneumonia or that the lungs are compressed by fluid in the chest cavity.

Additional sounds are heard in the lungs in some diseased conditions. For example, when fluid collects in the air passages and the air is forced through it or is caused to pass through tubes containing secretions or pus. Such sounds are of a gurgling or bubbling nature and are known as mucous rales. Mucous rales are spoken of as being large or small as they are distinct or indistinct, depending upon the quantity of fluid that is present and the size of the tube in which this sound is produced. Mucous rales occur in pneumonia after the solidified parts begin to break down at the end of the disease. They occur in bronchitis and in tuberculosis, where there is an excess of secretion.

Sometimes a shrill sound is heard, like the note of a whistle, fife, or flute. This is due to a dry constriction of the bronchial tubes and it is heard in chronic bronchitis and in tuberculosis.

A friction sound is heard in pleurisy. This is due to the rubbing together of roughened surfaces, and the sound produced is similar to a dry rubbing sound that is caused by rubbing the hands together or by rubbing upon each other two dry rough pieces of leather.

The Examination of the Digestive Tract

The first point in connection with the examination of the organs of digestion is the appetite and the manner of taking food and drink. A healthy animal has a good appetite. Loss of appetite does not point to a special diseased condition, but comes from a variety of causes. Some of these causes, indeed, may be looked upon as being physiological. Excitement, strange surroundings, fatigue, and hot weather may all cause loss of appetite. Where there is cerebral depression, fever, profound weakness, disorder of the stomach, or mechanical difficulty in chewing or swallowing, the appetite is diminished or destroyed. Sometimes there is an appetite or desire to eat abnormal things, such as dirty bedding, roots of grass, soil, etc. This desire usually comes from a chronic disturbance of nutrition.

Thirst is diminished in a good many mild diseases unaccompanied by distinct fever. It is seen where there is great exhaustion or depression or profound brain disturbance. Thirst is increased after profuse sweating, in diabetes, diarrhea, in fever, at the crisis of infectious diseases, and when the mouth is dry and hot.

Some diseases of the mouth or throat make it difficult for the horse to chew or swallow his food. Where difficulty in this respect is experienced, the following-named conditions should be borne in mind and carefully looked for: Diseases of the teeth, consisting of decay, fracture, abscess formation, or overgrowth; inflammatory conditions, or wounds or tumors of the tongue, cheeks, or lips; paralysis of the muscles of chewing or swallowing; foreign bodies in upper part of the mouth between the molar teeth; inflammation of throat. Difficulty in swallowing is sometimes shown by the symptom known as "quidding." Quidding consists of dropping from the mouth well-chewed and insalivated boluses of food. A mouthful of hay, for example, after being ground and masticated, is carried to the back part of the mouth. The horse then finds that from tenderness of the throat, or from some other cause, swallowing is difficult or painful, and the bolus is then dropped from the mouth. Another quantity of hay is similarly prepared, only to be dropped in turn. Sometimes quidding is due to a painful tooth, the bolus being dropped from the mouth when this tooth is struck and during the pang that follows. Quidding may be practiced so persistently that a considerable pile of boluses of food accumulate in the manger or on the floor of the stall. In pharyngitis one of the symptoms is a return through the nose of fluid that the horse attempts to swallow.

In some brain diseases, and particularly in chronic internal hydrocephalus, the horse has a most peculiar manner of swallowing and of taking food. A similar condition is seen in hyperemia of the brain. In eating the horse will sink his muzzle into the grain in the feed box and eat for a while without raising the head. Long pauses are made while the food is in the mouth. Sometimes the horse will eat very rapidly for a little while and then slowly; the jaws may be brought together so forcibly that the teeth gnash. In eating hay the horse will stop at times with hay protruding from the mouth and stand stupidly, as though he has forgotten what he was about.

In examining the mouth one should first look for swellings or for evidence of abnormal conditions upon the exterior: that is the front and sides of the face, the jaws, and about the muzzle. By this means wounds, fractures, tumors, abscesses, and disease accommpanied by eruptions about the muzzle may be detected. The interior of the mouth is examined by holding the head up and inserting the fingers through the interdental space in such a way as to cause the mouth to open. The mucous membrane should be clean and of a light-pink color, excepting on the back of the tongue, where the color is a yellowish gray. As abnormalities of this region, the chief are diffuse inflammation, characterized by redness and catarrhal discharge; local inflammation, as from eruptions, ulcers, or wounds; necrosis of the lower jawbone in front of the first back tooth; and swellings. Foreign bodies are sometimes found embedded in the mucous-membrane lining of the mouth or lodged between the teeth.

The examination of the pharynx and of the esophagus is made chiefly by pressing upon the skin covering these organs in the region of the throat and along the left side of the neck in the jugular gutter. Sometimes, when a more careful examination is necessary, an esophageal tube or probang is passed through the nose or mouth down the esophagus to the stomach.

Vomiting is an act consisting of the expulsion of all or part of the contents of the stomach through the mouth or nose. This act is more difficult for the horse than for most of the other domestic animals, because the stomach of the horse is small and does not lie on the floor of the abdominal cavity, so that the abdominal walls in contracting do not bring pressure to bear upon it so directly and forcibly, as is the case in many other animals. Beside this, there is a loose fold of mucous membrane at the point where the esophagus enters the stomach, and this forms a sort of valve which does not interfere with the passage of food into the stomach, but does interfere with the exit of food through the esophageal opening. Still, vomiting is a symptom that is occasionally seen in the horse. It occurs when the stomach is very much distended with food or with gas. Distention stretches the mucous membrane and eradicates the valvular fold referred to, and also makes it possible for more pressure to be exerted upon the stomach through the contraction of the abdominal muscles. Since the distention to permit vomiting must be extreme, it not infrequently happens that it leads to rupture of the stomach walls. This has caused the impression in the minds of some that vomiting cannot occur in the horse without rupture of the stomach, but this is incorrect, since many horses vomit and afterwards become entirely sound. After rupture of the stomach has occurred vomiting is impossible.

In examination of the abdomen one should remember that its size depends largely upon the breed, sex, and conformation of the animal, and also upon the manner in which the animal has been fed and the use to which it has been put. A pendulous abdomen may be the result of an abdominal tumor or of an accumultaion of fluid in the abdominal cavity; or, on the other hand, it may merely be an indication of pregnancy, or of the fact that the horse has been fed for a long time on bulky and innutritious food. Pendulous abdomen occurring in a work horse kept on a concentrated diet is an abnormal condition. The abdomen may increase suddenly in volume from accumulation of gas in tympanic colic. The abdomen becomes small and the horse is said to be "tucked up" from long-continued poor appetite, as in disease of the digestive tract and in fever. This condition also occurs in tetanus from the contraction of the abdominal walls and in diarrhea from emptiness.

In applying the ear to the flank, on either the right or left side, certain bubbling sounds may be heard that are known as peristaltic sounds, because they are produced by peristalsis, or worm-like contraction of the intestines. These sounds are a little louder on the right side than on the left on account of the fact that the large intestines lie in the right flank. Absence of peristaltic sounds is always an indication of disease, and suggests exhaustion or paralysis of the intestines. This may occur in certain kinds of colic and is an unfavorable symptom. Increased sounds are heard where the intestines are contracted more violently than in health, as in spasmodic colic, and also where there is an excess of fluid or gas in the intestinal canal.

The feces show, to a certain extent, the thoroughness of digestion. They should show that the food has been well ground, and should, in the horse, be free from offensive odor or coatings of mucus. A coating of mucus shows intestinal catarrh. Blood on the feces indicates severe inflammation. Very light color and bad odor may come from inactive liver. Parasites are sometimes in the dung.

Rectal examination consists of examination of the organs of the pelvic cavity and posterior portion of the abdominal cavity by the hand inserted into the rectum. This examination should be attempted by a veterinarian only, and is useless except to one who has a good knowledge of the anatomy of the parts concerned.

The Examination of the Nervous System

The great brain, or cerebrum, is the seat of intelligence, and it contains the centers that control motion in many parts of the body. The front portion of the brain is believed to be the region that is most important in governing the intelligence. The central and posterior portions of the cerebrum contain the centers for the voluntary motions of the face and of the front and hind legs. The growth of a tumor or an inflammatory change in the region of a center governing the motion of a certain part of the body has the effect of disturbing motion in that part by causing excessive contraction known as cramps, or inability of the muscles to contract, constituting the condition known as paralysis. The nerve paths from the cerebrum, and hence from these centers to the spinal cord and thence to the muscles, pass beneath the small brain, or the cerebellum, and through the medulla oblongata to the spinal cord. Interference with these paths has the effect of disturbing motion of the parts reached by them. If all of the paths on one side are interfered with, the result is paralysis of one side of the body.

The small brain, or cerebellum, governs the regularity, or coordination, of movements. Disturbances of the cerebellum cause a tottering, uncertain gait. In the medulla oblongata, which lies between the spinal cord and the cerebellum, are the centers governing the circulation and breathing.

The spinal cord carries sensory messages to the brain and motor impressions from the brain. The anterior portions of the cord contain the motor paths, and the posterior portions of the cord contain the sensory paths.

Paralysis of a single member or a single group of muscles is known as monoplegia and results from injury to the motor center or to a nerve trunk leading to the part that is involved. Paralysis of one-half of the body is known as hemiplegia and results from destruction or severe disturbances of the cerebral hemisphere of the opposite side of the body or from interference with nerve paths between the cerebellum, or small brain, and the spinal cord. Paralysis of the posterior half of the body is known as paraplegia and results from derangement of the spinal cord. If the cord is pressed upon, cut, or injured, messages cannot be transmitted beyond that point, and so the posterior part becomes paralyzed. This is seen when the back is fractured.

Abnormal mental excitement may be due to congestion of the brain or to inflammation. The animal so afflicted becomes vicious, pays no attention to commands, cries, runs about in a circle, stamps with the feet, strikes, kicks, etc. This condition is usually followed by a dull, stupid state, in which the animal stands with his head down, dull and irresponsive to external stimuli. Cerebral depression also occurs in the severe febrile infectious diseases, in chronic hydrocephalus, in chronic diseases of the liver, in poisoning with a narcotic substance, and with chronic catarrh of the stomach and intestines.

Fainting is a symptom that is not often seen in horses. When it occurs it is shown by unsteadiness of gait, tottering, and, finally, inability to stand. The cause usually lies in a defect of the small brain, or cerebellum. This defect may be merely in respect of the blood supply, to congestion, or to anemia, and in this case it is likely to pass away and may never return, or it may be due to some permanent cause, as a tumor or an abscess, or it may result from a hemorrhage, from a defect of the valves of the heart, or from poisoning.

Loss of consciousness is known as coma. It is caused by hemorrhage in the brain, by profound exhaustion, or may result from a saturation of the system with the poison of some disease. Coma may follow upon cerebral depression, which occurs as a secondary state of inflammation of the brain.

Where the sensibility of a part is increased the condition is known as hyperasthesia, and where it is lost—that is, where there is no feeling or knowledge of pain—the condition is known as anasthesia. The former usually accompanies some chronic diseases of the spinal cord or the earlier stages of irritation of a nerve trunk. Hyperasthesia is difficult to detect in a nervous, irritable animal, and sometimes even in a horse of less sensitive temperament. An irritable, sensitive spot may be found surrounded by skin that is not sensitive to pressure. This is sometimes a symptom of beginning of inflammation of the brain. Anasthesia occurs in connection with cerebral and spinal paralysis, section of a nerve trunk leading to a part, in severe mental depression, and in narcotic poisoning.

Urinary and Sexual Organs

In considering the examination of the urinary and sexual organs we may consider, at the beginning, a false impression that prevails to an astonishing extent. Many horsemen are in the habit of pressing upon the back of a horse over the loins or of sliding the ends of the fingers along on either side of the median line of this region. If the horse depresses his back it is at once said "his kidneys are weak." Nothing could be more absurd or further from the truth. Any healthy horse —any horse with normal sensation and with a normally flexible back—will cause it to sink when manipulated in this way. If the kidneys are inflamed and sensitive, the back is held more rigidly and is not depressed under this pressure.

To examine the kidneys by pressure the pressure should be brought to bear over these organs. The kidneys lie beneath the ends of the transverse processes of the vertebrae of the loins and beneath the hindmost ribs. If the kidneys are acutely inflamed and especially sensitive, pressure or light blows applied here may cause the horse to shrink.

The physical examination of the sexual and generative organs is made in large part through the rectum, and this portion of the examination should be carried out by a veterinarian only. By this means it is possible to discover or locate cysts of the kidneys, urinary calculi in the ureters, bladder, or upper urethra, malformations, and acute inflammations accompanied by pain. The external genital organs are swollen, discolored, or show a discharge as a result of local disease or from disease higher in the tract.

The manner of urinating is sometimes of considerable diagnostic importance. Painful urination is shown by frequent attempts, during which but a small quantity of urine is passed, by groaning, by constrained attitude, etc. This condition comes from inflammation of the bladder or urethra, urinary calculi (stones of the bladder or urethra), hemorrhage, tumors, bruises, etc. The urine is retained from spasms of the muscle at the neck of the bladder, from calculi, inflammatory growths, tumors, and paralysis of the bladder.

The urine dribbles without control when the neck of the bladder is weakened or paralyzed. This condition is seen after the bladder is weakened from long-continued retention and where there is a partial paralysis of the hind quarters.

Horses usually void urine five to seven times a day, and pass from 4 to 7 quarts. Disease may be shown by increase in the number of voidings or of the quantity. Frequent urination indicates an irritable or painful condition of the bladder or urethra or that the quantity is excessive. In one form of chronic inflammation of the kidneys (interstitial nephritis) and in polyuria the quantity may be increased to 20 or 30 quarts daily. Diminution in the quantity of urine comes from profuse sweating, diarrhea, high fever, weak heart, diseased and non-secreting kidneys, or an obstruction to the flow.

The urine of the healthy horse is a pale or at times a slightly reddish yellow. The color is less intense when the quantity is large, and is more intense when the quantity is diminished. Dark-brown urine is seen in azoturia and in severe acute muscular rheumatism. A brownish green color is seen in jaundice. Red color indicates a mixture of blood from a bleeding point at some part of the urinary tract.

The urine of the healthy horse is not clear and transparent. It contains mucous which causes it to be slightly thick and stringy, and a certain amount of undissolved carbonate, causing it to be cloudy. A sediment collects when the urine is allowed to stand. The urine of the horse is normally alkaline. If it becomes acid the bodies in suspension are dissolved and the urine is made clear. The urine may be unusually cloudy from the addition of abnormal constituents, but to determine their character a chemical or microscopic examination is necessary. Red or reddish flakes or clumps in the urine are always abnormal, and denote a hemorrhage or suppuration in the urinary tract.

The normal specific gravity of the urine of the horse is about 1.040. It is increased when the urine is scanty and decreased when the quantity is excessive.

Acid reaction of the urine occurs in chronic intestinal catarrh, in high fever, and during starvation. Chemical and microscopic tests and examinations are often of great importance in diganosis, but require special apparatus and skill.

Other points in the examination of a sick horse require more discussion than can be afforded in this connection, and require special training on the part of the examiner. Among such points may be mentioned the examination of the organs of special sense, the examination of the blood, bacteriological examinations of the secretions, excretions, and tissues, specific reaction test, and diagnostic inoculation.

ADMINISTERING MEDICINES

People commonly think of medicines as divided into two general classes; those for internal use, and those for external use.

Medicines for internal use are those that act through the circulation by being administered through the mouth into the stomach.

Medicines for external use are those that are applied externally to act in a local way, such as ointments, liniments and lotions.

But this is rather a limited conception of medicines, as there are curative agents that are used in various other ways, and could not be placed in either class.

Some are introduced into the system by hypodermic injection beneath the skin, or even directly into the veins or arteries.

Some are administered by inhalation into the lungs in the form of vapor or fumes.

Others are blown into the nostrils in the form of powder or spray.

Still others are introduced into the rectum in solution or in the form of a suppository, and pass into the system by absorption.

Doctors employ still other methods of medication which need not be mentioned here, for, after all, the internal and external medicines first spoken of are more important and more often used than all the others.

The easiest method of giving internal medicines, either liquids or powders, to horses is to mix the dose with bran mash or other soft foods. But this is not always practical. The odor or taste may be such that the animal will refuse to eat it, or he may be too sick to eat, or we may wish to give the remedy by itself so that it will pass into the system quicker and act more promptly, which may be done by one of the following methods.

Meaning of Medical Terms

Alternative: Property to change an unhealthy into a healthy condition.

Antacid: Property to neutralize acid condition of the secretion.

Antiseptic: Property to arrest germs or retard their activity.

Antispasmodic: Tending to allay or ward off spasms.

Anodyne: The property of relieving pain.

Aromatic: Highly flavored and having an agreeable odor.

Astringent: The property of producing contraction of soft tissues.

Carminative: Warming and mildly stimulating.

Cathartic: Causing free movement of the bowels.

Demulcent: Property of allaying irritation.

Diaphoretic: Tending to induce perspiration.

Disinfectant: Destructive to germ life.

Diuretic: Stimulating to the kidneys, increasing the secretion of urine.

Emetic: Tending to induce vomiting.

Expectorant: Tending to increase the secretion of mucous in the air passage.

Febrifuge: Tending to diminish fever.

Laxative: Mildly loosening to the bowels.

Narcotic: Tending to induce sleep.

Purgative: Actively cathartic.

Refrigerant: Tending to diminish the temperature.

Sedative: Soothing and cooling when used locally; tending to allay nervous excitement when given internally.

Stimulant: That which temporarily increases functional activity.

Stomachic: Mildly stimulating to the stomach.

Tonic: That which gradually and permanently improves digestion and assimilation, and imparts strength and tone to the whole system.

Vermifuge: Destructive to intestinal parasites.

Properties and Doses of Drugs

Different drugs possess different medicinal properties, or, in other words, act differently upon the system, or affect different organs or functions. One drug may have more than one property, or it may act in different ways according to the quantity used and the manner in which it is employed. By combining drugs a combination of properties may be obtained, and sometimes effects may be produced that are not characteristic of any of the drugs when used alone.

Below we give the properties and usual doses of some of the drugs commonly used in veterinary practice.

Acetate of Lead (same as Sugar of Lead): Sedative, astringent; dose for horses or cattle, half a dram to one dram. Used mostly in solution and locally.

Acetic Acid: Astringent, cooling; used mostly in lotions.

Aconite, Tincture of: Sedative, diaphoretic; dose for horses, fifteen to thirty drops; for cattle, twenty to forty drops.

Alcohol: Stimulant, narcotic, diuretic; dose for horses, one to four ounces; for cattle, three to six ounces. Used externally, astringent, cooling when diluted.

Aloes: Purgative; dose for horses, three-fourths of an ounce to an ounce; for cattle, one to two ounces. Should be given along with half an ounce to an ounce of ground ginger, which will help prevent griping.

Anise Seed: Stomachic, carminative; dose for horse, one ounce.

Aromatic Spirits of Ammonia: Stimulant, antispasmodic, antacid, diuretic; dose for horses, half an ounce to two ounces.

Arsenic, Fowler's Solution: Tonic, alternative; dose for horses, one-fourth ounce to one ounce.

Belladonna: Antispasmodic, anodyne, narcotic; dose for horses, (powdered leaves), two to four drams; fluid extract of the root, dose, half a dram to a dram.

Bromide of Potassium: Nerve sedative; dose, one to two ounces.

Buchu: Diuretic; dose for horse, half an ounce to one ounce of either the fluid extract or powder.

Cantharides: Stimulant, diuretic; horse dose, five to ten grains, used mostly as a local irritant or blistering agent.

Carbolic Acid: Antiseptic, disinfectant, anodyne, sedative, astringent; horse dose, half a dram to one dram. Used mostly in lotions and as a disinfectant.

Castor Oil: Purgative; horse dose, one pint.

Catechu: Astringent; horse dose, two to six drams.

Chloral Hydrate: Antispasmodic, sedative; horse dose, half an ounce to one ounce. Much larger doses are sometimes given. Should be well diluted.

Chloroform: Stimulant, anodyne, antispasmodic; horse dose, one to two drams. Anesthetic by inhalation.

Digitalis: Sedative, diuretic; horse dose, one-fourth to one-half dram (powdered). Tincture; two to four drams.

Epsom Salts: Purgative; best for cattle. Anesthetic intravenously, usually mixed with Chloral Hydrate.

Gentian: Tonic; dose for horses, one-fourth ounce to one ounce (powdered). Tincture; half an ounce to two ounces.

Ginger: Stomachic, stimulant; horse dose, one-fourth to one ounce.

Iodide of Potassium: Alternative, diuretic; horse dose, half dram to two drams.

Iodine: Alternative; horse dose, one-fourth dram to one dram. Tincture; used locally.

Laudanum: Same as tincture of opium.

Linseed Oil (Raw): Laxative; dose for horses, one to two pints.

Nitrate of Potash (Saltpeter): Diuretic, Febrifuge, alternative; horse dose, one-fourth to one-half ounce.

Nux Vomica: Tonic, stumulant; horse dose, one-fourth to one-half dram.

Opium: Sedative, narcotic, anodyne, antispasmodic; horse dose, (powdered), half a dram to two drams. Tincture (laudanum), horse dose, half an ounce to two ounces.

Pine Tar: Expectorant, antiseptic; horse dose, one-fourth to one-half ounce.

Resin: Diuretic; dose for horses, half an ounce.

Sulfate of Iron (same as Copperas): Tonic, astringent; horse dose, one-half to two drams.

Sweet Spirits of Nitre: Stimulant, antispasmodic, diuretic, diaphoretic; horse dose, one to two ounces.

Turpentine: Stimulant, antispasmodic, diuretic, and vermifuge in maximum doses; horses dose, one-fourth ounce to two ounces. Best given in eight times its bulk of raw linseed oil or mineral oil.

Whiskey: Stimulant, narcotic, diuretic; horse dose, four to eight ounces.

Doses for Young Animals

It is customary, in mentioning the dose of a drug or medicine, to name the quantity that is suitable for a grown or adult animal. Younger animals should receive less according to age. We offer the following general rules as a help in determining the proper doses for young stock.

For colt one to five months old, one-sixteenth of the adult dose. From five to nine months old, one-eighth of the adult dose. From nine to eighteen months old, one-fourth of the adult dose. From eighteen months to three years old, one-half of the adult dose. After reaching the age of three years, the adult dose may be given.

MEASURING MEDICINES

Liquids are measured in minims, drams, and ounces. A drop is approximately a minim. Sixty minims make one fluid dram, and eight drams make one fluid ounce, which is one-sixteenth of a pint. A teaspoonful of liquid is one dram, and a tablespoon is four drams, or one half an ounce. This is approximate of course, as spoons may vary somewhat in size.

Powders and dry drugs are weighed, the weights being grains, drams, and ounces. Grains correspond to the minims used in measuring liquids, there being sixty grains in a dram. Eight drams make an ounce, the same as in fluid measure. Dry materials cannot well be estimated by calling a spoonful so much grains or drams. A better plan is to weigh out a certain quantity, then divide it. For instance, suppose you have in mind to give two-dram doses of any powdered drug, and the quantity you have purchased is half a pound. Spread it out evenly on a sheet of paper, an divide into four equal parts. Then divide each of the four parts into four parts, then each of these into two parts, and you have it all made out into two-dram doses. By taking into consideration the quantity you have and the dose you wish to give, you can readily figure out the divisions to make.

METHODS OF ADMINISTERING MEDICINES

Medicine may enter the body through any of the following designated channels: First, by the mouth; second, by the air passages; third, by the skin; fourth, by the tissue beneath the skin (hypodermic methods); fifth, by the rectum; sixth, by the genito-urinary passages; and, seventh, by the blood (intravenous injections).

1. *By the Mouth.*—Medicines can be given by the mouth in the form of solids, as powders or pills; liquids, and pastes, or electuaries.

Solids administered as powders should be as finely pulverized as possible, in order to secure rapid solution and absorption. Their action is in this way facilitated and intensified. Powders must be free from any irritant or caustic action upon the mouth. Those that are without any disagreeable taste or smell are readily eaten with the food or taken in the drinking water. When placed with the feed they should first be dissolved or suspended in water and thus sprinkled on the feed. If mixed dry the horse will often leave the medicine in the bottom of his manger. Nonirritant powders may be given in capsules, as balls are given.

Giving a Ball

Pills, or "balls," when properly made, are cylindrical in shape, 2 inches in length and about three-fourths of an inch in diameter. They should be fresh, but if necessary to keep them some time they should be made up with glycerin, or some such agent, to prevent their becoming too hard. Very old, hard balls are sometimes passed whole with the manure without being acted upon at all. Paper is sometimes wrapped around balls when given, if they are so sticky as to adhere to the fingers or the balling gun. Paper used for this purpose should be thin but firm, as the tougher tissue papers. Balls are preferred to drenches when the medicine is extremely disagreeable or nauseating; when the dose is not too large; when the horse is difficult to drench; or when the medicine is intended to act slowly. Certain medicines cannot or should not be made into balls, as medicines requiring to be given in large doses, oils, caustic substances, unless in small dose and diluted and thoroughly mixed with the vehicle, deliquescent, or efflorvescent salts. Substances suitable for balls can be made up by the addition of honey, sirup, soap, etc., when required for immediate use. Gelatin capsules of different sizes are now obtainable and are a convenient means of giving medicines in ball form.

Drenching with a Syringe

This is an easy method of administering liquids, especially if the dose is small. Procure from your druggist an ordinary hard rubber syringe or metal dose syringe. The half ounce size will be all right. Fill with the remedy to be given, open the animal's mouth and empty the syringe far back toward the throat, not too forcibly. Repeat as often as required to give the proper quantity.

Giving an Electuary

In cases where the throat is sore and swollen so that neither a ball nor drench can be given with safety, the drugs may be made into a sticky mass with syrup or honey, then smeared upon the tongue and back teeth, where the mixture will be slowly dissolved and swallowed with the saliva. Such a preparation is called an electuary. Sharp and irritating medicines that might tend to inflame the membranes should not be given in this way. Electuaries are used mostly in giving soothing remedies to relieve a sore throat, and as the mass dissolves slowly a prolonged action upon the affected surfaces is obtained.

Giving a Ball

When balls are to be given we should observe the following directions: In shape they should be cylindrical, of the size above mentioned, and soft enough to be easily compressed by the fingers. If made round or egg-shaped, if too long or too hard, they are liable to become fixed in the gullet and cause choking. Balls may be given with the "balling gun" (obtainable at any veterinary instrument maker's) or by the hand. If given by the hand a mouth speculum or gag may be used to prevent the animal from biting the hand or crushing the ball. Always loosen the horse before attempting to give a ball; if tied he may break his halter and injure himself or the one giving the ball. With a little practice it is much easier to give a ball without the mouth gag, as the horse always fights more or less against having his mouth forced open. The tongue must be firmly grasped with the left hand and gently pulled forward; the ball, slightly moistened, is then to be placed with the tips of the fingers of the right hand as far back into the mouth as possible; as the tongue is loosened it is drawn back into the mouth and carries the ball backward with it. The mouth should be kept closed for a minute or two. We should always have a pail of water at hand to offer the horse after balling. This precaution will often prevent him from coughing out the ball or its becoming lodged in the gullet.

Drenching Horses

It is, very often, impossible to get balls properly made, or to induce owners or attendants to attempt to give them, and for these reasons medicines by the mouth are mostly given in the form of liquids. When medicine is to be given as a drench we must be careful to use enough water or oil to dissolve or dilute it thoroughly; more than this makes the drench bulky and is unnecessary. Insoluble medicines, if not irritant or corrosive, may be given simply suspended in water; the bottle to be well shaken immediately before giving the drench. The bottle used for drenching purposes should be clean, strong, and smooth about its neck; it should be without shoulders, tapering, and of a size to suit the amount to be given. A horn or tin bottle may be better, because they are not so easily broken by the teeth. If the dose is a small one the horse's head may be held up by the left hand, while the medicine is poured into the mouth by the right. The left thumb is to be placed in the angle of the lower jaw, and the fingers spread out in such a manner as to support the lower lip. Should the dose be large, the horse ugly, or the attendant unable to support the head as directed above, the head is then to be held up by running the tines of a long-handled wooden fork under the noseband of the halter or the halter strap or a rope may be fastened to the noseband and thrown over a limb, beam, or through a pulley suspended from the ceiling. Another way of supporting the head is to place a loop in the end of a rope, and introduce this loop into the mouth just behind the upper front teeth or tusks of the upper jaw, the free end to be run through a pulley, as before described, and held by an assistant. It is never to be fastened, as the horse might in that case do himself serious injury. The head is to be elevated just enough to prevent the horse from throwing the liquid out of his mouth. The line of the face should be horizontal, or only the least bit higher. If the head is drawn too high the animal cannot swallow with ease or even with safety. (If this is doubted, just fill your mouth with water, throw back the head as far as possible, and then try to swallow.) The person giving the drench should stand on some object in order to reach the horse's mouth—on a level, or a little above it. The bottle or horn is then to be introduced at the side of the mouth, in front of the molar teeth, in an upward direction. This will cause the horse to open his mouth, when the base of the bottle is to be elevated, and about 4 ounces of the liquid allowed to escape on the tongue as far back as possible, care being taken not to get the neck of the bottle between the back teeth. The bottle is to be immediately removed, and if the horse does not swallow this can be encouraged by rubbing the fingers or neck of the bottle against the roof of the mouth, occasionally removing them. As soon as this is swallowed repeat the operation until he has taken all the drench. If coughing occurs, or if, by any mishap, the bottle should be crushed in the mouth, lower the head immediately.

Do not rub, pinch, or pound the throat nor draw out the tongue when giving a drench. These processes in no way aid the horse to swallow and oftener do harm than good. In drenching, swallowing may be hastened by pouring into the nose of the horse, while the head is high, a few teaspoonfuls of clean water, but drenches must never be given through the nose. Large quantities of medicine given by pouring into the nose are liable to strangle the animal, or, if the medicine is irritating, it sets up an inflammation of the nose, fauces, windpipe, and sometimes the lungs.

2. Medicines are administered to the lungs and upper air passages by insufflation, inhalation, injection, and nasal douche.

Insufflation consists of blowing an impalpable powder directly into the nose. It is but rarely resorted to.

Gaseous and volatile medicines are given by inhalation, as is also medicated steam, or vapor. Of the gases used there may be mentioned, as the chief ones, sulphurous acid gas and, occasionally, chlorine. The animal or animals are to be placed in a tight room, where these gases are generated until the atmosphere is sufficiently impregnated with them. Volatile medicines—as the anesthetics (ether, chloroform, etc.)—are to be given by the veterinarian only. Medicated vapors are to be inhaled by placing a bucket containing hot water, vinegar and water, scalded hay or bran, to which carbolic acid, iodine, creolin, compound tincture of benzoin, or other medicines have been added, in the bottom of a long grain bag. The horse's nose is to be inserted into the top of the bag, and he thus inhales the "medicated steam." Care must be taken not to have this hot enough to scald the animal. The vapor from scalding bran or hay is often thus inhaled to favor discharges in sore throat or "distemper."

Injections are made into the trachea by means of a hypodermic syringe. This method of medication is used for the purpose of treating local diseases of the trachea and upper bronchial tubes. It has also been used as a mode of administering remedies for their constitutional effect, but is now rarely used for this purpose.

The nasal douche is employed by the veterinarian in treating some local diseases of the nasal chambers. Special appliances and professional knowledge are necessary when using liquid medicines by this method. It is not often resorted to, even by veterinary surgeons, since, as a rule, the horse objects very strongly to this mode of medication.

3. *By the Skin.* — Medicines are often administered to our hair-covered animals by the skin, yet care must be taken in applying some medicines—as tobacco water, carbolic-acid solutions, strong creolin solutions, mercurial ointment, etc. —over the entire body, as poisoning and death follow in some instances from absorption through the skin. For the same reasons care must also be exercised and poisonous medicines not applied over very large raw or abraded surfaces. With domestic animals medicines are only to be applied by the skin to allay local pain or cure local disease.

4. *By the Tissue Beneath the Skin (Hypodermatic Method).* — Medicines are frequently given by the hypodermic syringe under the skin. It is not safe for any but medical or veterinary practitioners to use this form of medication, since the medicines thus given are powerful and some are poisons except in proper doses. There are many precautions to be observed, and a knowledge of anatomy is indispensable. One of the chief precautions has to do with the sterilization of the syringe. If it is not sterile an abscess may be produced. Injections may be made into a vein when a person knows anatomy well.

5. *By the Rectum.*—Medicines may be given by the rectum when they cannot be given by the mouth, or when they are

not retained in the stomach; when we want a local action on the last gut; when it is desired to destroy the small worms infesting the large bowels or to stimulate the peristaltic motion of the intestines and cause evacuation. Medicines are in such cases given in the form of suppositories or as liquid injections (enemas). Foods may also be given in this way.

Suppositories are conical bodies made up of oil of theobroma and opium (or whatever medicine is indicated in special cases), and are introduced into the rectum or vagina to allay irritation and pain of these parts. They are not much used in treating horses.

Enemas, when given for absorption, should be small in quantity, neutral or slightly acid in reaction, and of a temperature of from 90° to 100°F. These, like foods given by the rectum, should be introduced only after the last bowel has been emptied by the hand or by copious injections of tepid water. Enemas, or cylsters, if to aid the action of physics, should be in quantities sufficient to distend the bowel and cause the animal to eject them. Simple water, salt and water, or soap and water, in quantities of a gallon or more, may be given every half hour. It is best that the horse retain them for some little time, as the liquid serves to moisten the dung and favor a passage. Stimulating enemas, as glycerin, should be administered after those already mentioned have emptied the last bowel, with the purpose of still further increasing the natural motion of the intestines and aiding the purging medicine.

Liquids may be thrown into the rectum by the means of a large syringe or a pump. A good "irrigator" consists of a funnel about 6 inches deep and 7 inches in diameter, which is to be furnished with a prolongation to which a piece of rubber hose, such as small garden hose, 4 feet long may be attached. The hose, well oiled, is to be inserted gently into the rectum about 2 feet. The liquid to be injected may then be poured in the funnel and the pressure of the atmosphere will force it into the bowels. This appliance is better than the more complicated and expensive ones.

Ordinary cold water or even ice-cold water is highly recommended by many as a rectal injection for horses overcome by the excessive heat of summer, and may be given by this simple pipe.

6. *By the Genito-Urinary Passage.* — This method of medication is especially useful in treating local diseases of the genito-urinary organs. It finds its chief applications in the injection and cleansing of the uterus and vagina. For this purpose a large syringe or the irrigator described may be used. Care should be used that only sterile or antiseptic solutions are introduced since drainage from these passages is poor and infection is easily introduced.

7. *By the Blood.* — Injections directly into veins or intravenous injections should be practiced by veterinarians only, for a number of reasons. This applies to other methods and all potent drugs that dosage and actions are not well understood.

Poulticing the Feet

The method of bandaging a poultice on must, of course, be varied according to the part of the body to which it is applied. It is probable that the feet are as apt to require poulticing as any other part, and the following is the easiest method of applying.

Make a bag of strong cloth somewhat larger than the foot and long enough to tie above the fetlock. Prepare your poultice and fill the bag with it to a depth of two or three inches. Put the foot into the bag and fill in around it with the poulticing material up to the fetlock, then tie the bag above the fetlock joint to keep it on. Wet the poultice with hot water several times a day, and change it once a day. When wetting it be sure that the water is not hot enough to scald. Do not tie so tight as to cut off circulation.

Poultices

Poultices are used principally to obtain prolonged application of heat and moisture to an affected part. Sometimes poultices are medicated by the addition of drugs, usually something possessing antiseptic or anodyne properties.

Flaxseed meal is perhaps the best material for making poultices. Hops and powdered slippery elm bark are also employed.

The action of a poultice is relaxing and soothing to the tissues, with a tendency to relieve inflammation and congestion, or hasten and promote suppuration.

Do not apply a poultice so hot that it will scald, or continue poulticing so long that the tissue becomes soft and flabby. A considerable quantity of material should be used so that the heat will be retained longer, and the poultice should ordinarily be changed or freshened up with hot water at intervals of two or three hours.

The Pulse

The pulse of the horse is best found where the artery crosses the lower edge of the jaw, about two inches forward from its angle. The pulse of cattle is found in about the same place, only a little more to the outside of the jaw.

In fullgrown animals at rest and in health the pulse of the horse is 36 to 46 per minute. The pulse of a new-born foal is three times as frequent as that of the horse, at six months twice as frequent, while in the two-year-old there are five beats to every four in the grown animal.

The pulse is increased by exertion, fear, excitement, etc. It is also more rapid during pregnancy after the fifth or sixth month.

Temperature

The normal temperature for a horse is 99 to 101 degrees Fahrenheit. At work on a hot day, the temperature may be a degree higher than at other times.

The normal temperature of cattle is 100 to 102 degrees. During heat or in advanced pregnancy, the cow or mare may show a temperature one or two degrees higher than her normal.

The temperature of animals is usually taken by introducing the clinical thermometer into the rectum. A temporary rise of one or two degrees need cause no concern, but continued high temperature denotes fever. In cases of high fever, a sudden drop to or below normal without general improvement in the other symptoms, is usually regarded as unfavorable. If there is general improvement, with perspiration and free action of the kidneys, the change is regarded as favorable. Where temperature rises as high as ten degrees above normal, recovery is doubtful.

Respiration

In the adult horse, the respiration is from nine to fourteen per minute when at rest. Young animals breathe faster than grown ones.

Exertion increases the respiration, but it drops back to normal when the animal has rested. If after driving or working a horse the respiration continues at a high rate for more than the usual time, note the pulse. If that is normal the condition is not serious, but a high pulse will denote that there is a derangement of some little consequence at least.

Inflammation of the Mouth

This may be due to some acrid or thorny plant in the hay or pasture, or to giving strong medicines without sufficient dilution, or to some foreign substance becoming lodged in the mouth or wedged between the teeth where it causes irritation, or to laceration of the tongue or cheek by the sharp edges of overgrown teeth, or to anything that can in any way injure or irritate the membrane.

The symptoms are swelling of the tongue, lips or cheeks, redness of the membrane, difficulty in eating or drinking, dribbling saliva, etc.

Ascertain and correct the cause of the trouble if possible. Allow the horse all the cool water he wants. Feed soft foods for several days until the inflammation has subsided.

Ulcerated Teeth

Sometimes an ulcer forms at the root of a decayed tooth. The symptoms are difficult mastication, foul smelling mouth, accumulation of decaying food around the affected tooth, the appearance of a knot upon the jaw, a cavity or black spot in the tooth, a fistulous opening in the jaw discharging pus, or there may even be a foul discharge from the nose when an upper tooth is diseased.

Have a veterinarian examine the case. He will likely find it necessary to extract the tooth, though some cases may be treated successfully and the tooth saved.

Wolf Teeth

There is a prevalent idea that the small and insignificant teeth commonly known as wolf teeth, that appear directly in front of the upper grinders, and sometimes the lower ones, have a damaging effect upon the eyes of a horse, or may even cause blindness. As a matter of fact, these teeth are just as harmless as they are useless. They may be extracted without injury, but will not harm if let alone. The fact that they are present at the time of shedding the colt teeth and cutting the permanent ones, during which period recurring inflammation of the eyes is apt to be frequent, is no doubt responsible for the mistaken belief that they are injurious. If the eyes become inflamed, use an eye lotion to relieve the condition.

Crib Biting

Crib-biting is doubtless merely a habit in most cases, and is frequently associated with the more serious vice of "wind-sucking" (swallowing air), which leads to digestive disorder and loss of condition. One plan of preventing it is to take out the manger and so arrange the stall that the animal will have no place on which he can set his teeth. Some try smearing aloes or other bitter drugs upon the parts where the animal takes hold, while others resort to use of a muzzle.

Lolling the Tongue

If the horse lolls his tongue only when the bit is in his mouth, it is merely an ugly habit and we know of no remedy for it. If the tongue hangs out all the time there is partial paralysis. Some cases of this kind may be helped or cured by giving half a dram of nux vomica and one dram of sulphate of iron in bran mash night and morning for two weeks, then discontinue for a week, after which repeat if necessary.

Lampas

This is an inflammation and swelling of the soft tissues just behind the upper front teeth. It is most common in young horses at about the time the permanent teeth are developing, and ordinarily does not require treatment. In older horses with teeth fully grown it indicates digestive derangement.

Scarify the part slightly with a knife for half an inch back of the teeth, then bathe with a solution of alum, one teaspoon in half a pint of water. If costiveness or stomach disorder is present, give a physic, an ounce of aloes or a pint and a half of raw linseed oil. If stomach trouble or general disorder is quite marked, get a proper diagnosis and treat.

Overgrown Teeth

Examine the horse's teeth occasionally and dress them down with a tooth-rasp if required. Owing to the lower jaw being narrower than the upper the wear is uneven, and the outer edges of the upper molars and the inner edges of the lower ones are apt to become overgrown and so sharp as to lacerate the cheek or tongue. Nourishment is the first essential to health in every living thing. Inability to properly grind the food is often responsible for bad condition in horses, and tonics without the required dental attention can be of little benefit in such cases.

Slow and tedious mastication, slobbering, dropping half chewed food from the mouth, tilting the head to one side while chewing, passing undigested grain, etc., are indications of tooth trouble.

Necrotic Ulceration of the Mouth

This disease is known to the profession as Necrotic Stomatitis, but we have applied the other name because it is more descriptive. It is not common among horses, but may affect any animal. In the beginning there is usually lassitude and weakness, the animal shows difficulty in swallowing, slobbers and refuses to eat, and swellings may appear beneath the jaws or about the throat. Examination of the mouth will reveal one or several grayish yellow ulcers, and a foul odor will likely be noticeable. The ulcers may be as small as a dime or as large as a dollar, with the appearance of a cheesy decay of the tissues. Sometimes the disease is not confined to the mouth, but extends to the throat and nasal cavities, often proving fatal.

Dissolve half an ounce each of alum and borax in a quart of water and swab the mouth with this solution twice daily. Mix half an ounce of salicylic acid with five ounces of glycerine, and swab some of this upon the ulcers after each cleansing. Where the ulcer is so located that you can get at it readily it is well to open it up, scraping out most of the cheesy substance before using the solution and salicylic acid mixture.

The ulcers are due to a germ called the Bacillus Necrophorus, and any slight abrasion or irritated condition of the membrane affords a chance for inoculation. Where the disease appears, thoroughly renovate the stables and use disinfectants freely. To guard against it, maintain cleanliness and sanitary conditions. Antibiotics are usually effective.

Salivary Fistula

This is not a disease, nor is it similar to fistulous diseases in which there is suppuration and a discharge of matter. It is a term that is applied where a salivary duct is opened by a wound so that the saliva flows out through the wound. This may occur in opening abscesses about the lower jaws of horses, as in a case of distemper, or from a kick, puncture or similar injury. The wound may heal with the exception of a small channel, through which the saliva flows, matting the hair about the opening.

Shave off the hair for an inch or so and apply collodion, which dries quickly, forming a thin skin. Strengthen this skin by applying several layers, one after another as fast as each dries. Allow the collodion to remain on as long as it will, and feed only soft foods for a few days. If when the collodion comes off the fistula is not closed, try it again, or try a smart blister over and around the opening, which may work better in some of the older cases.

Injured Maxillary Joint

This is the joint between the lower and the upper jaws, and its location is about midway between the eye and ear. It is sometimes injured by a sharp blow or kick, causing inflammation and swelling, so that the horse may be unable to masticate his food. In treating such an injury it is best to prevent movement of the jaw by putting a halter on the animal and tightening the nose band so that the mouth is kept closed. Bathe the part with hot water for half an hour at a time about four times a day. Dissolve half an ounce of acetate of lead in a quart of water, add two ounces of tincture of arnica, and apply some of this lotion each bathing. When the swelling and inflammation have been reduced, apply a mild blister. One dram powdered canthardies mixed with an ounce of lard will answer. Feed then oatmeal gruel while the tight-fitting halter is on, which the animal can suck between his teeth, then mashes and other soft foods for a time thereafter.

Inflammation of the Parotid Gland

This is sometimes called mumps. It may accompany distemper, colds, etc., or may be due to injury or to being confined in hot and poorly ventilated stables. The gland, which is situated below the ear, is hot, swollen and painful, and the horse holds his head in a stiff manner, chews slowly when eating, and may have more or less general fever.

Apply hot poultices, or even cloths wet in hot water. Feed only soft foods. If after the inflammation has subsided a hard swelling remains, use a mild blister or apply tincture of iodine.

When a case is not attended to early, suppuration may occur. Let the matter come well to the surface and form up a point before opening, as in making a deep cut you are liable to sever a duct.

Choking in Horses

A greedy or hungry horse may bolt his oats and choke, or he may choke on almost any food that he attempts to swallow without chewing.

Give a little linseed oil or sweet oil, then rub up and down the gullet to break up and scatter the mass. Give the oil several times if necessary. If none is at hand, give water instead. This treatment usually relieves, but is sometimes necessary to open the gullet and remove the offending material, then close the incision with silk thread or catgut. After such an operation, give only liquid foods for a time. Such drastic action should only be attempted by a veterinarian.

Fistula of the Withers

The word Fistula means a tube or pipe, and fistulous diseases are those characterized by one or more deep-seated abscesses of a chronic nature, with slender channels or pipes extending to the surface through which the pus is discharged.

Fistula may occur in any part of the body, but usually affects the withers, where some call it Thisalo, or the poll, where it is called Poll Evil, and less frequently the foot, where it is called Quittor. Where merely the term Fistula is used in referring to a case, it is to be assumed that Fistula of the Withers is meant.

The Cause

It is accepted as an established fact that Fistula of the Withers, as well as the other forms of fistula we have mentioned, is always due to an injury of some kind. Even a slight bruise, such as might be sustained in rolling upon a small stone or other hard substance, will sometimes produce it.

The withers, being a prominent elevation in the contour of the animal, are especially liable to injuries, and being formed by the prolongations or spines that extend upward from the backbone and terminate abruptly in the flesh, even moderate violence is apt to bruise the tissues at the ends of these bones. Furthermore, the tissues about the withers, and also the poll, are not of the highest organization, and are consequently inferior in their power of recovery when injured.

It is probable, too, that a humorous or deranged state of the blood may render an animal more susceptible to fistulous diseases. Both Fistula and Poll Evil being present in the same animal, as they occasionally are, or a tendency for either disease to recur upon slight provocation, even when all signs of the previous attack have been eradicated, suggests this probability. Instances of the kind,

however, are rare. Ordinarily there is nothing to indicate that the horse is not normal constitutionally, and most horses when properly healed are no more liable to the disease than those that have never had it.

We have often been asked whether Fistula can in any way be contagious, some stating that several cases have broken out among their horses within a short interval, though previously they had had no trouble with it.

For such an occurrence there must be some explanation other than contagion, as there is nothing to justify a belief that the disease can be transmitted from one animal to another. Perhaps there is on the premises a low shed that has gradually been filling up with litter, so that in playing about it and running in and out the animals strike and bruise the withers; or, it may be that one of the horses is of a quarrelsome disposition and has taken to biting the others, the withers affording a good place for him to take hold. It may be, too, that somebody is careless as to how the collars are fitting, or there may be a variety of other causes worthy of being investigated.

The First Stage

Fistula begins with a low form of deep-seated inflammation involving the injured tissues, which gradually break down, forming a pus cavity.

A swelling appears upon one or both sides of the withers, which is usually the first indication of trouble, though sometimes it is observed a day or two earlier that there is soreness about the part.

If the swelling is quite hot and sensitive the case will likely develop rapidly, but if there is little or no excess of heat and apparently no soreness, the inflammation is apt to be deeper seated and of a lower order, and considerable time may elapse before suppuration occurs. In the case of slow development no attempt should be made to open or drain the swelling.

The Developed Stage

Sometimes the swelling fluctuates a little, but usually it remains about stationary or slowly increases until one or more openings form. In some cases a great quantity of pus is discharged when the bunch first breaks, the swelling diminshes somewhat and the openings may heal or partially heal, then after a few weeks the part rises and breaks again. In other cases the discharge is not so profuse, but more continous.

Fistula is not a disease that runs its course or cures itself. Gradually the surrounding tissues become involved in the destructive process, and to provide a permanent channel for escape of the foul accumulations a lining of tough membrane forms in the openings, which are then called pipes. These pipes extend in various directions, leading to diseased parts deep down in the flesh or even between the shoulder blades. As more and more tissue becomes diseased, new openings may form, there sometimes being fifteen or more pipes discharging pus so profusely that it flows down to the animal's hoofs. The disease does not confine itself to the soft tissues, but the bone also becomes involved in a slow decay, and there is no better way to describe a bad case than to apply the term that many have used in writing of their cases to us, and say that "the horse is literally rotten."

The Termination

Not all cases take on the extreme form that we have just described.

Sometimes there will be little or no swelling, only one or two pipes, and but a very moderate discharge of pus, yet no tendency to heal, and in this condition the animal may live for years, or death may occur at any time, most frequently by blood poisoning taking place.

Usually, however, the disease progresses, rapidly or slowly and unless cured the termination will be death by blood poisoning, or by paralysis through the spinal cord becoming affected, or by sheer exhaustion, or the animal is humanely destroyed to end his misery.

Some Wrong Ideas

It is wrong to suppose, as many do, that as soon as the swelling is observed a knife should be plunged into it. If you use the knife at all, which is seldom necessary, wait until the disease has become well centered, and a soft spot upon the swelling indicates that pus has formed and is not far below the surface. You may be sure that nature is doing the best she can to correct the trouble, and by opening the part too soon you interfere with rather than assist her efforts, and are apt to find no pus at all, but only a peculiar watery seepage of the tissues.

It is also a mistake to suppose that where pus has formed there must be an opening for drainage downward and outward from the bottom of the cavity. The pus is not the disease, nor will its presence interfere with the healing when a healthy state of the tissues has been established. Neither will the pus burrow down into the tissues, extending the area of disease. Its tendency is toward the least resistance, which is upward or toward the surface in a case of Fistula. Where the pus seems to go deeper or lower down, it is merely a case of disease going there first and forming it. The only exception is that in an occasional rare case pus may get between the skin and flesh, and the skin being tough and easily lifted from the flesh, it may work along under it instead of breaking through.

But the most absurd mistake of all is to regard the pipes as being the disease. The pipes are there for a good rather than an evil purpose, and are needed while the diseased condition exists. Treat to cure the disease, and not to destroy or remove the pipes. They will disappear when there is no further use for them. A large percentage of these cases may be successfully treated and cured by a veterinarian. The treatment, however, as in Poll Evil, often has to be continued for many weeks. In cases where surgical operation is necessary, permanent scars may be left.

49

Treating Incipient Fistula

When the swelling appears, note whether it is hot and sensitive. If it is, bathe the part with cold water for twenty to thirty minutes three times a day for several days until the temperature is reduced. If there is no excess of heat the cold water applications are not required. Antibiotics are quite effective. Brucella vaccine has been used.

Poll Evil

Read all that is said regarding Fistula of the Withers, remembering that Poll Evil is fistula of the poll, having the same general characteristics and requiring the same treatment. Constant irritation by a tightly fitting halter or bridle may start this condition.

The poll is the region behind the ears, and the swelling may appear upon one of both sides, developing in practically the same manner that Fistula does.

Owing to the proximity to the brain and spinal cord, sudden death occurs from Poll Evil oftener than from Fistula.

 Sometimes where the joint between the head and first bone of the neck, or the joint between the first two bones of the neck, becomes affected the animal's neck will be stiff, and in an occasional case the damage is such that more or less stiffness remains after a cure is effected. The only wonder is that this does not occur oftener, when we consider that the usual seat if Poll Evil is in direct contact with the bone, and that there is permanent stiffness in probably less than one per cent of all cases. The horse may become "touchy" about the head and ears, making it difficult to halter or bridle him. Much can be done to prevent both of these conditions by eliminating possible sources of injury. Prevention is much easier than cure.

Sunstroke

Sunstroke is due to violent or too prolonged exertion under a burning summer sun. When the day is hot, rest your horse and give him water often. If he lags or staggers, take him to a shade place at once, give him a long rest, and if possible a stimulant, half a pint of whisky or two ounces of aromatic spirits of ammonia in half a pint of water.

If the attack is severe and the horse lags, droops his head, stops, pants violently and falls to the ground in an unconscious state, lose no time in dashing cold water upon him, not only upon the head and neck, but over the entire body. Give him the whisky or aromatic spirits of ammonia every hour, and continue incessantly the applications of water until either the animal dies or consciousness returns. If recovery ensues, the horse should have rest for a month, with wholesome food and plenty of cold water to drink. For ten days or so give one dram sulphate of iron each morning in bran mash, and two drams nitrate of potash in drinking water each evening.

Spasms or Cramps

Either name is applied to involuntary muscular contraction, a muscle or set of muscles becoming very hard and rigid, and the animal powerless to move them. This may occur as a symptom in connection with some specific disease, but sometimes comes on by itself and without apparent cause, and it is cases of the latter kind that we are now referring to.

The cramp may come on suddenly, last for but a few minutes and never return, or there may be a tendency to cramp at short intervals. In other cases the cramp may last for hours or even days, then pass off suddenly, there being no certainty as to whether it will return or not. It is probable that the trouble is due to some affection or distrubance of the nerve centers.

If the cramps are of considerable duration or attacks recur, give the horse a physic, one ounce each of aloes and ginger dissolved in a pint or more of hot water and allowed to cool.

51

Follow with half a dram of nux vomica and one dram of sulphate of iron night and morning in bran mesh for about ten days. Apply soap liniment to the affected muscle, rubbing in well once or twice a day.

Tetanus or Lockjaw

Lockjaw is an affection of the nerves and muscles resulting from inoculation with the tetanus germ, which produces the most virulent toxin known. It is apt to follow a nail puncture or any similar wound that closes or heals first on the outside. The reason for this is that the tetanus germ remains inert in the presence of the oxygen that is in the air, but multiplies if the outer part of the wound closes so that all air is excluded. Consequently an open sore or large open wound is not conductive to lockjaw, but even so slight a prick that it passes unnoticed may produce it. Before the tetanus germ was discovered, it was supposed that lockjaw sometimes resulted from constitutional causes, this theory arising from the fact that the disease developed in animals that, as they thought, had received no injury. The germs cannot crawl and enter a wound of their own accord, nor can they propagate by coming in contact with a sore and sticking fast. They are imbedded in the flesh by the instrument that does the injury, and this, together with what is said above, explains why even small punctured wounds are dangerous and should have careful treatment.

The symptoms are general stiffness and hardness of the muscles of the jaws, neck, loins or hind legs. The tail may be held erect, or the neck stiff with nose poked forward, and the haw or membrane at the inner corner of the eye will extend partially over the eyeball, and the animal is easily excited, which tends to aggravate the various symptoms.

As yet no reliable treatment has been devised; anyway, none has become generally recognized as a cure, so various methods are employed and the ailment is frequently fatal. We will mention three treatments, each of which is said to have given good results.

Pure carbolic acid in five per cent solution, one dram administered every two hours by hypodermic injection into the neck or shoulders. After twenty-four to thirty-six hours, administer less frequently until symptoms subside.

Another method is to give a large quantity of bromide of potassium, two-ounce doses four time a day, and continue until the muscles relax.

The third is the serum treatment, injecting tetanus anti-toxin according to the directions supplied with it.

Keep the patient in a quiet and darkened place where there will be nothing to excite him.

Large doses of penicillin are sometimes effective.

Azoturia

Suppose that a horse has been at heavy work and has been allowed an abundance of nourishing food. Then comes a period of rest and he stands in the stable, perhaps only a few days, still eating hearty rations. When he is to be used again he comes from the stable full of life and energy, but presently hangs back, appears stiff in the hind parts, shows lameness, a profuse sweat breaks out, the muscles of the loins and hips swell and become very hard, and if urine is passed it is very highly colored. A little later the animal may lose all control of the hind legs, go down, and will be unable to rise. Death is apt to follow in a few hours or days, or the horse may improve and recover. This is Azoturia.

If you are driving or working a horse that has been idle several days and observe signs of stiffness in the hind parts, stop immediately and let him stand an hour or two, for exercise aggravates the attack. Likely you can then get him back to the stable, for as a rule the trouble comes on before you get very far away. Then give him a purgative dose of aloes and feed bran mashes or other light food for a few days.

In severe cases where the animal goes down, call a veterinarian if there is one within reach. If not, use copious injections of warm soap suds to clear the bowels, cover the loins with a blanket wrung out of boiling water, and a dry blanket on top of it to retain the heat. Change the blankets every twenty minutes or so.

Give one ounce each of sweet spirits of nitre and aromatic spirits of ammonia in a pint of cold water every hour until four doses have been given. Allow all the cold water the animal will drink, and as much salt as he will eat. Draw urine with a catheter if necessary. Antihistamines have shown good results in some cases. One ounce of chloral hydrate relieves the pain.

When the horse gets on his feet give him a dose of aloes and feed moderately on mashes.

Regular daily exercise will prevent Azoturia. When a horse is idle feed him accordingly, and when putting him to work again break him in gradually.

Poisoning from Plants

Animals are sometimes taken with peculiar symptoms, scarcely resembling any known disease, and death may follow, the cause remaining a complete mystery. It is probable that a considerable percentage of such cases are due to eating some poisonous plant in the pasture, or possibly in the hay.

We recall one instance where thirty animals, horses, mules and cattle, died in one pasture within a few weeks, and though the carcasses were all removed to an adjoining pasture and some of them were neither buried nor burned, not an animal in the second pasture became affected. Whether the mystery was ever solved we do not know, but such an occurrence would suggest the presence of some poisonous weed in the deadly pasture, or, as seems less probably, local germ infection of some unknown kind.

The following has been suggested by the Department of Agriculture, and is probably the best general antidote for plant poisoning. For a horse, fifteen to twenty grains each of permanganate of potash and aluminum sulphate, dissolved in a pint to a quart of water. Twice this quantity may be given to cattle. The dose may be repeated every twelve hours until three or four doses have been given if necessary. The solution must be fresh, and cannot be made up beforehand as it deteriorates very quickly. Be sure that the drugs are completely dissolved before you give it.

Though it is rather difficult to illustrate or describe plants in such a way that they may be readily recognized, we will refer briefly to a few that are more or less troublesome. A veterinarian should be called as soon as any poisoning is suspected. There are specific antedotes for most poisons.

Sorghum

There remains considerable to be learned upon the subject of sorghum poisoning. That under some conditions the plant may be poisonous to stock seems to be well established, though it is often eaten freely without bad effect. It is probable that the small, scrubby and stunted plants are most apt to produce poisoning, and cattle seem to be more susceptible than other animals. Sorghum poisoning acts very quickly, and the affected animal usually dies before anything can be done in the way of treatment. When turning stock into a field in which sorghum is growing, it might be a wise precaution to risk only a single animal first. Frost on growing sorghum seems to enhance formation of the deadly prussic acid.

Poison Hemlock

This plant occurs principally in the Eastern States, very little of it being found in the Mississippi Valley. It grows in a scattering way, there usually being only a plant or two in one place, and is very poisonous. It varies in height from two to six feet, has a smooth hollow stem with purple spots, leaves somewhat like parsley, and clusters of white blossoms appear in July or August. The leaves have a rank and disagreeable taste and odor. The poison is contained in the leaves and seeds, and also the root late in the season.

The most noticeable symptoms produced by poison hemlock are usually general and increasing weakness, more or less evidence of pain, excessive flow of saliva, loss of appetite, and partial blindness. When fatal, death results from paralysis of the respiratory organs.

Water Hemlock

This plant is known by several names, among them being spotted cowbane, spotted parsley, wild hemlock, and snake weed. It grows mostly on low and marshy ground, and is found from the Eastern Coast to the Rocky Mountains. It is a stout weed two to five feet high, has rather an upright or erect appearance, the stalk is hollow and marked with purple, and the blossoms are white and formed in clusters. The stalk springs from a cluster of large fleshy roots, which are the most poisonous part of the plant. The symptoms produced are similar to those of Poison Hemlock, and in addition there will likely be convulsions.

Oregon Water Hemlock

This species of hemlock is found in Oregon and other states of the northwest. It grows principally in damp or marshy places, and has white flowers that appear in midsummer. It is somewhat bushy in appearance, leaf stems springing from the root at the ground. The root is large and rather odd in formation and it is this part that is most poisonous.

The symptoms are nausea, straggling gait, pains in the abdominal regions, convulsions, etc. This is a very dangerous poisoning and recovery is doubtful.

Rattlebox

This is a small, fuzzy plant, seldom growing higher than eighteen inches, and having rather long, narrow and tapering leaves, each growing on a very short stem by itself. The blossoms resemble those of the common pea, and the seeds form in pods of a very dark color and an inch or so in length. These seeds loosen and rattle in the pods when ripe, hence the name. It is found throughout a large section of the country, and is probably most abundant in the vicinity of the Missouri River. It has caused considerable loss, and seems to be more dangerous in hay than in the pastures.

The poison acts slowly in the system, and the animals appears sleepy, shows some difficulty in breathing, and gradually declines. Ordinarily no treatment is needed, but it should be seen to that he gets no more of the rattlebox. If considerably affected a good general tonic may be given to assist the animal in regaining his strength.

Stemless Loco

The stemless loco is another variety of the weed, found over about the same territory as the wooly loco. It is more erect, has fewer branches and is not so bushy in appearence. The foliage springs from the root at the surface of the ground, the leaves are longer, narrow and quite pointed, and the seed pod has but a single cell instead of two.

The two varieties produce similar if not identical symptoms. The poison acts slowly, and when a horse is affected he loses flesh, becomes nervous, has an unsteady gait, and apparently becomes deranged mentally. Death follows in two to eight months unless he is prevented from eating more of the plant, which he will do if he can get it, as he acquires a strong liking for it. The effects of the poisoning are seen for a long time, even in cases that recover. As already stated, there is as yet no satisfactory treatment for loco poisoning.

Wild Cherry

The leaves of the wild cherry, and especially those on the young shoots or sprouts, contain considerable prussic acid, which is a very active poison when a sufficient quantity is taken. Few animals will eat these leaves to the extent of poisoning themselves, but occasionally one does and death follows quickly by paralysis of the respiratory organs. The symptoms are rapid and difficult breathing, staring eyes and a frightened appearance, week pulse, and the breath has a peach-pit odor. Wilted leaves are most harmful. If seen in time, a veterinarian can give an intravenous antedote that is very effective, but time is of the essence in this as in most poisoning cases. With prussic acid they generally have only a few hours to live without treatment.

Wooly Loco

Loco is a source of much trouble and loss upon the Western plains, and is more or less common throughout the semi-arid regions of the country. Considerable disputing has been done as to whether the plant actually contains a poisonous principle, various theories being advanced to account for the symptons it produces. It now seems to be generally accepted that loco is poisonous, though up to this time no antidote has been found.

The wooly loco, here illustrated, grows from six to twelve inches high, there being a considerable cluster of soft silvery white foliage branching out from a single stem slightly above the surface of the ground. The flowers are mostly purple, resembling pea blossoms, and the seeds grow in a pod composed of two cells.

MINOR AILMENTS OF HORSES

In order to prevent complications of disease arising out of apparently simple ailments or injuries, all animals affected should be treated as early as possible. If a veterinarian is not available considerable care can be given by the average horseman if he is able to recognize the symptoms. Following are some of the most common ailments encountered and the first aid treatments recommended. If an improved condition is not readily evident after first aid treatments call a veterinarian immediately.

Heat Exhaustion

Overheating and sunstroke. These are noncommunicable disturbances of the nervous system due to heat.

1. *Cause:* Caused by long continued hard or fast work during very humid weather, especially among animals not in good condition or having heavy coats.

2. *Prevention:* Do not overtax the strength of the animal. Watch animals for early symptoms. Clip animals that have heavy coats. Water frequently on hot days and give the horse an ample supply of salt.

3. *Symptoms:* Thumps, a condition described in a later paragraph, often precedes overheating. The animal that has been sweating freely will cease to sweat and will be dull and the gait is staggering or wobbly, especially in the hindquarters. If halted, the animal stands with the legs spraddled; breathing very rapidly and shallow; nostrils dilated; expression drawn and anxious: nasal membranes bluish red in color; and trembling of body muscles. The body feels hot to the

Plate VI

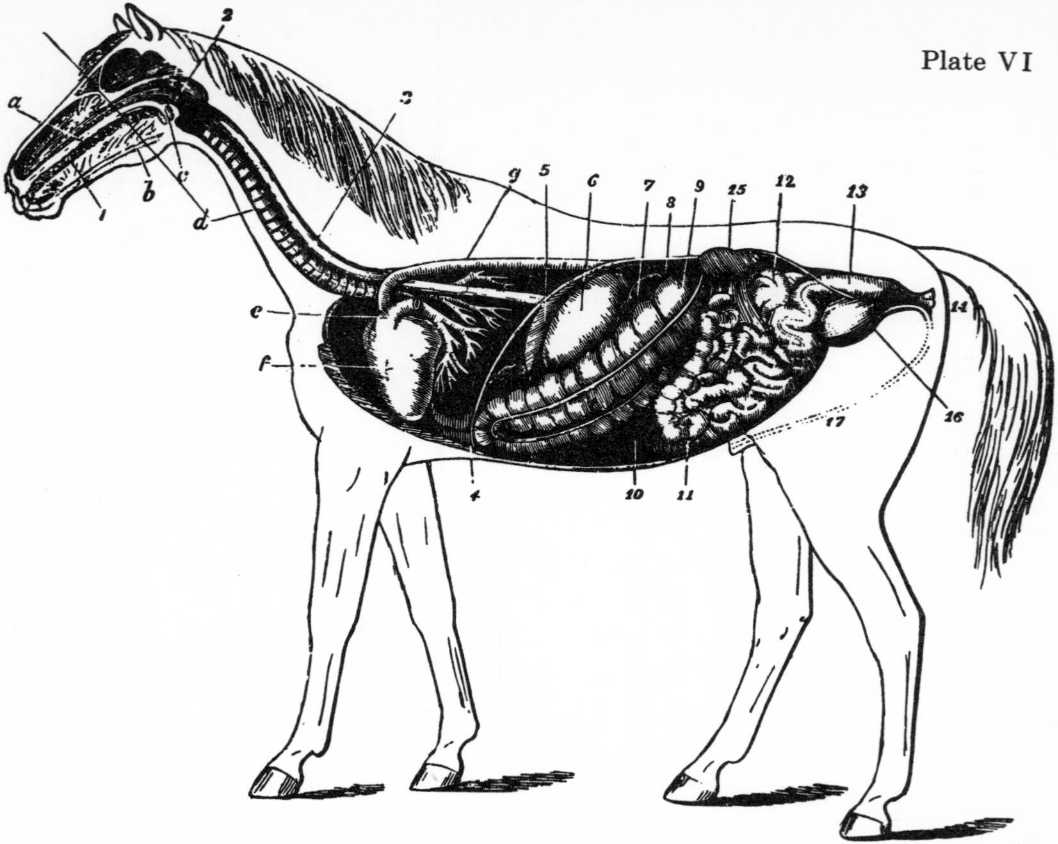

DIGESTIVE AND MALE URINARY APPARATUS OF A HORSE—*after Megnin.*

EXPLANATION OF PLATE VI.

Digestive Apparatus of the Horse.

1. Mouth.
2. Pharynx.
3. Œsophagus.
4. Diaphragm.
5. Spleen.
6. Stomach (left sac).
7. Duodenum.
8. Liver (upper extremity).
9. Great colon.
10. Caecum.

11. Small intestine.
12. Floating colon.
13. Rectum.
14. Anus.
15. Left kidney and ureter.
16. Bladder.
17. Urethra.
A. Hard palate.
B. Tongue.
C. Soft palate.

D. Trachea.
E. Pulmonary artery (divided).
F. Heart.
G. Posterior aorta.

hand and the temperature will be from 103 to 109 degrees F.

4. *Nursing and First-aid Treatment:* Prompt first-aid treatment is of utmost importance. Stop the animal at once in the shade if any is nearby. Remove the equipment and apply large quantities of cold water to all parts of the body but especially to the head, sides of the neck, groin, and flanks. Wash out the mouth and nostrils with cold water. Give the animal three or four swallows of water every few minutes. Under this treatment the temperature will drop quite rapidly, and as improvement is noted move the animal about very slowly and rub the body to prevent chilling. As soon as the temperature is near normal, the animal may be moved slowly into the barn. The use of cold water in rectum prohibits obtaining of correct temperature readings which are very important. If temperature is lowered too much, the animal is apt to die of shock.

Thumps

Thumps are spasms of the diaphragm.

(1) *Cause:* Overwork or fast work during hot weather especially among animals not properly conditioned.

(2) *Symptoms:* General symptoms of fatigue with spasmodic jerking noticeable in the belly and flanks; frequently a distinct thumping sound will be heard.

(3) *Nursing and First-aid Treatment:* If riding away from the stable, halt the animal and if the temperature is elevated, reduce it by sponging the body with cold water and then have the animal ridden or led into the stable at the walk.

Exhaustion

(1) *Causes:* Over exertion; excessive or prolonged heavy work; lack of condition.

(2) *Symptoms:* After the animal arrives in stable, he may lie down and refuse his feed, especially his grain, yet drink considerable quantities of water. The temperature may be

slightly elevated and the pulse may be weak and thready. Sweating may be quite noticeable and possibly patchy, yet the body feels cold and clammy.

(3) *Nursing and First-aid Treatment:* Make a comfortable place for the animal to lie. Cover the body with a blanket to prevent chilling. Hand rub the legs. Give small amounts of water frequently. A period of rest is all that is needed to recuperate from excessive fatigue.

Colic

A general term applied to abdominal pain caused by digestive disturbance either spasmodic and flatulent or gas colic.

(1) *Causes:* The causes of both types of colic are very similar, but gas colic is more frequently caused by foods fermenting in the digestive tract. General causes are indigestible or spoiled feed, sudden changes in feed, overeating, eating while fatigued, working too soon after feeding, watering while exhausted or hot bolting the feed, overeating of green feed, and watering too soon after feeding. Windsucking or "cribbing" is frequently a cause of gas colic. Collections of sand in the bowel may result in repeated attacks of colic.

(2) *Prevention:* Close attention to the principles of feeding and watering will prevent most cases of colic.

(3) *Symptoms:* Pain as indicated by restlessness, pawing, stamping of the feet, looking around at the flanks, kicking at the abdomen, lying down, rolling, sweating, and frequent attempts to defecate usually resulting in the passage of but a few pellets of dung or a discharge of gas. In spasmodic form, the attacks are often intermittent with short periods of a few minutes of apparent freedom from pain. In the gas type of colic, the digestive tract is filled with gas, the belly is distended, and breathing is difficult.

(4) *Nursing and First-aid Treatment:* Place the animal in a well-bedded box stall. Get a veterinarian at once, if possible. Do not attempt to keep the animal from rolling, etc., unless he is throwing himself to the ground so violently that it is evident he may rupture some organ. Give frequent

rectal injections of 2 or 3 gallons of warm soapy water. Wring blankets out of hot water and wrap around the belly and flanks as hot as can be borne without burning the hands or animal. Water may be given in small amounts. Withhold all feed until at least 12 hours after all pain has disappeared and then feed lightly for 2 or 3 days.

Diarrhea

(1) *Causes:* Spoiled feed, overfeeding, of "washy" feeds, sudden changes of diet; and nervousness.

(2) *Prevention:* Careful attention to kind, quality, and quantity of feed and methods of feeding. Exclude "washy" feeds from the diet of animals which tend to scour.

(3) *Symptoms:* The droppings are frequent and of semi-fluid nature. If the condition continues long, the animal looses flesh and appetite is wanting.

(4) *Nursing and First-aid Treatment:* Correction of diet in mild cases will be sufficient. A veterinarian should be called in cases that do not show immediate results.

Azoturia

(1) *Cause:* Caused by violent exercise following idleness and heavy feeding.

(2) *Prevention:* When conditioned animals accustomed to regular work are given a period of complete rest for longer than a day, reduce the grain ration by at least one-half. When animals are exercised after a period of rest, they should be walked for at least 20 minutes after leaving the stables and not called upon to do more than a very small amount of fast work the first day.

(3) *Symptoms:* Increased excitability, profuse sweating, and rapid breathing are the first symptoms. Very soon the animal begins to stiffen in his hindquarters, drag the hind legs and knuckles over in the hind fetlocks. If continued in work the animal will become completely incapable of sup-

porting weight on the hind legs and fall to the ground, and in such cases the chances of recovery are remote. The urine is scanty and red or coffee-colored.

(4) *Nursing and First-aid Treatment:* Stop the animal immediately when the first symptoms are noticed. Remove the saddle or harness and cover with three or four blankets. Keep the animal standing, if possible; if not, provide a good bed. Heat some oats or common salt, place in a sack and spread over the loins to relieve the pain. If hot water is available, a hot blanket wrung out, placed over the back and loins, and covered with dry blankets is very beneficial. After a few hours the average case can be moved slowly to the stable, provided the distance is not too great. At this time he should be given a purgative which may be obtained from a veterinarian and be fed on bran mashes, grass, and hay for a few days.

Laminitis (Founder)

(1) *Causes:* Overeating grain, eating improper or spoiled feeds, colic, exhaustion, overexertion, long continued work on hard-surfaced roads, and drinking cold water while sweating.

(2) *Symptoms:* Intense lameness, which appears quickly. In mild cases the animal moves stiffly, taking short, rapid steps with the forefeet and with the hind legs carried well forward under the body to relieve the forefeet from the weight of the body. Usually only the forefeet are affected and the affected feet are very hot. The pulse and respiration are greatly accelerated and temperature may reach 105 degrees F.

(3) *Nursing and First-aid Treatment:* Remove the shoes from the affected feet and place the animal in a well-bedded box stall. Cover the affected feet and legs as high as the knees and hocks with several layers of burlap and keep saturated with cold water. (In this case the shoes need not be removed.) Laxative diet is indicated. Feed bran mashes and a little hay. Early treatment is an important factor. Cases

that are not cured in 4 or 5 days are likely to develop into chronic laminitis which is practically incurable. As soon as the acute pain has diminished, moderate walking exercise each day is beneficial. Following the attack, shoe with a bar shoe over a leather pad covering a tar and oakum pack. The horse should be induced to lie down. Moisture can be applied to the feet by packs as soon as the fever in the feet is noticed.

Scratches

An inflammation in the back of the pasten region.

(1) *Causes:* Wet muddy, and filthy surroundings; failure to dry legs that have become wet from slush, rain, or washing; pasterns not thoroughly cleaned while grooming; short clipping of hair on the back of the pastern. Most prevalent during wet, cold weather.

(2) *Symptoms:* Redness, heat, pain and swelling of the skin on the back of the pastern. Later the surface of the skin becomes moist and raw, and dust and dirt dry with the secretions to form a scabby mass sticking to the skin and hair. The skin may crack. Usually there is lameness.

(3) *Nursing and First-aid Treatment:* With soap and warm water carefully soak off all accumulated dirt and dried secretion. Rinse with clean, warm water and dry. Apply a white lotion pack under a bandage twice daily. Rest the animal on clean, dry standings and feed laxative feeds. After the moistness of the skin has decreased apply dry powdered boric acid or tamic acid held in place by cotton in a loose bandage. Avoid the use of water after the first cleansing.

Thrush

(1) *Causes:* Failure to clean out the depths of the commissures and cleft of the frog, lack of frog pressure, filthy standings, dryness of the feet, and cuts or tears in the horny frog are all contributing causes.

(2) *Prevention:* A hoof that is properly groomed once each day will not develop thrush. A thorough washing of the under surface of the hoof once a week will materially assist in prevention of this disease.

(3) *Symptoms:* Cracks, depressions, or fissures in the horn of the frog in which is found a thick, dark colored discharge with a very offensive odor. The cleft of the frog and the sides of the frog at the depths of the commissures are the parts usually diseased.

(4) *Nursing and First-aid Treatment:* Clean and wash the hoof. With a sharp hoof knife, trim away all diseased and torn horn and all ragged pieces. With cresolis solution (one and one-half teaspoonfuls to a cup of water) and stiff brush thoroughly scrub the horn. After it has dried, paint the area with iodine. Repeat the washing and iodine treatment daily until the horn begins to appear dry and then apply pine tar.

Tendonitis

Tendonitis is an inflammation of the large tendons on the back of the leg in the cannon region.

(1) *Causes:* A strain of these tendons; long toes and low heels; violent efforts and sudden checks, as in jumping or galloping over rocky, uneven ground; long-continued exertion in which the muscles tire and are more easily strained; lack of fit condition; tight bandaging.

(2) *Prevention:* Proper balance and shoeing of the feet. Have the animal in good, fit condition. Avoid other causes of the injury.

(3) *Symptoms:* Lameness; heat and swelling in the tendon, sensitiveness of the tendon to pressure. The tendons of the forelegs are far more frequently affected than are those of the hind legs. The tendons in the cannon region may be affected their entire length or only in a part of their length.

(4) *Nursing and First-aid Treatment:* Absolute rest is most essential. Shower the leg with cold water from a hose or apply cold or ice water packs throughout the day, and for the night apply a white lotion pack over the injured tendon.

After the acute swelling and tenderness have disappeared, bathe with hot water and massage, then rub the tendon briskly with tincture of iodine once daily.

Rope Burn

This is an injury usually occurring on the back of the pastern.

(1) *Causes:* Tying with the tie rope too long is the most frequent cause. Often caused by the animal getting his foot, usually a hind foot, over his own or an adjacent horse's tie rope or entangled in a picket line guy rope. An improperly made or improperly used side line of casting rope often results in rope burns.

(2) *Symptoms:* A simple chafe or abrasion of the skin. It may involve the underlying tendon. Lameness is usually a symptom.

(3) *Nursing and First-aid Treatment:* General methods of treatment same as for scratches (in a preceding paragraph) except that white lotion packs should not be used if the injury is more than a surface one.

Lameness

(1) Lameness may best be detected at the trot. When an animal is lame it takes as much weight as possible off the injured leg and places it on the opposite one. If lame in a foreleg, the animal will be seen to nod its head every time the sound foot comes to the ground. If lame behind, the hock of the sound leg comes higher and dips lower than that of the lame one, and the head may nod as the lame foot strikes the ground. Animals lame in both fore and hind legs take short strides with both; they idle along instead of striding out.

(2) Most cases of lameness occur at or below the knee and hock. The foot is the most common seat. Lameness in the shoulder is comparatively rare. In all cases where no apparent or sufficient cause can be detected the foot should be thoroughly examined.

Fractures

A fracture is a broken bone.

(1) *Causes:* Most fractures result from kicks inflicted by other animals. The bone forming the point of the hip may be fractured by falling on the side or by striking it against the side of a door.

(2) *Symptoms:* When any long supporting bone of the leg is completely fractured, the leg dangles helplessly and will bear no weight. When the bone forming the point of the hip is fractured the animal may show but few symptoms other than lameness, difficulty in advancing the hind leg on that side, tenderness and swelling over the seat of injury, and a noticeable lowering of the point of the hip on that side.

(3) *Nursing and First-aid Treatment:* Complete fractures of any of the supporting bones of the legs of horses or mules are generally considered incurable, and the destruction of the animal is usually advisable. Fracture of the bone forming the point of the hip will heal provided the animal is given a complete rest for a month or six weeks.

Sprains

A sprain is a joint injury usually without any break or injury of the overlying skin.

(1) *Causes:* Twisting or pulling of the joint or bending the joint beyond its normal range of action resulting in stretching or tearing of the ligaments.

(2) *Symptoms:* Marked lameness; heat and swelling over the joint; tenderness on pressure or manipulation.

(3) *Nursing and First-aid Treatment:* Treatment should be the same as outlined for Tendonitis.

Wounds

(1) *Classification.* Wounds are diveded into—
    a. Incised wounds or cuts.

b. Lacerated wounds or tears.

c. Punctured wounds or holes.

(2) *Treatment:*

a. Cleanliness of the wound itself, of the dressing and the dresser is of the greatest importance.

b. To stop bleeding: Stoppage of bleeding is the first point to be attended to. Tight bandaging above and below the wound or a pad on the wound is usually sufficient to control the flow. If a large blood vessel is cut and the end exposed, it should be tied around with clean thread which has been soaked in antiseptic.

c. *To clean:* Cut the hair from the edges of the wound and remove all dirt, clots of blood, splinters, and foreign bodies of all kinds. This may be done by carefully syringing the parts with clean warm water or a warm antiseptic solution.

d. *To close:* Sutures and bandages are used for this purpose, but no wound that has been dirty must ever be entirely closed. Sutures may be used in parts where there is little flesh, such as around the forehead, eyelids, and nose. They are less useful in the fleshy parts, because the movements of the muscles and swelling cause them to pull out.

e. *Drainage:* Drainage at the lowert part of the wound is necessary for the removal of pus. In horizontal wounds a small vertical opening must be made below the line of the stitches.

f. *Dressing:* Wounds should be dried carefully with gauze or cotton, treated with an antiseptic, covered with dry gauze or cotton, and a bandage applied; or cotton soaked in antiseptic may be put on and held in position by a bandage, care being taken to avoid undue pressure. If the location will not permit bandaging, the injured parts may be treated with an antiseptic and covered with a clean piece of cloth or gunny sack, the inside of which may be lined with a piece of gauze large enough to cover the wound. Bandaging for too long a period may prevent the area from covering itself with skin, resulting in proud flesh. After a wound has begun to granulate (fill in with repair tissue), it will often heal much better if no dressing or bandage is placed in contact with the wound, provided it is not irritated by flies.

g. *Rest and Restraint:* If the injury is slight, the animal may continue at work; otherwise he may be kept in a box stall, cross-tied, or subjected to some other form of restraint.

h. *After Care:* All wounds should be kept dry and dressings should be changed only often enough to keep the wound clean. As little washing as possible should be done, and the parts should be sopped instead of rubbed.

i. *Flies:* The healing of wounds that cannot be covered is sometimes retarded by the presence of flies. The edges of such wounds, and also the surface if not too moist, may be covered lightly with pine tar.

j. *Pround Flesh (Excessive Granulations):* In sluggish, slow-healing wounds small, rounded fleshly masses are called proud flesh. The growth may be kept down by removing with scissors to the level of the skin and treated with boric acid, tincture of iodine, powered burned alum or by searing to the level of the skin with a heated iron, care being taken to see that the surrounding skin is not burned. Inoculation for Tetanus (lockjaw) should be considered in any case where there is chance of infection.

Contusions (Bruises)

A contusion is an injury of a part without breaking the overlying skin.

(1) *Causes:* Blow from a blunt object. Being kicked is a common cause.

(2) *Symptoms:* When over a muscle, they produce soreness and lameness and, if severe, may rupture a blood vessel which will result in a fluctuating swelling caused by an accumulation of blood usually just under the skin. Such injuries are most common on the thigh and buttocks. Contusions over a joint may be mistaken for a sprain of the joint.

(3) *Nursing and First-aid Treatment:* Rest and general method of treatment as outlined for tendonitis. In bruises where a fluctuating swelling results that does not reduce in a week or ten days, the swelling may be opened with a knife

at its lowest point to allow the fluid contents to escape. After opening, the external parts should be kept clean and the external wound painted with iodine once daily.

Summer Sores

(1) *Cause:* Apparently due to the effects of irritation of an ordinary wound by flies. They invariably occur during hot weather when flies are most prevalent.

(2) *Prevention:* Protect all wounds from flies by appropriate dressings or medicinal application.

(3) *Symptoms:* The wound tends to form proud flesh rapidly, and the surface of the area is porous and expels a considerable amount of thin discharge. Near the surface of the proud flesh and in its depths may often be found small, hard, grayish or yellowish bodies having much the appearance of cracked corn.

(4) *Nursing and First-aid Treatment:* Remove pronounced growth of proud flesh. Thereafter treat as other wounds with special protection from flies.

Eye Injuries

(1) *Causes:* Eye injuries are usually due to blows, scratches, or punctures from brush, forage, etc., and to small objects lodging on the front of the eyeball or under the lids.

(2) *Symptoms:* Watery eye, flow of tears from the eye, reddened membranes, and partial or complete closing of the eye are symptoms of all forms of injury. If the cornea or clear part of the eyeball itself is injured, the cut or wound may be visible, and surrounding it the eye will become milky white in color. Ordinarily foreign matter merely lodged behind the lids does not cause the eyeball to become milky in color.

(3) *Nursing and First-aid Treatment:* If there is any foreign body under the lids, flood it out with clean water using a syringe, or remove by the careful use of a tightly rolled

swab of cotton or gauze. Then flood the eye several times daily with boric acid solution prepared by dissolving two level teaspoons of boric acid in a cupful of warm water. Use an eye dropper for this purpose. Cover the eye with a pad of cotton about 6 inches square covered with gauze, and hold in position with strings tied about the head and to the halter, or sew the pad on the inside of an improvised head bandage made from a grain sack. In bad cases, soak the pad in boric acid solution before applying. Keep the animal in a dark place.

Treads and Overreaching

(1) *Causes:* Treads are injuries or wounds in the coronet on the front or sides of the feet which may be self-inflicted or inflicted by the shoes of other animals. They are caused frequently by animals crowding in stables, through doors, and in shipment. Overreaching wounds are selfinflicted and are injuries to the bulbs of heels, pastern, or fetlock, caused by the animal's hind foot striking the part. Those injuries are most frequently inflicted when landing after jumping an obstacle, at the extended trot, and at times at the gallop. Wounds similar to overreaching wounds are often caused on the heels of the hind feet by another horse crowding up on the animals from the rear.

(2) *Prevention:* The nature of some cases suggests the means of prevention. Shoeing with rocker-toed and high heels which speed up the action of the forefeet is often beneficial. Jumping horses, in which the injury cannot be prevented otherwise, should be jumped with bell boots.

(3) *Symptoms:* Treads wounds usually are in the coronet and the skin, and often some of the horn at the top of the hoof is torn. There is usually heat and swelling in the part. Most overreaching wounds occur at the bulbs of the heel; the skin above the horn is more bruised and scraped than cut; and the horn at the heel is torn loose and may be separated from the sensitive tissues, or the wound becomes infected.

(4) *Nursing and First-aid Treatment:* For either injury clip the hair around the wound and clean thoroughly with cresolis solution, removing all foreign material. With scissors cut off all loose flaps of skin or tissue and, with a hoof knife or rasp, thin somewhat the horn in the region of the injury. Saturate a small piece of cotton with iodine and bandage tightly over the injury. Dress in this manner daily. When the wound appears dry and is healing, cover with tar and a small pad of oakum and bandage tightly.

Interfering Wounds

Interfering wounds are self-inflicted wounds made on some part of the inside of the leg, usually the fetlock, by being struck by the hoof or shoe of the opposite leg.

(1) *Causes:* Defective conformation, such as toeing out, cow-hocked, and narrow breasted; defective shoeing; and traveling over uneven footing. Fatigued animals are more likely to interfere behind.

(2) *Prevention:* Corrective shoeing, etc. If not correctable, use leather or felt interfering boots, or pad the part with oakum held in place with a bandage.

(3) *Symptoms:* The injury may vary from a slight roughing of the hair at the coronet or inside of the fetlock to a deep wound causing marked lameness. At the moment of interfering, an animal will often carry the leg for a few steps without putting weight on it, then go very lame for a few steps and soon proceed without lameness.

(4) *Nursing and First-aid Treatment:* Treat the same as other wounds. Apply a thick, padded dressing to avoid further injury.

Penetrating Wounds of the Foot

(1) *Causes:* Most penetrating wounds of the foot are caused by the animal stepping on nails or screws or by a misdirected shoeing nail.

(2) *Nursing and First-aid Treatment:* If the nail is still imbedded in the horn, clean all dirt from the bottom of the foot by washing and then wash with cresolis solution before removing it. Remove the nail or other object, and with a knife, thin the horn over a fair-sized area surrounding the penetration and make a final opening about ⅛ to ¼ inch in diameter through the horn to the sensitive tissue. Saturate a rather small piece of cotton with tincture of iodine and place it on the wound. Over this place a pad of oakum covering part of all of the bottom of the hoof and hold in place with strips of tin or light sheet metal of such length and width that their ends can be engaged between the hoof and the shoe on the inside and entirely around the shoe. Do not probe the wound in the sensitive tissue and do not compress the dressing so tightly that the secretions are dammed back into the wound. Dress daily with iodine until the wound appears to be dry and healing and then apply a tar dressing under an oakum pack about every 3 days until no further dressing is necessary. Inoculate for tetanus (lockjaw) in any case of penetrating wound.

Dry Feet

(1) *Causes:* Lack of frog pressure, lack of exercise, dry weather, allowing the shoes to remain on the feet too long, and a loss of the wax-like horny covering (periople) of the horny wall.

(2) *Prevention:* Make provision for frog pressure and exercise and animal regularly. During dry weather, pack the bottom of the hoof with wet clay, or turn horse on pasture.

(3) *Symptoms:* The first symptom is the hardness and drying of the horny frog. While dryness in itself may not cause lameness, it is an active cause of contracted heels, corns, thrush, etc.

(4) *Nursing and First-aid Treatment:* The first stop should be to correct errors in shoeing and the second to restore and maintain the normal moisture content of the horn. Moisture may be restored to the horn by packing the feet daily with

wet clay, by standing the animal in a shallow clay mud bath, by wet packs on the feet, or by standing in a foot bath. Turning on grass which is wet or has dew on is helpful, too. Treatment for Quarter Crack: Soften the horn of the wall by wet packs, bran poultices, or standing the animal in water for a few days. After this clean out the crack and cut away the overlapping edges of the horn. For an inch or more on each side of the crack and for 1½ inches or more downward from the coronary band, rasp the wall as thin as possible without injuring the "quick" or drawing blood. For a quarter crack, trim away the bearing surface of the wall from a point ½ inch in front of the crack back to and including the buttress so that the affected quarter does not come in contact with the shoe. Shoe with a bar shoe, with good frog pressure, over a leather pad with tar and oakum. Keep the wall soft with daily application of tar, especially over the crack. A little tar rubbed vigorously into the coronary band once a week will stimulate the growth of horn.

Sore Backs

Sore Backs are probably the greatest cause of disability among riding horses.

(1) *Causes:* Improper saddling, poorly fitted saddles, dirty or improperly folded saddle blankets, careless riding such as lounging in the saddle, unevenly placed loads, and poor conformation.

(2) *Prevention:*

a. The individual rider must be very careful that the adjustment of his saddle is correct and that his blanket is clean and accurately folded. Riders must sit erect in the saddle at all times. Riding on the cantle or standing in one stirrup is sure to bring saddle sores.

b. Intelligent application of the principles of correct saddling can usually overcome poor conformation or poorly fitted saddles. Small pads made from old blankets or strips of felt tacked on the bars of the saddle take the place of lack of flesh.

(3) *Treatment:*

a. Ascertain and remove the cause. In fresh cases where the skin is not broken it is sometimes beneficial to apply cold water baths with gentle hand rubbing. This should be followed by the application of wet packs saturated with cold water and held in position by means of a surcingle or bandage.

b. Injuries to the withers and ridge of the spine should be irrigated or bathed with cold water but without pressure and without massage.

c. Slight galls, chafes, or abrasions are treated with white lotion or powered boric acid.

d. "Sitfasts" are patches of dry dead skin and may involve deeper tissues. They are caused by continuous pressure of the saddle, cinch, or collar. When sitfasts appear, apply warm baths or warm poultices until the dead skin becomes loose. Then remove all dead and bruised tissue with forceps and a knife and treat with iodine and boric acid.

e. If it is necessary to continue to ride an animal with a sore back, means must be devised to relieve pressure from the affected part.

Prevention and Control of Communicable Diseases

(1) *General Health:* Maintain animals in good condition, feed well, groom well, keep in clean surroundings, do not overwork, protect from undue exposure, and they will resist many forms of infection. Animals in rundown condition are very susceptible to disease.

(2) *Segregation:* Animals should be divided into three groups; affected, suspected, and healthy. The suspected animals include all those which have been in contact with the diseased. Attendants, watering and feeding arrangements, and all equipment should be included in the separation and should be kept separate until the outbreak is over. Once an animal is placed in the affected group it should remain there until all danger is over.

(3) *Disinfection:* Strict cleanliness of stalls, equipment,

77

water troughs, feed boxes, and feed bags is a good safeguard against the spread of disease. Stables, equipment, etc., which have been in contact with diseased animals should be disinfected with cresolis solution. Articles that can be boiled may be thoroughly disinfected in this manner.

Influenza

This is a very communicable disease, also known as shipping fever, affecting chiefly the respiratory system. It is spread by both direct and indirect contact.

(1) *Cause:* Influenza is caused by the animal's eating or breathing some of the body discharges of a diseased animal, particularly the nasal and bowel discharges.

(3) *Prevention:* Cleanliness of surroundings and good condition of animals. Quarantine of newly acquired animals for 21 days. Segregation of diseased animals. Disinfection of stall and equipment.

(3) *Symptoms:* The first symptoms noticed are depression, great weakness, loss of appetite, rapid breathing, hacking cough, and possibly a slight watery nasal discharge. At this stage the temperature is elevated (101.5 degrees to 106 degrees F.), and the mucous membrane of the eyelid will have a brick red color tinged with yellow. Later the nasal discharge becomes more profuse and usually thick and yellow. Pneumonia is often a complication. Young animals frequently develop strangles at the same time they have influenza.

(4) *Nursing and First-aid Treatment:* Isolate the diseased animal. Absolute rest and good nursing are very important. Allow plenty of sunshine and fresh air but protect the body from drafts. Keep the animals warm with blankets and leg bandages during cold weather. Induce the animal to eat, as the disease is very wasting and it is important to maintain the strength with feed. Give plenty of water. Do not give cathartics. Preventative vaccines should be given prior to exposure. These are usually given in a series within the last 2 weeks before exposure.

Coughs and Colds

Animals suffer from coughs and colds quite similar to the same conditions in man. They are mildly infectious inflammations of the membranes of the nose and throat.

Strangles and Distemper

This is a communicable disease most often seen in your animals, affecting chiefly the glands in the regions of the throat. It is spread by both direct and indirect contact.

(1) *Cause:* This disease is caused by the infections (nasal, abscess, or other body discharges of a diseased animal) coming in contact with the nasal membranes or the digestive tract.

(2) *Prevention:* The instruction given for prevention of influenza applies also to this disease. The greatest danger of spread is by infected watering and feeding utensils. One attack usually renders the animal immune. There is a fairly effective vaccine available.

(3) *Symptoms:* Early symptoms are loss of appetite, increased temperature, pronounced moist cough, profuse watery nasal discharge which later becomes thick and yellow, head and neck extended stiffly, and a hot and painful swelling between the jaws. The swelling usually develops after about a week into an abscess containing very thick yellow pus. In more serious cases abscesses develop in other parts of the body.

(4) *Nursing and First-aid Treatment:* Segregate sick animals and see that they have absolute rest. Clothe the body according to the weather and prevent drafts but provide plenty of fresh air. Paint the swelling between the jaws with tincture of iodine once daily. Tempt the appetite and provide feed that is easily chewed. Clean the discharge from the nostrils two or three times daily with cresolis solution of strength for washing wounds, and after abscess opens, clean two or three times daily with same solution.

Oxyuris curvula

Sclerostoma armatum.

Spiroptera microstoma.

Sclerostoma tetracanthum.

Ascaris megalocephala.

INTESTINAL WORMS.

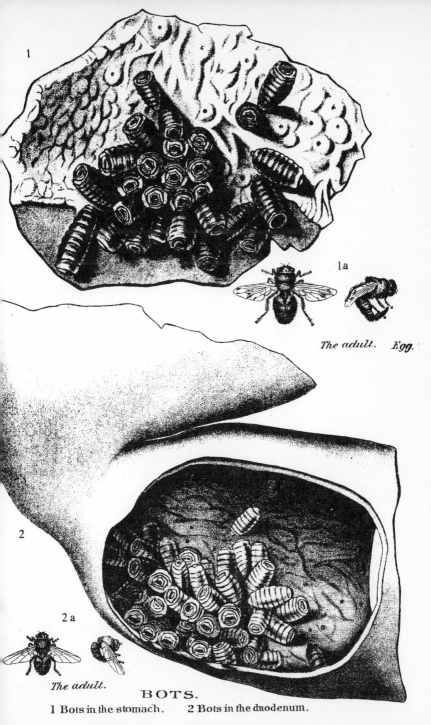

The adult. Egg.

The adult.

BOTS.
1 Bots in the stomach.   2 Bots in the duodenum.

(1) *Causes:* Exposure to wet or cold, particularly when tired or heated; damp or poorly ventilated stables; sudden changes in weather.

(2) *Symptoms:* Dryness and redness of the nasal membranes followed by a watery discharge which in a day or so becomes grayish and thickened. (Normally with the mature horse the temperature should be 99-100 degrees, the pulse about 38 beats per minute, and the respiration rate about 15 per minute.) If the throat is affected, the cough is at first dry and later moist. The nasal discharge is odorless. In the early stages the animal is somewhat listless and may run a slight temperature, 100 to 102 degrees F.

(3) *Nursing and First-aid Treatment:* From early symptoms it is difficult to tell whether the condition is a simple cold or the beginning of influenza or possibly strangles. For this reason the animal should be handled as if he had influenza. Simple colds will usually respond to rest and a mild, laxative diet. The animal must be protected from cold and drafts or overheating.

Lice

Horses may be infested with three species of lice that bite and suck blood from the animal causing much discomfort. The horse itches severely and continual rubbing against solid objects causes a loss of hair. The lice avoid sunlight and seek the darker colored portions of the body. They are readily seen on tufts of hair pulled out of the coat. Treatment consists of thorough grooming and washing in 4 or 5 percent creolin solution. Baths can only be given during favorable weather and often it is advisable to clip lousy horses in the spring.

Mange

Mange resembles lousiness but it is caused by a mite that cannot be seen by the naked eye. Mange is also accompanied by more or less change in the texture of the hide. It becomes thick and scaly. Mange yields readily to treatment of lime sulphur dip.

Internal Parasites

There are many kinds of internal parasites or worms that infest horse. The commonest are the round worms, red or blood worms, and bots. Round worms are very large, from 6 to 8 inches in length. They live in the intestines of the horse and sometimes may be seen in the manure where they have passed out.

The red worms are very small and can barely be seen. They spend part of their life in the intestines, and part in the blood stream. They are particularly dangerous because in many cases they locate in the large blood vessels and cause a partial stoppage. They do this frequently in the arteries supplying the intestines, and the reduced blood supply is a frequent cause of colic. Horses may go lame from plugged arteries.

Bots

Bots are located in the stomach. The bot fly deposits its eggs on the long hair of the horse. From here they enter the mouth and then reach the stomach as bots.

The symptoms of internal parasites are unthriftiness, lack of condition, weakness, and paleness of the eyes. The hair is long and rough and colts become pot bellied. Young horses and colts are more affected than older ones.

The treatment of internal parasites is a serious question. Any drug that will kill the parasites is also poisonous to the horse. A dose may be given that will destroy the parasites and not injure the horse. This may vary from horse to horse. Also the proper time of year must be chosen in many cases, or the drug may be ineffective. Many horses have been severely damaged and even killed by improper treatment for worms.

For this reason the safest way is to have a diagnosis made and treatment prescribed by your veterinarian who is trained in the proper procedure. There is nothing that will pay bigger dividends to the horseman than having his horses properly treated for parasites. The horses will do better on less feed, there will be fewer attacks of colic, and they will have more endurance and vigor.

Symptoms of Disease

The most common indications of disease are partial or complete loss of appetite; abdominal temperature; accelerated breathing; increased pulse rate; listlessness; dejected countenance; profuse sweating; stiffness; nasal discharge; cough; diarrhea; constipation; pawing; rolling; lameness; inflamed membranes; unhealthy coat of hair; loss of hair; itching; or unnatural heat or swelling in any part of the body.

Nursing in General

The chief points to consider in nursing are:

a. *Ventilation* — Allow plenty of fresh air but protect from drafts. Avoid extremes of temperature and in the field provide shelter from wind and rain. Utilize grass plots and corrals whenever possible.

b. *Clothing* — The amount of clothing must be regulated by the climate. In winter woolen bandages on the legs are useful, and as many as three or four covers may be used. In summer fly sheets are extremely comforting.

c. *Bedding* — A good clean bed induces an animal to rest more and produces a soft springing surface for foot cases. It should be shaken up several times daily and be kept free of urine-soaked straw.

d. *Stalls* — A roomy box stall, well beded, should be used whenever possible. Keep a bucket of water in the stall and change the water frequently.

e. *Shoes* — The shoes may be removed and the feet leveled

if the animal is to remain in a stall for more than a few days.

f. *Exercise* — Convalescent patients should receive just as much exercise as each individual case permits. However, absolute rest is one of the very best treatments.

g. *Grooming*   (1) Animals that are weak and depressed should not be worried with unnecessary grooming. Such animals should be carefully hand-rubbed at least once a day, and their eyes, nostrils, and docks should be wiped out with a sponge or soft cloth. The feet should be cleaned. (2) Animals that are only slightly indisposed should be groomed in the usual way. (3) Animals with tetanus should not be cleaned at all.

h. *Feed* — Some sick animals retain a good appetite. The principal things to observe in their cases are that they are not overfed, that droppings are kept soft, and that they have plenty of water. Sick animals with impaired appetites require special attention. They often relish a change of diet, such as a bran mash, steamed oats, chopped alfalfa, grass, roots, and apples. Feed small amounts often; do not allow uneaten portions to remain in front of them; keep mangers and feed boxes clean; sprinkle a little sweetened water over the hay and grain.

HEALTH OF THE COLT

Mare and Foal

Pregnant mares should be given more care than the average horse receives in order to assure one of the best possible foals for the time, money, and effort spent. Such animals should be handled with judgment and patience as many of them tend to slow up and become, as is often termed "logy". Mares in foal should be given plenty of exercise in light work or turned in pasture when not at work. Mares should not be worked where there is danger of slips and overstrains. Stalls for pregnant mares should be amply large enough to allow the mare to lie down or get up with ease, and these should not be located near that of a vigorous tormenting stallion. The ration of the mare should be adequate to keep her in good flesh. If internal treatment for worms and other parasites is necessary it should be done in the late fall or early winter.

Care at Foaling Time

The commonly accepted gestation period of the mare is 330 to 340 days. As the foaling time approaches the mare should be kept in a clean, well bedded box stall at night. In warm weather a pasture lot free from other livestock is ideal. If a storm should threaten, the mare must be taken inside. If a night watch is kept it is well to see the mare every hour.

Shortly before parturition the mare will become restless and uneasy. She will repeatedly lie down and get up again.

When actual labor starts the mare will usually lie down stretched out on her side and strain. Sometimes they keep on their feet the entire time. Labor should normally last but a few minutes and if help is necessary a competent veterinarian should be called early in order to save the life of the foal. Foals seldom live more than three hours after the first contractions begin.

Colts may be born with the fetal membranes covering the body. This is sometimes called being born with a veil. If such happens, this should be quickly removed from the nostrils and breathing stimulated by brisk rubbing or artificial respiration.

As soon as the mare rises and takes possession of the foal, it is well to leave the stall and allow her full charge unless extra attention is necessary. Sometimes nervous mares or those with their first foal need some help to start the colt nursing. Soiled straw and membranes should be taken immediately from the stall. Retained membranes should be removed within 8 to 12 hours after foaling. The mare is very susceptible to infection in any manipulation. Removal of retained membranes should only be attempted by one who is trained in anatomy and can secure surgical cleanliness.

Care of Foal for the First Few Days

The umbilical cord should break normally at birth or when the mare rises. In case the stump remains too long or the cord fails to rupture it may be pinched off with clean fingers about two inches from the belly wall. No time should be lost in applying tincture of iodine to the umbilical stump. It is well to apply this once daily until the stump is dried up. The tincture of iodine may be placed in a short wide-mouthed bottle such as a vaseline bottle, and this held over the stump of the cord.

Bowel movement should take place in the foal within 6 to 8 hours after birth. If bowel movements are not normal it will be necessary to treat the baby colt by rectal injections and medicine by way of the mouth. Foals with an obstructed bowel are very sick and need quick relief.

To hold a colt, it should be grasped with one arm around the chest and the other around the rump. This is the most practical method and affords the least pressure on the delicate bones and joints.

Foals are much easier to handle than three year olds and they should be broken to halter, feet picked up, and taught to lead or stand. These lessons well learned by the foal are never forgotten, and breaking two years later is made much easier. Allow the colts to run with mares on clean grass pastures as much as possible.

Navel Ill

Navel ill is a bacterial or germ infection in the blood stream that may be present before birth or be obtained through an open navel after birth. It is a disease of the new born and is especially prevalent in colts kept in dirty stalls or colts born in fly season.

This condition affects the entire body but tends to localize in the navel and joints. It is a serious disease and demands preventive or immediate attention. Even with the best of care recovered animals may be left with a leg weakness as shown by enlarged hocks, etc.

Navel ill may sometimes be prevented by vaccinating the mare two or three times before foaling. This is usually done at 6 weeks, 4 weeks, and 2 weeks before foaling. If the mare has not been vaccinated, it may be wise to vaccinate the colt with two or three injections. If the foal becomes dumpy or stiff, your veterinarian should be called at once. Certain drugs or sometimes blood from the mare can be injected into the blood stream, and frequently are of great value, but they must be used early to be of benefit.

Scours or Diarrhea in Colts

The digestive tract of the new born is very sensitive and

easily disturbed. Scours may be caused by an infection from the mare's udder or improper composition of the milk. The first milk the mare gives to the colt is thought to be benficial in preventing scours. Too much milk per feeding—usually in hand fed colts—will cause scours. Navel infection sometimes leads to scours. Try to determine the causes and eliminate these, as the first step in treatment. A medium dose of mineral oil followed by bismuth subnitrate is generally effective for simple cases of diarrhea. In persistant cases the colt becomes weak and professional help in the early stages will pay big dividends.

LAMENESS

Lameness is any irregularity in gait which results from moving with pain or difficulty because of some defect. Severe lameness may make a horse worthless; any lameness lowers his value.

Severe lameness may often be detected by examining the horse in the standing position. If the lameness is severe enough, he will refuse to place any weight whatsoever on the affected limb. "Pointing," or placing the limb in an unnatural position indicates that pain exists in that limb.

Most lameness may be detected at the walk, although the symptoms are usually accentuated at the trot. Since the individual is forced to carry most or all of his weight on the sound limb, there is always a sinking or "nodding" of the hip or head as the sound limb strikes the ground. When the lameness is in the left foreleg, for example, the head will "nod" as the right foot is planted on the ground but will jerk up as the left or lame leg touches the ground. Lameness in the rear limbs may be detected in the same manner by observing the motion of the hips. The hip opposite the lame leg always drops as the sound foot hits the ground. Always observe the horse carefully from in front, from behind and from the side.

Lameness in both front legs is indicated by stiff stilted action and short stride, which often gives the impression of stiffness in the shoulders. The head is carried higher than usual without "nodding." The hind feet are lifted high while the front feet scarcely leave the ground as the horse moves. When at rest, the weight of the body is constantly shifted from one foot to the other and the hind feet may be cramped under the body in an attempt to relieve the pain in the front feet. Such symptoms are characteristic of navicular disease.

Symptoms of lameness in both hind limbs are short stride, awkward gait and lowered head. The front feet are raised higher than usual as the horse walks. It is very difficult or impossible to back a horse that is lame in both hind legs. When at rest the horse is very uneasy and constantly shifts his weight from one leg to another.

A swinging leg lameness is a symptom of pain resulting from advancing the limb. This type of lameness usually results from inflammation occurring above the knee or hock. A supporting leg lameness is characterized by pain when weight is put upon the limb. The source of this lameness is usually located below the knee or hock.

Shoulder lameness occurs occasionally but is less frequent than most horsemen believe. As the affected limb is advanced, pain is produced, resulting in a short stride and dragging of the toe of that limb.

The exact location of the lameness is usually more difficult to determine. Many common unsoundnesses of the limb may be observed by carefully comparing the general outline of the opposite legs. Swellings or bony growths can usually be detected in this manner. Inflammatory areas can usually be detected by pressing the region firmly with the fingers. Many cases require the services of a veterinarian for a correct diagnosis.

Unscrupulous dealers often resort to many methods of relieving symptoms of lameness. If the lameness is slight, the sound foot is sometimes made equally lame by cutting the hoof to the sensitive portion in order to make the gait appear normal. Drugs are sometimes injected to deaden the nerves of the foot in order to relieve the pain which causes the animal to limp. Holding the rein close to the head when leading may prevent "nodding."

The possible causes of lameness in horses have never been numbered.

An exhaustive treatise upon the one subject of lameness would probably require an entire book larger than this one.

As to the prevalence of lameness, it has been said that half of the average veterinarian's income is derived from treating ailments at or below the knees and hocks of horses. Granting that this may be an exaggeration, it still serves to illustrate the importance of the subject.

Though the possible causes of lameness are many, the probable or common causes are comparatively few, and these are spoken of separately farther on.

Locating Lameness

Lameness being of many kinds and due to many causes, it is sometimes difficult to tell in what part the trouble is located.

We offer the following suggestions for what help they may afford, and not as a set of infallible rules for determining the location of lameness.

Observe how the horse stands as well as how he travels.

Note his manner of standing when he is quiet in his own stall where the floor is level and there are no exciting influences.

If one fore foot is advanced eight or ten inches in front of the other, and the animal shows a tendency to retain this position, or assumes it again shortly after having been induced to shift, there is apt to be soreness or tenderness in the heel, or in the back part of the limb somewhere a little higher up.

If the animal stands with knee and fetlock bent, resting the foot on the toe without advancing it in front of the other, the lameness is probably in the shoulder or elbow joint.

Where a horse stands with both front feet forward throwing the weight on the heels, and the hind feet are advanced farther under the body than they naturally would be, there may be soreness in the front part of the feet.

If there is a tendency to rest one limb more than the opposite one, there is probably something wrong with the limb that is being favored.

When a lame animal rests on all four limbs, the pastern of the lame limb is apt to have a more upright position than the other.

In exercise, the lameness is apt to be most apparent at a

slow trot. Make your observations when the animal has been at rest rather than when warmed up; or, as is sometimes best, warm him up pretty well, then let him stand perfectly quiet for a half hour or so to cool off.

Have a man lead him, allowing plenty of free rein instead of holding close to the bit. Some horses will not carry the head in a natural manner when being led, so let the leader take first one side, then the other, in order that this may not deceive you.

If there is lameness in one limb, the animal will throw less weight upon it, and will lift the foot of the lame leg from the ground as quickly as possible. The sound may be a help in detecting this, as the lame foot strikes the ground with less force.

If the lameness is in a fore leg the head and fore part of the body will likely show a quick upward motion when the lame foot comes in contact with the ground, with a corresponding drop when the sound foot strikes the ground and takes the weight. At the instant when the lame foot takes the ground and the head is thrown upward, a tendency to drop the hip on the opposite side may be noticed, but this would not indicate lameness behind.

Where there is lameness in both fore limbs the animal steps short, strikes the ground lightly and makes the interval that the feet are on the ground as short as possible. The shoulders keep a rather stiff and upright appearance and the head is apt to be carried high. In endeavoring to make the hind feet carry more of the weight, they are brought well forward under the body, which arches the loins somewhat and gives the croup or rump a drooping appearance.

Lameness in one hind limb is accompanied by a greater rising and falling motion of the hip on the lame side when the animal travels.

If there is lameness in both hind limbs the animal will be reluctant about backing, the head will be carried low with a probable tendency to poke the nose forward, and the fore-feet will be kept rather backward and under the body instead of reaching forward. The impact of the hind feet upon the ground will be light, and the interval of contact will be short.

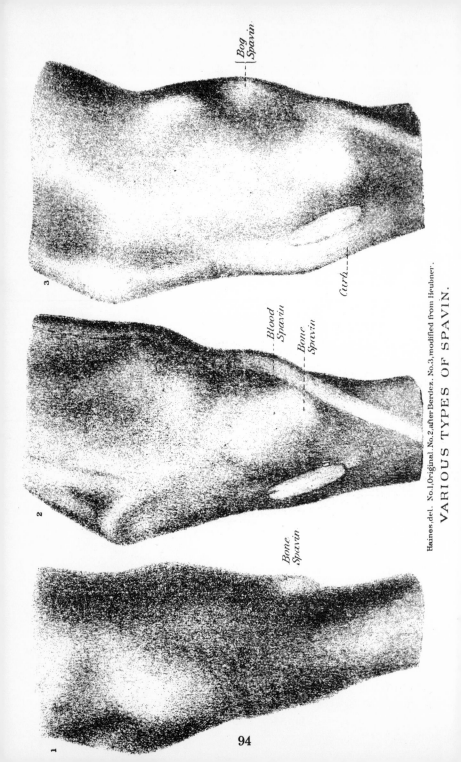

Bone Spavin

Blood Spavin

Bone Spavin

Bog Spavin

Curb

Haines.del. No.1.Original. No.2.after Berdez. No.3,modified from Heubner.

VARIOUS TYPES OF SPAVIN.

94

Sound hock.

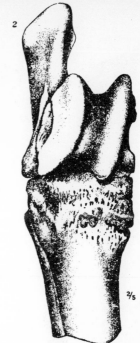

Cured spavin.

Spavin.

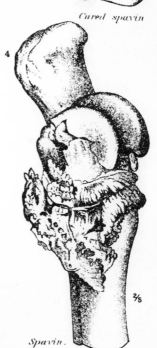

Spavin.

BONE SPAVIN

95

Lameness in front and behind on the same side produces a swaying, ambling gait.

Lameness in front and behind on opposite sides causes the horse to travel somewhat as he would if only one of the legs were lame, though the defect in gait is more marked.

When a horse is lame in two legs, he is usually more disposed to avoid trotting than where but one leg is lame.

Bone Spavin

Bone or "Jack" Spavin is a disease of the small flat bones at the lower part of the hock joint, and is marked by lameness and the formation of a bony deposit. It is a prevalent ailment and probably ruins many horses.

The part affected is the inner side of the hock, rather low down and a little forward of the center of the leg, at about the point shown in the drawing. The true hock joint is not  usually involved, but may be in some of the very bad cases. The somewhat characteristic lameness is apt to be present in some degree before the enlargement becomes noticeable, though often the development of the blemish is observed before lameness is apparent, and some little time may elapse before it becomes troublesome. Sometimes, too, there may be the external appearance of Bone Spavin without lameness developing, and we advise letting these cases alone.

A sprain, often very slight, is the usual beginning of Bone Spavin. Inflammation and the throwing out of the bony substance follows. Any horse is liable to develop a spavin, but some are rather predisposed to bony blemishes, and it is said that such a tendency is more or less hereditary. This being accepted as correct, Bone Spavin and Ringbone will become less prevalent only when the common practice of using blemished animals for breeding purposes is discontinued.

When an animal having Bone Spavin is made to move over in the stall, he will likely move the lame leg in a stiff manner, throwing the weight mostly on the toe, and may make a quick hitch with the sound leg. When taken out of the stall the same stiff limping is observed, but often for a few steps only. If allowed to stand for a half hour, the lameness occurs again in starting. If made to turn quickly in a short circle, the animal flinches and may even hop on three legs a little distance. as the case develops the lameness does not work off so readily, and finally exercise may aggravate instead of diminish it, the horse sometimes becoming entirely unfit for service, or even too lame to get about in grazing.

The enlargement is hard on bony, usually shaped like the bowl of a spoon, and may attain the size of a hulled walnut.

Treating Recent Bone Spavin

Taken in the very start, an application of strong blister will completely overcome the lameness, and will usually cause the bunch to be absorbed as well. No scar results and the limb in left as clean as before the blemish appeared.

Even if the trouble is of three to six months' standing, we would advise using this remedy if the animal is young, or if especially desirous of avoiding a scar. Keep the horse as quiet as possible in the stable for four weeks or more, making the first application rather toward the forward edge of the enlargement, then after the proper interval apply again, just back of where you did before so that you reach the back edge of the formation. After that, if further treatment is needed, apply a little higher or a little lower than the center of the bunch, as may seem best, no particular location being especially essential. Cover only a small surface each time; ordinarily in such a case we would advise that each treatment cover a spot about the size of a one-cent piece.

Treating the Older Cases

When Bone Spavin is well developed and has become firmly established, use Ringbone Paste. We would consider a case well developed and the Paste the proper treatment if either the lameness or the enlargement has been observed for six months or more. If the horse is old or the lameness quite severe, it is well to use the Paste even if the case is of less than six months' duration.

Rest is essential in connection with this treatment, and the horse should remain quiet in the stable. The time required varies in different cases, but is usually four to six weeks.

Most cases of Bone Spavin are cured with one treatment, though the lameness may hang on for several weeks after the outward effects of the remedy have passed off. A few cases require a second treatment, and an occasional one may even need a third, but do not attempt to rush matters by applying again at once if the lameness does not seem to be improved by the time the part is fully healed. Wait a few weeks and you will likely find that the lameness is subsiding, and that no more of the remedy will be required. If the lameness passes off and the bunch remains, let well enough alone, for it is usually considered well enough and all that can reasonably be expected is when an animal is made serviceably sound.

Occult Spavin

In Occult or Blind Spavin the characteristic Bone Spavin lameness is present, but no enlargement or bony deposit is to be observed. If in doubt as to whether the lameness is located in the hock, lift the foot so as to bend the hock joint as far as it will go, hold it in that position a minute or two, then let it down and start the horse quickly. If the trouble is there he will show a more decided lameness for a few steps.

Occult Spavin is apt to be tedious and rather difficult to cure, as the trouble is deep seated, usually affecting the surfaces between the flat bones of the lower part of the hock.

Splint

This is a bony deposit on the inside of the foreleg below the knee, the distance from the knee varying in different cases. It may occur upon the outside of the leg as well, but such cases are quite rare. If the enlargement is not high up against the knee, and is well forward and out of the way of the tendons, it is not apt to give much trouble. Sometimes the animal will show no lameness on soft ground, but become very lame upon a hard road, and carry the head in a drooping fashion.

Old cases that are causing no lameness should be let alone, as the bunch is apt to be too thoroughly hardened to be absorbed away. If there is a lameness, or if you want to remove a recent growth, note whether the part is feverish. If it is, use the sedative lotion (formula given) for a few days to reduce the heat, then apply a blister, repeating it a time or two if required. This will almost invariably remove the lameness, and, except in the old cases, cause the bunch to be absorbed as well. No scar remains.

Ringbone

Ringbone is a bony formation, sometimes just above the hoof, and sometimes higher up and on the upper pastern bone. The enlargement may extend nearly around the part, or may be in front or upon the side only. Lameness sometimes appears before an enlargement is noticed, while in other cases the enlargement exists some little time before causing lameness. Some regard Ringbone upon the forefoot more difficult to cure than when upon a hind foot, for the reason that the pasterns are more upright and the forelegs carry nearly two-thirds of the animal's weight.

We will not dispute that there may be some truth in this, though our own observations do not tend to confirm such a theory.

To enter fully into the treatment of Ringbone would be to repeat much that we have said concerning the treatment of Bone Spavin. If there is merely an enlargement and no lameness, let it alone. There are a few

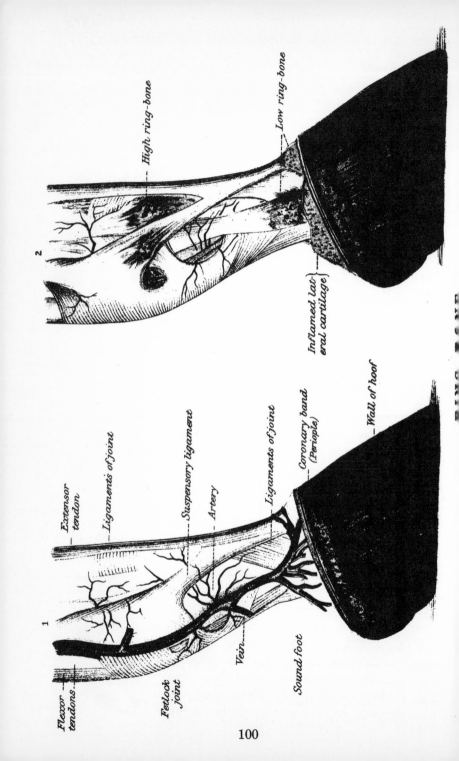

RING-BONE

1

Flexor tendons
Fetlock joint
Vein
Sound foot
Extensor tendon
Ligaments of joint
Suspensory ligament
Artery
Ligaments of joint
Coronary band (Periople)
Wall of hoof

2

High ring-bone
Low ring-bone
Inflamed lateral cartilage

cases that never cause trouble so treat these cases early.

Where Ringbone is just developing on a colt or young horse and is accompanied by lameness, blister and rest.

The cases that are pretty well established and causing lameness should be treated with Ringbone Paste. This remedy seldom fails even in the very old cases that have been fired or unsuccessfully treated in various other ways. Do not apply it all over the enlargement, but upon one small spot. One treatment in this way is often sufficient to cure, even though the blemish extends well around the foot. Use your own judgment in selecting the spot. If the enlargement is principally in one place, cover a surface only the size of a dime as advised for Bone Spavin. If the bunch is longer than it is wide, extending around the foot partially or entirely, it will be all right to place the paste in an oblong position, narrower than the dime and enough longer to involve about a third more surface. Keep the horse quiet and after the part is healed repeat on a different surface if necessary. If the animal has more than one Ringbone, treat only one at a time.

Sidebone

Sidebone is practically the same formation as Ringbone, though some authorities make a slight distinction. All agree, however, that the same treatment is required. In appearance it differs from Ringbone in that the enlargements are upon the sides of the foot and do not meet in front, and sometimes only one side is enlarged. Where the animal is not lame no treatment is advised. If it is a very recent case on a young horse, showing little lameness and slight development, use the Blister, treating alternately one side then the other, if both sides are affected, at intervals of a week or so. If well developed and lameness is quite marked, use the Ringbone Paste, treating one side first, then the other after the first has fully healed. Too much treatment at one time may make the horse shift too much weight to the other legs with bad effects.

Sedative Lotion

The formula here given is a valuable remedy to have about the stable. It is inexpensive and can be prepared by any druggest. For recent sprains, feverish joints, hot swellings, etc., it is the best possible application.

Muriate of Ammonia .... 2 ounces
Acetic Acid .... 1 ounce
Nitrate of Potash .... ½ ounce
Alcohol .... 2 ounces

Water sufficient to make one pint.

In this form the lotion is too concentrated to use, and should be diluted with eight parts of soft water. Apply freely two to four times a day until the temperature of the part is reduced to normal. Do not attempt to rub it in, but simply saturate the hair thoroughly.

Curb

 This is an enlargement of the ligament at the back part of the hock, due to sprains, kicks, etc. It occurs rather low down, and in the beginning is usually accompanied by heat and tenderness. In some cases there is lameness only in the earlier stages, while in other the blemish may continue troublesome. Where an old curb does not lame the horse we do not advise treatment of any kind, as after a time the enlargement becomes solid and permanently fixed.

In the early stages, notice whether there is heat in the part, and if there is use the sedative lotion to reduce it. Then apply a blister. If there is little or no heat, it will not be necessary to use the lotion. In the fairly recent cases, this treatment will overcome the lameness and reduce the enlargement completely, but where the blemish has become well set the appearance of the part may not be improved. Allow rest until the horse recovers. The hocks of some animals have rather a curby appearance that is entirely natural, and must be regarded as a slight deformity rather than un-soundness.

Sprains and Swellings

In cases of ordinary sprains and swelling accompanied by heat and soreness, we would direct your attention to what is said under the heading of "Sedative Lotion." If, after all in-flammation has been removed from the part, the lameness or enlargement does not disappear within a week or so, Blister in the manner directed for ordinary blemishes, re-peating the applications as may be required. Steroid therapy is beneficial.

Bog Spavin

This is a soft, yielding, bulging enlarge-ment occurring in front and a little to the inside of the true hock joint, and is formed by excessive secretion of the lubricating fluid or joint oil. From the feeling of the bunch some are led to inquire whether it should not be opened, but to open it would be to risk ruining the animal.

There are two wrong ideas concerning Bog Spavin that have some prevalence. One is that the blemish never lames a horse; the other is that it is necessarily permanent and in-curable. These theories, however, may readily be accounted for where one's observations have been limited to a few cases.

In order to make the matter clear, we will say that Bog Spavin occurs in two forms, and will speak of each in the light of our own experience and observations. The first form is merely an excessive secretion of fluid or a dropsical condition of the part, producing no lameness and objection-able only on account of its ugly appearance and the conse-quent disadvantage when the horse is offered for sale. The second form is just the same in appearance, but involves actual disease or inflammation of the joint, and is accompanied by lameness that may be only moderate or very severe.

In cases like the first mentioned we do not urge treatment, owing to the uncertainty of removing the blemish. Nevertheless, a large percentage of them can be removed, and our estimate is that a good Blister is effective about three times out of four in such cases, but we cannot say in advance which will yield and which will not. Ordinarily, we would discourage treatment if the animal is of the large-boned type, or if the blemish is so small as to be of little consequence.

It is not uncommon for boggy bunches to appear on young colts. We do not advise treating these, as they usually disappear later on of their own accord. A little brisk rubbing with the hand occasionally is said to be benefical.

In cases of the laming type, keep the animal quiet and use the sedative lotion if there is heat in the part. After a few days when the heat has been removed, or at once if there is little or no excess of heat, apply a Blister. By this treatment the lameness will be overcome, and the blemish will usually be reduced or removed entirely, the latter being more probably in cases of this type than in those where there is no lameness except in some of the older cases where the bunch has become quite hard.

Wind Galls

Every horseman is familiar with the bulging enlargements called Wind Galls or Wind Puffs. They are quite common and appear on either side of the tendons above the fetlock joint. As they are usually harmless and frequently obstinate, we do not strongly advise treatment unless the horse is lame. If there is lameness, treat with Iodine or a Blister.

Blood Spavin

Most of the so-called cases of Blood Spavin are Bog Spavin. Blood Spavin is seldom very conspicuous, and is both harmless and incurable. It is merely a dilation of the vein that passes over the part where spavin occurs.

Capped Hock

This blemish appears on the point of the hock and is caused by kicks and bruises. Treat the same as Curb, first using the sedative lotion if there is heat in the part, then applying a Blister. Repeat the treatment a time or two if required. Would not advise treating old case not attended by lameness, as removel of the blemish would be very doubtful.

Thoroughpin

Read what is said concerning Bog Spavin, which may apply to Thoroughpin as well, the two blemishes being practically the same in character, but differently situated. It is not uncommon for both Bog Spavin and Thoroughpin to occur on the same hock, and such cases are apt to be rather tedious, so much of the hock being affected.

The seat of Thoroughpin is at the upper and back part of the hock, as shown in the drawing, and the enlargement may appear upon one or both sides. Often by pressing upon one side the accumulation of fluid may be forced through to the other. In treating Thoroughpin Blister on one side, then after a week or ten days treat the other side in the same manner, alternating in this way a few times if necessary. Where Bog Spavin is present as well, rotate the applications, applying to one enlargement at a time and allowing a week or so to elapse before treating another. Any condition envolving the hock joint will require a great deal of patience to be effective because there are so many moving structures in close proximity.

Stifle Lameness

Lameness may develop in the stifle joint from a kick, sprain or injury of any kind. Usually the animal stands with the leg in a half bent position, the foot resting on the toe. The lameness is not alike in all cases. The leg may be brought forward with a sudden jerk, or the motion may be a stiff, awkward swing. Often a swelling or enlargement forms, either at the point of the stifle or a little farther back.

Rest is essential in overcoming this difficulty. Keep the animal as quiet as possible, and apply a good Blister, either in front or upon the outside of the part as may seem best, repeating the treatment at intervals of ten days or so. It is not necessary to apply to any exact or particular spot, as the effect of the remedy is somewhat distributed, but keep within the vicinity of the seat of trouble. Some of these cases may prove a little tedious, but sufficient rest and some perseverance will usually bring them out all right. If there should be considerable heat in the part, it would be well to begin the treatment by using the sedative lotion for a few days.

Dislocated Patella

Dislocation of the patella or knee-cap is sometimes an accident attending a slip when a horse is rising in his stall. The animal stands with the leg extended backward and is unable to bring it to its natural position. Fasten a rope about the fetlock, pass the other end through a collar or strap around the horse's neck, and while a strong man or two draws the foot forward by means of the rope, stand behind the horse, with one hand on the inside of the stifle joint and the other on the outside, pressing the patella into its place. If dislocation occurs frequently, treat the same as stifle lameness or inject a blister.

Sometimes a young animal will be troubled with the patella slipping out and in with a snapping sound at every step. This is due to a weak or relaxed state of the muscles that should hold this bone in place. Keep the animal quiet in the stable and treat as for stifle lameness, which will have a stimulating and strengthening effect upon the muscles.

Inflammation of the Hock Joint

A kick or sprain is apt to set up violent inflammation in the hock joint, accompanied by great swelling and lameness. If not relieved the result may be serious, and as such accidents are always liable to occur, it will be well to know what to do. The treatment should be directed toward keeping down the inflammation. Put the animal in a comfortable stall and pack the joint loosely with cotton batting, then keep the cotton constantly wet with the sedative lotion. If after three days the condition is not improved, discontinue the lotion and apply hot poultices. If matter should form, let it break of its own accord, then wash the opening with a solution of chloride of zinc, one dram to a pint of water. After the part heals, if lameness yet remains, apply a blister. Steroids and antibiotics are the best professional treatment, better if applied in the early stages.

Sprained Tendons

Drawing heavy loads is a common cause. The horse digs his toes into the ground and throws great stress upon the back tendons of the legs. Sprain of the tendons is indicated by swelling, heat and lameness. Kicks and bruises may also produce the same effect, and should be treated in the same manner. Sometimes the swelling is so light as to hardly be detected, yet there is considerable lameness. Pressure causes flinching, however, and in this way the injury may be located.

If heat and swelling are present, use the sedative lotion, applying freely three or four times a day. If the lameness hangs on, or if the case is an old and chronic one, apply a blister, repeating the treatment upon a different spot at intervals of two or three weeks, meanwhile allowing rest. In severe cases a high-heeled shoe is advisable.

Callous Enlargements

Frequently a callous enlargement or thickening of the skin follows barb wire cut or other injury. These blemishes may in most instances be reduced by applying a smart blister each time, repeating the applications as often as may be required. Should it fail to take hold actively enough, rub it in with a little friction. There is nothing that will grow hair on an old and bare scar.

Collar Boil

This name is often applied to hard lumps forming under the skin of the shoulder where the collar rests. A blister is successful in most cases of the kind, causing the bunches to disappear by absorption. Apply to a small surface, repeating on different spots as may be necessary. This should be done at some time when the animal is not required for work, or else used only in breast harness that exerts no pressure upon the part. The same applies to saddle sores.

Shoe Boil

 Shoe Boil or Capped Elbow is a growth or tumor at the point of the elbow joint, caused by pressure upon the heel of the shoe when the animal lies cow-fashion with his legs bent under him. This manner of lying is sometimes induced by the stall being too narrow. If it is, widen it and he will likely assume a different position. Shortening the heel of the shoe, especially on the inner side, will sometimes be sufficient to remove the cause, or it may be necessary to pad the foot each night. Treat the bunch with a blister at intervals of two weeks or so until reduced. The primary object is to remove the cause and most of these will heal up of their own accord without treatment.

Construction of the Foot

Before entering upon the common causes of lameness in the foot, it will be well to consider, at least in a superficial way, the general structure of this part.

The foot is not the dead and insensitive thing that its external appearance suggests. Within the horny box that we call the hoof are bones, ligaments, tissues, blood vessels and nerves that are as much alive and just as sensitive as those that go to make up other parts of the horse. First, let us think of the coronary band around the top of the hoof, from which continually grows the wall of the foot. If any part of this band becomes injured in a permanent way so as to interfere with its formation, the wall of the foot will always be weak below that point.

The wall of the foot, a fibrous horny substance, is hardest upon the surface, and provided with a thin varnish-like coating to prevent both the escape of moisture from within and the absorption of moisture from without, and it is evident from this that rasping high up on the surface of the wall should be avoided by the smith in shoeing.

Beneath the wall is the quick or sensitive laminae, in which inflammation from disease, a shoe-nail prick or other injury, may cause intense pain and lameness.

The horny sole is produced from the sensitive sole beneath it, the process being continuous to provide for wear. It is composed of numerous horny layers that become harder as they approach the surface. Stone bruises or punctures may injure the sensitive sole.

The frog is a V-shaped yielding formation with a horny surface, extending forward from the heel, with cavities, called clefts, at either side, and a third and smaller one dividing it at the back part. The purpose of the frog is to act as a cushion, and in order to do this it must bear a little weight when the foot is upon the ground, which is to be considered in shoeing. Beneath the horny frog is the sensitive frog, subject to disease or injury.

Finally, let us remember that inflammation of the sensitive interior of the foot is apt to be especially painful, owing to

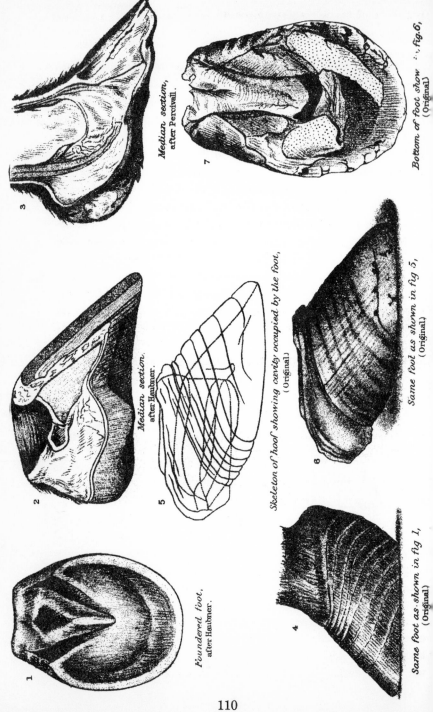

Median section, after Percivall.

Bottom of foot shown in fig. 6. (Original)

Median section, after Haubner.

Skeleton of hoof showing cavity occupied by the foot. (Original)

Same foot as shown in fig 5. (Original)

Foundered foot, after Haubner.

Same foot as shown in fig 1. (Original)

pressure of the almost unyielding hoof that resists swelling.

Acute Founder or Laminitis

This disease is an inflammation of the sensitive laminae and sensitive sole, or may in bad cases involve still other parts of the internal foot. Some animals, especially those having badly formed feet, seem rather predisposed to this ailment. It may arise from a great variety of causes, and in consequence it is one of the common ailments. Eating wheat or rye, even in moderate quantity, will sometimes produce it or it may be due to eating too much of any kind of food, drinking cold water when heated, over-exertion on hard roads, bruises, punctures, shoe-nail pricks, badly fitted shoes, etc., or it may appear without any special cause being apparent.

Laminitis occurs most frequently in one or both feet, though the hind feet are sometimes affected. Some cases recover completely, while in others the foot is permanently injured and becomes badly deformed.

Where both forefeet are affected the animal extends them forward, resting the weight upon the heels, and brings the hind feet well forward under the body. If both hind feet are affected, they will have a forward position to get the weight upon the heels, and the forefeet will be placed backward and made to support as much of the weight as possible. Where only one foot is affected, the animal will relieve it of weight. The breathing is fast and heavy, with nostrils dilated, and the pulse is usually rapid and strong. If made to move the horse will groan and sway and finally slide his feet, though very reluctantly. The hoofs of the affected feet are hot, and if tapped lightly the animal will evince great pain.

Sometimes the horse will be found lying down instead of standing. Do not make him get up. If he is standing, induce him to lie down if possible. Give him a nice bed of straw, and if he still persists in standing, take a rope or strap and pass one end under him then a man at each side raises the rope tightly against his belly, as though to carry a part of his weight. Gradually the animal takes advantage of the help given, and tries to rest on the rope. At the proper time let the rope go and he is apt to drop down. Feeling the relief that lying down affords, he is apt to remain down quite a while, and thereafter no encouragment with the rope will be required.

Ordinarily it is better to begin treatment by removing the shoes as gently as possible. Then dip cloths in hot water and wrap them about the feet, changing them every ten or fifteen minutes for a half to three quarters of an hour, then for a like period use cold applications instead, alternating in this way for about four hours. Follow with hot poultices until the soreness passes off. After two to four weeks when the inflammation has subsided, use a blister lightly upon the coronets, covering a surface an inch or so long and repeating upon different surfaces at intervals of two or three weeks. This will overcome any remaining sensitiveness and tend to ward off Chronic Founder. Allow a long rest at pasture or in a roomy box stall with soft earth floor or plenty of straw.

Some stand the horse in a tub of hot or cold water instead of applying the wet cloths, but it is always advisable to get him off his feet while the inflammation and pain are so intense. Antihistamines are sometimes effective if used early.

Chronic Founder

Chronic Founder is apt to follow the acute attack, through slight inflammation remaining after a cure seems to have been effected, or as a result of injury done the internal structures of the foot by the excessive feverishness and congestion. There is usually more or less lameness, and the feet gradually shrink, sometimes becoming very much deformed, In a majority of cases a complete cure can never be effected, though by proper treatment and care the animal will be able to render good service. Note what is said about Contraction of the Feet and treat Chronic Founder accordingly. Keep the animal off the hard roads. Recently plastic casts are used with good results.

Contraction of the Feet

Contraction of the Feet may be due to anything that causes a shrinking or wasting away of the soft structures within the foot. Standing on hard floors, alternate soaking and drying of the hoofs, allowing the wall at the back part of the foot to become overgrown and turned in, too much paring about the sole and frog, bad shoeing, injuries, etc., tend to produce this condition.

In undertaking a cure the first thing essential is to remove the cause if possible. Remove the shoes and place the horse in a stall having a soft, moist earth floor. Apply a blister upon the coronet, covering a surface about an inch long, and repeating after two or three weeks upon a different surface. This will help through its stimulating effect, and the treatment may be prolonged as required. Several months' rest is advisable, especially in the bad cases. Put on a level bar shoe when the horse is ready for work.

In very bad cases precede this treatment by applying poultices for a couple of weeks, or allow the horse to stand twelve or fourteen hours a day with his feet in a pool of clay mud.

Navicular Disease

Another name that is sometimes applied to this disease is Coffinjoint lameness. The part affected is the Navicular Bone and its surrounding tissues, and anything that may tend to set up inflammation in the back part of the foot may produce it. It is most common among fast road horses that have good action and strike the road hard with the feet.

Usually the first symptoms observed is that the horse when quiet in his stall will place one forefoot forward about eight or ten inches with the heel slightly raised; or, if both feet are affected, he will advance first one then the other. In traveling there may as yet be no lameness apparent, but the horse does not reach out as he should and is liable to stumble frequently. Gradually lameness develops, at first disappearing with exercise and only returning after the animal has been standing a time. Later on the lameness is more aggravated, the heel may contract, and the muscles of the shoulder or chest may waste away, producing Sweeny or what some call "Chest Founder." Upon examination heat in the back part of the foot is usually detected, and the animal flinches from pressure in the hollow of the heel, or when the wall in the region of the quarter, or the sole at each side of the frog, is tapped with a hammer.

Treatment, except in some of the recent cases, is usually unsatisfactory. Remove the shoe. If inflammation is quite marked, stand the horse in wet clay or poultice the foot until it is reduced. If there is little or no heat, or after you have reduced it as above, apply a good blister on the heel freely enough to blister. At intervals of about two weeks repeat on different spots about the heel or sides of the pastern. Some cases are apparently cured in this manner, but we cannot promise definite results. Even though the lameness is entirely relieved, a return of the trouble is always probable. Rest for a year is the best cure.

Corns

Ninety-nine corns in every hundred are due to faulty shoeing, and the remedy is to remove the cause. Corns occur on the forefeet and are indicated by lameness, the animal placing the affected foot forward and resting it on the toe when standing. Examining the foot you will find heat on the inside of the hoof at the heel and on pressing or striking the part the animal will flinch. Remove the shoe and pare off a little of the sole at that point, and you will find a red spot. In bad cases where matter forms, there is great lameness, and the matter may find its way out at the top of the hoof. In long-standing cases the result is usually contraction of the heel.

After removing the shoe poultice the foot to soften the hoof, overcome the inflammation and take out the soreness. Rasp the wall of the hoof level and put on a level bar shoe, rasping away a little of the wall at the corn to relieve it from pressure. Pare the corn very little, if at all, and do not apply caustic or strong medicine of any kind. Use the bar shoe until the sole of the foot becomes strengthened, then use a flat shoe and do not pare the sole, and you will have no more trouble with corns.

Seedy Toe

Sometimes the wall at the front part of the foot separates from the sensitive laminae, producing a hollow space. Such a condition is called Seedy Toe. It rarely causes lameness, and when lameness occurs it is probably due to sand or dirt getting into the cavity and causing irritation.

Treatment is seldom effective in uniting the parts. Put on a shoe having a broad toe clip, and fill in between the clip and separation with tar and oakum. Keep the hoof soft by occasional poultices, and blister the coronet at intervals to stimulate the growth of horn.

Quittor

Quittor is the name given to a fistulous disease of the foot resulting from bruises, pricks in shoeing, pebbles working up into the clefts of the frog, or any injury causing suppuration within the foot. It is marked by swelling upon the coronet, lameness, and finally fistulous openings upon the heel or at the top of the hoof. If there is considerable inflammation and soreness, apply poultices for a few days until relieved. Treat with antibiotics and a good wound dressing, meanwhile keeping the horse quiet.

Quarter Crack

Quarter Crack or False Quarter is due to derangement of that portion of the coronary band just above it. For instance, an injury to the coronary band may destroy its power to produce healthy horn, and at that point the wall of the foot is weak and imperfect. These cracks are usually widest at the bottom, as shown in the illustration.

If there is lameness, poultice the foot to reduce the inflam-  mation, then put on a bar shoe so fitted that there will be no pressure upon the wall at the affected part. Apply a blister upon the coronet above the crack, which in many cases will stimulate the production of healthy horn, the exceptions being those in which the functions of the coronary band are permanently impaired.

Sand Crack

Sand Crack is a split in the upper part of the hoof where the wall is thin, due to a dry and brittle condition of the horny substance. It may appear suddenly, and usually occurs on the front or inside quarter of the foot. When weight is thrown upon the foot the crack may spread and the sensitive tissue bulging into the opening, may be caught and pinched when the foot is raised and the crack closes. This causes inflammation and lameness.

Apply poultices to soften the hoof and take out any inflam- mation or soreness that may be present. Put on a bar shoe so fitted as to relieve that part of the wall from pressure. With a sharp knife cut out a piece of the hoof clear to the quick at the upper end of the crack, which is likely to be at the coronary band. Fill the place with tar to keep out the dirt. This cutting, if carefully and properly done, removes the pressure at that point and gives the new hoof a chance to grow out sound. Apply a blister to the coronet above the crack once a month.

Thrush of the Foot

Thrush is a diseased condition of the frog of the foot. It may be caused by injury, bad shoeing, filthy stables, and by long continued wet weather and mud, the feet scarcely getting a chance to dry. The disease is marked by a very foul-smelling discharge from the clefts of the frog. In bad cases the horny frog may even become detached from the sensitive frog.

Clean out the clefts. You will likely find them very deep and extending into the sensitive parts of the foot. If the case is a bad one or the horse is lame, apply a poultice for a few days.

Treat with a good fungicide and sanitation.

Canker

Canker affects the frog, and may sometimes spread to the sole of foot. It is accompanied by a thin and very foul-smelling discharge, and the frog becomes much enlarged, soft and spongy, there being rapid growth of a peculiar horny, fungus like substance that bleeds quite freely when it is pared. Canker probably results from causes similar to those that produce Thrush. The presence of some form of vegetable parasite being an added feature. It is a disease that is difficult to cure, but most cases will yield to the following treatment:

Apply poultices for two or three days, changing them twice daily, and adding a little carbolic acid to the water used in making the poultice, about a teaspoon to each pint. Then pare down the frog, cutting away all the unhealthy growth that you can without too much bleeding. After the bleeding has stopped apply terchloride of antimony, commonly called butter of antimony, covering all the diseased surfaces. Repeat about every other day, cleaning the part each time by scraping the surface carefully. When the unhealthy growth seems to have disappeared completely, discontinue the antimony and use tincture of iodine lightly, once daily or every other day, until the part assumes a healthy appearance. Keep the horse in a clean place, and if necessary in order to keep out the dirt and protect the sore, cover the part with cotton batting or oakum and fasten it on.

Nail Injuries in Shoeing

Sometimes in shoeing a nail is driven too close to the sensitive sole, causing pressure and soreness. Where lameness develops a few days after the animal has been shod and no other cause can be found, tap the heads of the nails or the wall at each nail lightly with a hammer. The offending nail may often be detected in this way, and ordinarily its removal will be all that is required.

Should the nail strike the sensitive sole the smith will observe it at the time, withdraw the nail and reset it, but the injury done may be sufficient to cause inflammation and sometimes suppuration. If this occurs, remove the shoe and apply poultices for a few days. Should the lameness fail to pass off, open the part by paring along the course of the nail to allow the matter to escape, then continue the poulticing until the soreness subsides. These injuries are most apt to occur in horses having thin and weak hoofs. Give penicillin and tetanus shot.

Punctured Wounds in the Foot

The treatment of wounds of this character should depend somewhat upon the nature and extent of the injury. Deep punctures especially should have the early attention of a veterinarian who can judge as to the probable damage done and treat accordingly, for if the bone, coffin joint or flexor tendon is injured, results more or less serious are apt to follow. Shallow punctures may also bring serious consequences, especially if caused by a rusty and dirty nail. In such cases it is well to enlarge the opening slightly by paring out a little of the sole, then if you have a Veterinary Healing Oil handy, a few drops injected or otherwise introduced will, if it reaches the bottom of the wound, destroy any germs that may have been implanted, and also tend to prevent inflammation. If there is apparent soreness or any sign of inflammation, poultice the foot and see that there is a sufficient opening for matter to escape. Give penicillin and tetanus shot.

Elephantitis or Milk Leg

Elephantitis and Milk Leg are names sometimes given to chronic enlargement of the leg from the hock down, resembling Lymphangitis in appearance, and usually being a result of that disease. The animal may not seem to suffer from the ailment, and the swelling remains about stationary, fluctuating but little if at all. Not much can be expected from treatment in such cases, as the lymphatics are permanently injured. Tincture of iodine applied to limited surfaces once or twice a week may prove helpful.

Lymphangitis or Water Farcy

This is an acute inflammation of the lymphatics. It is most common among heavy draft horses, and most frequently follows a few days rest after having been at hard work on heavy feed. It may also be due to  over-feeding, sudden exposure, general disorder, etc. It often comes on in a night, and in the morning the animal will be found shivering, breathing heavily, and stiff in one or both hind legs. Soon a general fever comes on, the pulse is rapid, and the glands high up on the inside of the thigh are enlarged and tender. In a few hours the lymphatic vessels of the leg begin to swell, and the limb may become two or three times its natural size. If the inflammation is not relieved in a day or two, suppuration may occur in the glands and the animal may die of blood poisoning, or the lymphatic vessels will be so impaired that the leg will remain permanently enlarged.

In very mild cases moderate exercise may throw off the attack. If more severe, and especially if due to heavy feeding and lack of exercise, dissolve an ounce of aloes and an ounce of ginger in half a pint of boiling water, add half a pint of cold water, and give as a drench. Give also twenty drops of tincture of aconite every two hours until the pulse approaches normal. Three time a day for two or three days, give a quarter ounce of nitrate of potash in drinking water. Bathe the swollen leg for an hour at a time with hot water at intervals of three or four hours, and after each bathing apply the sedative lotion (formula given on another page). After a day or so when the inflammation is well reduced, exercise the animal lightly for half an hour two or three times daily. Feed bran mashes or other easily digested foods.

Sweeny

Sweeny is a very common trouble, and is especially liable to occur in young horses that have but recently been put to work. The usual form of Sweeny results from a sprain of the muscle that fill the posterior cavity on the outside of the shoulder blade, and at first there may be heat, swelling and some lameness, followed by rapid wasting of the muscle. Very often this shrinking of the muscle is the first symptom observed, and in some bad cases the shoulder blade becomes so denuded that there appears to be no flesh at all between the skin and the bone. Sweeny should be treated early, as in old cases a fatty degeneration of the tissues may occur, rendering complete restoration of the muscle impossible.

A Sweenied condition of the shoulder may also result from Ringbone, or any form of lameness that interferes with the natural activity of the shoulder muscles, and in such cases it is necessary to give attention to the cause. Hip Sweeny may likewise be due to lameness farther down, or to an injury, or it may result from an attack of Azoturia. Treat with internal blister.

Shoulder Lameness

Lameness in the shoulder is indicated by the animal carrying his head low, dragging the toe on the ground, swinging the foot outward in bringing it forward, or standing with the joints bent and heel raised, but without advancing the lame foot in front of the other. Such lameness may be of a rheumatic nature, or due to strain or injury of some sort. In cases where there are no outward signs, such as heat or swelling it is often very difficult to locate the seat of lameness.

If the part is hot and swollen, apply two or three times a day the sedative lotion, formula for which is given on another page. Where there is no heat or swelling, use the blister in the same manner, applying where, in your judgement, it is most needed. Complete rest must be given until all lameness has disappeared. Steroids are usually effective.

Broken Knees

This name is given to bruises or abrasions of the knees such as may occur in falling. Slight injuries of the kind require no treatment, but if the knee is considerably bruised and swelling follows, bandage the part loosely and keep it wet with a solution of acetate of lead, one ounce to about three pints of water. Tie the horse high so that he will not attempt to lie down. If the wound is deep, extending through the skin, bend the knee to the position it was in when injured, and if you see any dirt wash it away with a stream of tepid water or a soft, clean sponge. Do not probe the wound. Trim the hair from any loose flaps of skin, draw them together and fasten with strips of adhesive plaster. If swelling and inflammation follow, use the lead solution as above. In bad cases it may be advisable to put the animal in a sling. Such an injury may ruin a horse if severe enough to break bones, lacerate the tendons, or open the joint so that the lubricating fluid escapes.

Knee-Sprung

Some cases of Knee-Sprung are hereditary, even existing

from colthood up, and nothing can be done for them. Most cases are due to sprain or other injury, or to some over-exertion or continued hard usage, causing the back tendons of the leg to become contracted. It is first noticed that the animal is weak or unsteady at the knees, with a probable tendency to stumble. As the tendons become more contracted, it is readily seen that the knee is not brought up to its natural position in standing, and in bad cases the animal stands with the knees bent forward to a very conspicuous extent.

It is only the reasonably favorable cases that we advise treating. Where the trouble is due to wire cut or any injury that may have lacerated the tendons, or if the horse is somewhat advanced in age and has had hard usage, we would advise letting the case alone. But if the subject is a young animal and the trouble is just coming on, or has appeared within a year and is moderate only, treatment will as a general rule prove effective. Use Steroids.

Cocked Ankle

This is a knuckling over or breaking forward at the pastern, indicating some weakness of the ligaments. It is sometimes induced by overwork, or by allowing the foot to become overgrown so that it does not rest in a natural position upon the ground. If there is any apparent cause, correct it. If the foot has been growing long at the toe, shaping it up properly and putting on a shoe slightly elevated at the heel may be beneficial. Allow rest, and if there seems to be any heat in the part, apply a loose bandage for a few days and keep it wet with cold water. Follow with light applications of a blister at intervals of two or three weeks. Bent Ankle, sometimes seen in young foals, is of a different character. They usually straighten up with age.

Rheumatic Lameness

Rheumatic Lameness is most common in the shoulder, but

also affects other parts. It is apt to have a shifting tendency, changing from one leg to another, and may sometimes be accompanied by swelling. There may also be more or less general stiffness, dullness or lack of energy, all the symptoms being aggravated by exposure to cold and dampness.

Rheumatism is due to an irritating principle, causing inflammation of the joints and muscles. Stimulating liniments may afford some temporary relief, but a cure requires that the cause be eliminated.

It is well to first empty the bowels with a dose of physic, a pint and a half to two pints of raw linseed oil, then give aspirin, a dose each evening in bran mash for a week or ten days, then every other day for a couple of weeks to obtain a thorough action upon the system. Half ounce doses of nitrate of potash, given in drinking water once a day for several days, may also be helpful. Steroids help many cases.

Fractures of the Bones

This is a subject that we shall touch upon only briefly, because in the larger animals treatment is seldom advisable, except in cases of simple fracture, and if possible professional attention should be given them. By simple fracture is meant a single break and not a shattering of the bone, and without wounding or lacerating the flesh about the part.

If, for instance, the case is simple fracture of a horse's leg, the ends of the broken bone should be brought into proper position and secured as promptly as possible. Tear long strips of muslin about three or four inches wide, wet with starch and wrap smoothly around the part. After sevral layers have been put on, apply splints of thin wood or stiff leather, bandaging them firmly in place with the starched muslin. The bandage should extend clear down to the foot, otherwise there is apt to be a serious swelling and inflammation in the lower parts, and should also extend well above the fracture, holding all joints below and the first above in a fixed position if possible. If swelling exists before the bandage is applied, it may be necessary after a few days to readjust the bandage, which should be done with the utmost care.

It is also necessary to put the animal in a sling and keep him there until the bones have united, which is apt to be six weeks, and the bandage should remain on about as long. After that, rest should be given for two or three months.

Constructing a Sling

A simple manner of constructing a sling for a horse is as follows: Secure four stout posts in an upright position, having one on each side behind, and the forward pair at about the breast. A pole or piece of timber strong enough to bear considerable weight without bending, is then fastened from each forward to each rear post, at a height about half way up the animal's side. When the horse is within the frame a crosspiece may be fastened in front and behind. The next thing required is some stout cotton canvas, or, new grain sacks may answer the purpose. Fasten securely to the poles at each side, bringing it close up under the body so that he may settle down into it and rest at will.

Balky Horses

To use the whip on a balky horse usually makes matters worse. Ordinarily it is best to divert the animal's attention by some quiet and gentle means. Sometimes this may be done by lifting a forefoot and tapping the nails of the shoe with a hammer or stone, then drop the foot quickly and give him the command to go. Another suggestion is to have one man hold the lines while a rope is passed behind the horse's knees, then a man on each side holding an end of the rope walks forward with it, so that the horse will have to go forward to keep from falling. A couple of drops of carbon disulphide placed just above the hoof on the heel of each front foot will cause the balker to keep raising his feet and thus not be able to plant his feet and balk.

Heaves

This name has reference to a specific ailment among horses that is marked by a characteristic manner of breathing. Broken Wind is another name that is cometimes applied, but as it is also used in referring to other forms of difficult or unnatural breathing, it conveys no definite meaning other than that there is something wrong with the respiration.

Heaves is a prevalent ailment and when fully developed may readily be recognized by almost any one familiar with horses. The first symptom is apt to be a short, dry half-suppressed cough, usually most noticeable after a little exertion, or after feeding or watering. As the case develops the peculiar breathing or heaving becomes marked, and in some instances the coughing diminishes at this stage. In the act of respiration, the air may be drawn into the lungs with the usual ease and freedom, but a sort of double exertion, quite noticeable in the flank, seems required to expel it, and often this is accompanied by a wheezing sound.

Not a Lung Disease

All authorities agree that Heaves is closely allied with digestive derangement, and the general conclusion is that the heaving is a reflex nervous contraction of the lungs induced by stomach disorder, and not in itself a lung disease.

That this should be so there is little wonder, when we consider the close nervous conjuction of the organs involved. The nerve supplying the lung passes also to the stomach, so that derangement of this organ may easily, and in a very marked way, distrub the breathing through what is known as reflex nervous action.

Some authorities state that post mortem examination of animals that have for a long time suffered with Heaves, revealed a noticeable change in the lung tissue. Others report having repeatedly made the most careful microscopical examinations, and have invariably found the lung structure normal. From this it would appear that where change was observed, it was propably due to previous inflammation during a severe cold or some other acute attack, or possibly a result of the long continued unnatural breathing. That it could have been the cause of the heaving, is successfully disputed by the fact that in some old cases of Heaves the lungs were found normal.

Further indication that Heaves is a manifestation of stomach disorder may be found in the fact that an abundance of bulky food, or even copious drinking, will aggravate the heaving, and especially if the horse is put to work before the stomach has had time to relieve itself.

Roaring

Roaring, thick wind, or noisy respiration may be due to anything that partially obstructs the air, anywhere along its passage to and from the lungs, and it may be temporary or chronic, curable or incurable, depending upon the nature of the obstruction. Roaring and Heaves are distinct ailments, not even similar in character, though sometimes both are present together.

The different types and causes of Roaring are many. Most of the chronic cases are due to paralysis and wasting of the muscles of the larynx, particularly on the left side. In other cases there is a thickening of the membrane in the nasal passages, due to a chronic catarrhal condition, or resulting from inflammation during a severe cold or an attack of Distemper. Sometimes, too, the trouble is due to a polypus or fleshy tumor, or even a bony tumor in the nose. Temporary Roaring may accompany any acute inflammation of the membranes, or may be caused by an abscess in the head.

Treatment, of course, should be suited to the cause. If there is a catarrhal affection of the membranes, the roaring may cease if that is overcome or relieved. If the membranes somewhere in the air passages are permanently thickened, there is little hope that anything will benefit. If there is paralysis of the muscles of the larynx, the case is, as a rule, incurable. Light blisters upon small surfaces about the larynx have been employed, but usually without any marked success. Operations upon the larynx have in some cases over-come the trouble.

Cold in the Head

Horses are subject to colds, and they "catch" them in much the same manner that people do, and these colds often develop into a cough. Many think of a cold and a cough as being the same thing, but thinking it over you will remember that the cold comes first, and the cough follows a little later.

The general symptoms of cold in the head are sneezing, watering of the eyes, redness of the membrane in the nostrils, and the horse will likely appear dumpy and have a little fever. Put him in a comfortable stable, blanket him, and give him warm bran mashes and a dose of raw linseed oil. Let him have all the water he wants to drink. Antibiotics will control the secondary invaders. Use separate feed and water pails. In obstinate coughs, a little pine tar placed back on the tongue once or twice a day is some benefit.

Sore Throat

Simple sore throat in horses presents symptoms similar to Distemper and Influenza, though as a rule there is less con-stitutional distrubance, especially in the mild cases. The nose is raised and protruded, head carried stiffy and more in a line with the neck than usual, there is swelling of the throat or beneath the ears, difficulty in swallowing, coughing, the animal is sensitive to pressure on the throat, etc. Bad cases may be accompanied by inflammation of the membrane of the nose, rapid pulse and high fever.

Give rest in a clean, dry well ventilated stable. Blanket the animal, and bandage the legs if they seem cold. Give soft foods and appropriate antibiotics. If the case is severe, apply poultices for a day or two. Steam the nostrils as for the Distemper. Mix four drams solid extract of belladonna, one dram tannic acid, and four drams bisulphite of soda with five ounces syrup of honey. Smear the back teeth twice a day with a piece of this mixture the size of a small hickory nut. In an occasional bad case it is necessary to have a veterinarian open the windpipe five or six inches below the throat and insert a tracheotomy tube in order to prevent death by suffocation.

Chronic Coughs

When a cough takes on a chronic form, lingering beyond the period of a cold or other acute ailments in which the membranes are irritated and inflamed, it may be due to several causes. There may be a thickened condition of the membranes, such as is frequently caused by colds, Distemper, etc., and if so, practically nothing can be done; or, the cough may be a forerunner of Heaves, in which case the treatment for Heaves should be given. If due to a chronic irritation in the throat, lungs or bronchial tubes, a little pine tar placed back on the tongue once or twice a day may benefit. The use of selected antibiotics as indicated, will tend to restore the membranes to a healthy state.

Catarrh

Chronic catarrhal conditions may result from a cold, or any disorder that affects the membranes of the air passages. The conspicuous symptom is a discharge from the nose, and when this is thin and of a bluish color it is termed nasal gleet. In bad cases where the sinuses of the face and head are bulged and filled with matter, some cutting may be required, and it is best to consult a competent veterinarian. Steaming the nose, as for Distemper, may often be resorted to with benefit. This can usually be prevented by early treatment with antibiotics or sulfa drugs your veterinarian prescribes. In all exposure conditions greater satisfaction will result from early treatment.

Bronchitis

This is an inflammation of the larger air tubes that supply different parts of the lungs. It may accompany or follow sore throat or Distemper, or may occur by itself. The horse is dull, droops his head, breathes rapidly, lacks appetite, and coughs. The mouth is usually hot and dry, and the pulse rapid, and by placing the ear over the region of the lower part of the windpipe, a rattling sound will be heard. After a few days there is a whitish discharge from the nose. If this discharge assumes a dirty reddish color, the pulse becomes fast and weak and the breathing more rapid, recovery is doubtful.

First Aid: Place the animal in a comfortable stable, well ventilated, but away from drafts. Blanket well, and if the legs are cold, rub them briskly and wrap them with bandages. Feed bran mashes. Call your veterinarian as soon as possible.

If there is considerable fever and a rapid pulse, give fifteen drops of tincture of aconite every four hours until the pulse is more normal. Give a quarter ounce of nitrate of potash in drinking water three times a day, continuing through the course of the attack. Steam the nostrils, as recommended for Distemper, three or four times daily. When all the acute symptoms have passed off and the animal is recovering, give half a dram of nux vomica and one dram of sulphate of iron, night and morning, in bran mash.

Chronic Bronchitis

A chronic inflammation or catarrhal affection of the bronchial passages sometimes results from an acute attack of Bronchitis, or may come on gradually from other causes. It is marked by a wheezing sound, which may usually be heard distinctly by placing the ear against the chest, a slight cough, shortness of breath upon exertion, and sometimes considerable whitish discharge from the nose.

A combination of antibiotic and sulfa drugs along with a

tonic recommended by your veterinarian, good food and care are essential.

Bleeding from the Nose

This does not often occur in animals, but is sometimes brought on by over-exertion, or an injury to the membrane of the nose. Usually the bleeding is from one nostril, but may be from both, and the blood is of a dark color and is not frothy. Secure the head in an elevated position. Apply cold water to the back of the head and upper part of the neck. Spray a strong solution of alum into the nostrils with an atomizer, or blow flour up the nose. In bad cases, and where the bleeding is from one nostril, plug the nostril with a sponge or cotton, having a string fastened to it so that it may be withdrawn when the bleeding stops. Never plug both nostrils. Vitamin K may prevent this condition.

Bleeding from the Lungs

Bleeding from the lungs may be distinguished by the bright red color and frothy appearance of the blood, and the animal is apt to cough considerably in raising it. Where the bleeding is excessive, death or suffocation may occur. The cause may be over-exertion, acute congestion of the lungs, tuberculosis, or any thing that may produce a rupture of the lung tissue. In slight cases, merely keeping the animal quiet will be sufficient. If the bleeding is more severe, your veterinarian can give coagulant drugs to thicken the blood if called in time.

Distemper or Strangles

This is a contagious disease of colts and your horses, and it usually affects an animal but once. It runs a more or less definite course, and treatment is usually directed to nursing the patient through, rather than attempting to break up the disease, or interfering with its natural trend. Vaccines will help prevent it.

The symptoms are coughing, discharge at the nose, soreness of the throat, and the animal stands with the head poked forward. In drinking, some of the water is apt to flow back through the nose. Later on an enlargement forms between the jaws or back of the jaws.

Place the animal in a warm, dry and wellventilated stable. Put a blanket on him and bandage the legs. Give soft and easily digested foods, such as scalded oats and bran. If the soreness of the throat is severe or breathing is difficult, put a little turpentine or piece of camphor gum in a pail of boiling water, hold it under the animal's head and throw a blanket over the head and pail so that the steam will be inhaled. Repeat this three or four times a day. If fever is quite noticeable, give half an ounce of nitrate of potash once a day in drinking water. Apply hot poultices to the tumor, and when it becomes soft and forms up a point, open it to allow the matter to escape. Continue the poultices for a few days after the tumor is open. If great quantities of matter accumulate in the nose, continue the steaming with hot water and turpentine as already suggested. Owing to the general weakened condition, it is best not to give a physic. If the bowels do not act freely enough, give injections of soap and warm water. After the acute stage is over and the animal is well on the road to recovery, light exercise may be given, but care should be taken not to overdo it, and exposure to cold should avoided, as that might bring on a relapse. If the glands about the throat remain enlarged, apply tincture of iodine or iodine ointment. Where the disease leaves an animal in a disordered and debilitated condition, a good tonic may be used to advantage. After Distemper a horse should not be put to work until he has fully regained his strength. Roaring is the most frequent bad effect of a permanent character produced by Distemper. Selected antibiotics are most helpful and are especially beneficial if treatment is started before the disease has progressed to far into secondary stages.

Influenza or Pink Eye

This is a contagious germ disease known to many as "Pink Eye." It usually occurs during the spring and fall months, and has at times been very prevalent. The symptoms are general weakness, lassitude, fever, quick pulse, inflamed membranes, redness of the eyes, sneezing, discharge from the nose, cough, sore throat, etc. The animal is apt to be thirsty, and sometimes will eat hay readily, but refuse grain.

Give entire rest in a comfortable and well-ventilated stable, blanket the patient and bandage his legs. Allow plenty of cold water, and feed bran mashes, scalded oats, etc. If the cough is severe, put a piece of camphor gum as large as a walnut in a pail of boiling water and compel the animal to inhale the steam by holding the pail under his nose and covering head and all with a blanket. Continue this about twenty minutes at a time, three or four times a day. If the eyes are much inflamed, an eye powder in a puffer tube or eye spray should be used daily as long as necessary. Half-ounce doses of nitrate of potash should be given daily in drinking water. Care and nursing are more important than medicines in most cases of Influenza. Should the attack leave the animal in a debiliated state, a good tonic and plenty of good feed will give marvelous results.

Goiter

Goiter is an enlargement of the glands situated on each side of the throat just back of the angles of the lower jaw. It is most prevalent in sections where there is much limestone, and considerable lime in the drinking water, but is not confined to these parts. At first the swellings may be somewhat soft, becoming more solid as they increase in size. In bad cases the animal's breathing may be affected.

Apply tincture of iodine. Give internally iodine of potassium, one dram a day in bran mash for two or three weeks. If after a time the animal loses appetite and there is a watery discharge from the eyes and nose, discontinue for a week or so. It is also well to give the animal rain water to drink. Your veterinarian can prescribe a good iodine for long use.

Tumors in the Nose

Tumors of various kinds may form in the nose of animals, and usually their presence is not suspected until they have attained such a size as to interfere with the respiration. Where a snoring sound accompanies the breathing and gradually grows worse, and the obstruction seems to be in the nostril rather than in the throat, have a veterinarian make an examination. If a tumor is found it will have to be removed by surgery. The causes of noisy breathing in horses are more fully discussed under "Roaring."

Hints on Feeding Horses

Avoid working a horse more than six hours without feeding. His stomach is small in comparison with the size of his body, and is usually emptied within five hours after feeding. After that the horse weakens rapidly unless fed soon.

Variety in rations helps to keep a horse at his best. A mixture of corn and oats, two parts of oats to one of corn, is an excellent working ration. It is still better if the corn is cracked and scalded one meal in advance.

Give little corn to road or race horses. Feed them oats principally if you want them to show snap, nerve force and spirit. For growing colts there is nothing that will take the place of oats and bran.

Over-ripe, woody hay is not easily digestible, and may bring on derangement of the stomach. Millet hay is not good for horses, and should be fed sparingly if at all. Clean alfalfa or clover hay is very nutritious, and much of the prejudice against it is unjust. No matter what kind of hay you are feeding, give only as much as the horse will eat up clean each time. Doing this will prevent waste, the horse will thrive as well and there will be less probability of digestive troubles.

The common practice of watering horses before feeding is all right. Ice cold water is not good for stock, and a tank heater is a good thing to have in the winter.

When a horse is tired, after a hard day's work or a long drive, give him a little hay to take the sharp edge off his appetite before giving him his grain. If he is hot and thirsty, do not let him fill himself with cold water, but after he has eaten a little hay, water him and give him his grain.

When a horse has been at hard work on heavy feed, then stands idle in the stable a few days, reduce his rations accordingly. Failure to do so may bring on Azoturia or other serious trouble.

It is well to make a practice of feeding bran mashes occasionally, on Saturday nights for instance. A tablespoon of ground ginger stirred into the mash will have a stimulating and appetizing effect and will be appreciated by a tired horse. A pint of linseed meal will add nutrition and increase the laxative effect. A light feed of oats or other grain may follow the mash if desired.

Do not forget that animals require salt, but ordinarily it should not be mixed with the food. Horses that get enough salt are less apt to have worms.

Making Bran Mash

Bran Mash is a favorite food for sick horses, excepting in some ailments where there is irritation of the bowels. It is easily digested and has a mild laxative effect, which is often very desirable. To properly make a bran mash, proceed as follows: Take a pail and scald it out thoroughly. Even if the pail is already clean, the scalding is good because it warms it up. A wooden pail is best because it retains heat better than a tin one. Put the bran into it and add a little salt. Pour on boiling water sufficient to make a thick mass. Do not make it thin and sloppy, as the horse will not like it so well. Stir thoroughly, then cover the pail and let it stand twenty minutes or so. It should be only moderately warm when given to the animal.

Physic for Animals

Laxatives and purgatives are no less important in veterinary practice than they are in the treatment of human ailments.

The health of every part of the body, whether man or animal, depends first of all, upon the processes of assimilation and elimination, upon constant nourishing and constant cleansing, and if the system is sluggish and clogged with refuse, the cleansing is a matter of first concern, and in many minor cases is all that is required.

The purgative remedies most commonly given to horses are the following:

Aloes; three-quarters of an ounce to one ounce, mixed with a littel ginger and made into a ball, or given as a drench by dissolving along with half an ounce to an ounce of ginger in half a pint of boiling water, then adding half a pint of cold water.

Raw linseed oil; a pint and a half to two pints, given as a drench. Never give boiled oil, as it is poisonous.

Castor oil; one pint, as a drench.

For colts; Castor oil; two ounces and upward according to age.

It is often preferable to empty the bowels by injections of warm water with a little soap in it. Ordinarily, two to six quarts should be used for a horse, but in some cases much larger quantities are injected. The work may be accomplished by means of an enema syringe, or by using a rubber tube, half an inch or so in diameter, one end of which is attached to a pail in such a manner that the water will flow through the tube when the pail is elevated.

Colic

Colic is the most dangerous ailment of horses that occurs with such frequency as to place it in the class of common disorders. In spite of his best efforts, some cases will have a fatal termination, and it is doubtful whether any other ailment in the whole category of veterinary disease is accountable for more anxiety or greater loss.

The causes of Colic are many and various, and the ailment itself takes on various forms, the two common ones being what is known as Spasmodic Colic and Flatulent Colic, which are spoken of separately farther on. Colicky symptoms may be produced by almost any disorder causing acute pain in the stomach or bowels, and even the most experienced are unable to diagnose all such attacks with minute accuracy. There may be an accumulation of indigestible substances acting as an obstruction, or a part of the intestine may become tucked in, twisted or knotted, thus stopping the passage, and it is only after the death of the animal that such conditions may be definitely determined.

Try to prevent an animal from behaving too violently when suffering from Colic, especially if the attack is of the flatulent type. Thowing himself to the ground, rolling, etc., adds to the danger of rupture in the stomach, bowel, or diaphram.

If, in a case of Colic, the pulse becomes so small, quick and rapid as to be almost imperceptible, with evidence of more violent pain, and the horse breathes more rapidly, perspires very freely, and the legs and ears are cold, recovery is extremely doubtful. A little later the animal may sit for a few minutes at a time on his haunches, or may stand rather quietly and appear more at ease, but retain a distressed and anxious countenance. Sometimes, and most frequently at about this stage, a kind of vomiting will occur, a fluid-like substance being expelled at intervals, and principally through the nose. If all these symptoms appear, they may be regarded as strong indications that rupture of the stomach has occurred, and if it has, there can be no other than a fatal termination.

It should not be assumed from the above that when an animal dies during an attack of colic it is always due to rupture. In probably a majority of instances, post mortem examinations would reveal no rupture anywhere, suffocation being a frequent cause of death. The primary aim should be to remove the gas or stop fermentation.

Treating Mares in Foal

Mares in foal are often subject to colicky symptoms, sometimes due merely to this condition, though actual and severe attacks of Colic may also develop. It is advisable, under such circumstances, to avoid the use of such remedies as would otherwise be given, at least until you are satisfied that the case is a desperate one that requires more active measures. Try an ounce of common baking soda and half an ounce of ground ginger. Dissolve in half a pint of hot water, then add half a pint of cold water and give as a drench, repeating the dose in an hour if necessary.

Ordinarily, no matter what the ailment may be, it is better to avoid remedies of all kinds as much as possible when an animal is pregnant. Some of the best veterinarians claim that no drug or medicine, unless given in very excessive quantities, can produce abortion. Nevertheless, under such conditions, the system may be unusually sensitive or excitable, and that unexpected developments might follow even moderate medication. If bad, call your veterinarian.

Spasmodic Colic

Among the common causes of Spasmodic Colic are the following: Indigestion, overwork, change of food, over-feeding, chilling by sudden exposure, drinking cold water too freely upon an empty stomach, etc. In many cases, however, no particular cause is apparent.

The attack usually comes on suddenly, the animal paws with his forefeet, shifts about, looks around at his side, and may make frequent attempts to urinate. Then the pain ceases and he stands quietly as though nothing were wrong, and may even resume eating.

After a short interval another spasm comes on, likely more severe than the first, and the animal repeats these actions, also lying down, rolling on his back, getting up, lying down again, etc. In some severe cases a sweat breaks out, the breathing is fast and heavy, and the eyes are staring.

The alternate cramps and periods of relief continue. The attacks become less frequent and less severe and the animal recovers; or, the reverse may follow, the pulse becomes rapid and weak, a cold sweat breaks out, the legs tremble and are cold, the belly is tense, the brain becomes deranged and the horse dies.

The earlier you treat the case the better are your chances of saving the animal. Your veterinarian has a number of antispasmodic drugs that are very helpful. After the animal has recovered from the attack, always allow rest for several days, feeding moderately on easily digested foods.

A horse having Colic should not be driven, but should be allowed room enough so that he may move around a little.

If you haven't a colic cure give the following: One ounce chloral hydrate dissolved in a little water and added to eight ounces of raw linseed oil. To this add one ounce of turpentine, shake the mixture thoroughly and give as a drench. If relief does not follow in an hour, give another dose.

Another remedy is one ounce sulphuric ether and one ounce tincture of opium in half a pint of water every half hour until relieved. Follow with a dose of raw linseed oil if required. Use also the injections of soap and warm water.

Don't Mistake Symptoms

Inflammation of the Bowels is sometimes mistaken for Spasmodic Colic. We here compare symptoms in order to guide you in making a diagnosis.

Inflammation of the Bowels comes on gradually, and is generally preceded by increased pulse and temperature.

Spasmodic Colic attacks suddenly and is not preceded by fever, and the pulse remains natural until the case is somewhat progressed.

In Inflammation of the Bowels, the legs and ears are generally cold, and the pain is constant, there being no periods of relief.

In Spasmodic Colic the legs and ears are natural, but may

become cold in the last stages of a severe attack, and there are intervals of relief from pain when the animal will remain quiet.

A horse may lie down when suffering from Inflammation of the Bowels, but is not apt to roll so violently as in Spasmodic Colic. The membranes of the mouth and nose are congested and quite red, the mouth is hot and dry and the animal is thirsty.

In Spasmodic Colic the mouth is moist, and the membranes of the mouth and nose have their natural color.

As Inflammation of the Bowels advances, the belly becomes tucked up and hard, and pressure with the hand causes the horse to flinch.

In Spasmodic Colic, pressure upon the bowels seems to relieve rather than increase the pain.

Flatulent Colic

The causes of Flatulent Colic are similar to those of Spasmodic Colic. Eating a large quantity of green food when not accustomed to it, is a common cause.

The symptoms develop more slowly than in the spasmodic form. The horse may appear dull and sluggish, may paw some, and may or may not lie down. Gas accumulates in the stomach and intestines, and the abdomen is distended, producing a drum-like sound when struck with the hand. The symptoms now become more distressing, and, unlike Spasmodic Colic, there are no periods of relief. The breathing is difficult, and the horse is apt to perspire freely. Unless relieved, death may occur at any minute. In urgent cases tapping the colon is sometimes resorted to, but an inexperienced person should not attempt it.

Give a teaspoonful of Colic Cure, and in one hour repeat the dose unless the symptoms are pretty well relieved. Injections of warm, soapy water will also be helpful in this form of Colic.

If you haven't a Colic Cure, give a dose of raw linseed oil, and follow with two tablespoonfuls of bicarbonate of soda and a like quantity of ground ginger in a quart of warm water. Use injections of warm water and soap, then add an ounce of turpentine to eight ounces or raw linseed oil, and inject into the rectum.

Colic from Indigestion

Some horses are subject to frequent attacks of colicky pains arising from indigestion, and sometimes a severe case of colic develops from such a beginning. Give a dose of a Colic Cure, and follow a little later with a dose of raw linseed oil. If the attack is rather severe, use also injections of warm, soapy water to start the bowels.

To guard against further attacks, avoid over-ripe, woody hay and other foods not easily digested. Let the diet be largely of oats, or foods having a slightly laxative tendency, also give a bran mash occasionally. If the teeth are over-grown and uneven, have them dressed down.

Sand Colic

This is the name given to colicky disorders due to the presence of sand in the stomach or bowels. Grazing on sandy ground where the grass is short, eating grain off the ground, drinking from shallow ponds or streams, or the habit some animals have of eating dirt, may account for the sand being taken in . Various symptoms may arise, and it may be difficult to determine the exact nature of the trouble unless sand is found in the feces. There may be indigestion, frequent diarrhea, colicky pains, or the sand may accumulate until it acts as an obstruction in the bowels. Many cases, especially of the latter kind, are fatal.

Prevent the animal from eating more sand. Feed easily digested, laxative foods. Give a dose of raw linseed oil. If the bowels seem to be obstructed, inject large quantities of warm water. If there is considerable pain, give a dose of Colic Cure.

Inflammation of the Bowels

This ailment is not especially common, and the cause is usually obscure. It is apt to have a fatal termination, and is sometimes mistaken for Spasmodic Colic. See the comparison of symptoms immediately following our mention of that disease.

Eliminate the cause. Treat with a bland diet and rest. Bran is not a very good food in such a case, as it is apt to irritate the bowels.

Hide Bound

This is not a disease, but results from general disorder and impoverishment of the system. It is common among farm horses that have stood idle in the stable and had insufficient care during the winter. Though the appetite may be good, the food is not properly digested and assimilated, the blood is impure, the animal is thin in flesh, the skin is tight over the ribs and the hair tends to stand erect.

In a case of this kind you can hardly go amiss by beginning treatment with a dose of physic. Then give a good tonic and tone up the system. Nothing else puts a horse in condition so quickly, and the good that it does is lasting.

Indigestion in Horses

Though loss of appetite is a common symptom of indigestion, some horses suffering from stomach derangement are extremely greedy and will eat almost anything. Rough coat, general weakness and paleness of the mucous membrane are usually observed. Give a moderate amount of clean and easily digested food. A light dose of physic in the beginning is advisable in most cases. If no response, call your veterinarian.

Constipation in Horses

Continued feeding of dry foods that are lacking in nutritious elements, may establish a tendency to constipation. Marked cases of the kind are usually attended by indigestion, and general bad condition of the animal. Regulate the diet, allowing green pasture, or feeding bran mashes, oats, roots, etc. Give also about four ounces of raw linseed oil daily for a time, which will have a mild loosening effect upon the bowels. If there is indigestion, rough coat or general disorder, use any good tonic, a dose each evening for about ten days, then every other day for a time.

Diarrhea in Horses

Diarrhea is usually due to something in the food or water that does not agree with the animal. Find and remove the cause if possible. If the case is severe and great quantities of very liquid substance is passed, the animal showing marked signs of exhaustion, the trouble must be stopped as soon as possible. Give bismuth subnitrate in one to two ounce doses. If condition continues get professional help.

Dysentery or Bloody Flux

This is the name applied where Diarrhea taken on a more violent form, and is accompanied by straining or griping pains, and the presence of blood or a mucous-like substance in the feces. It may prove fatal within a few days, or the animal may live for several weeks or months, finally dying of exhaustion unless the disease is checked. As a general rule, treatment is unsuccessful except in some of the cases that receive early attention. Where blood is passed, it indicates ulceration, and the case is especially dangerous. This form of the disease is often called Bloody Flux.

Add two ounces of an astringent to a pint and a half of raw linseed oil and give as one dose. After three of four hours, give one ounce each of turpentine and tincture of iron in a quart of boiled flaxseed. Repeat the latter dose two or three times a day. Cleanse the bowels with warm water injections, then inject a pint of thin starch gruel, to which has been added half a dram of carbolic acid, two drams of sugar of lead, and one ounce of artringest. Put the horse in a comfortable place, and if he seems chilly, blanket him and bandage the legs. Allow plenty of clean drinking water. Feed a teacupful of boiled flaxseed mixed with ground oats, and a little good, clean hay. After two or three days, if any further treatment is required, give an ounce each of tincture of iron, tincture of gentian, and tincture of ginger, three times daily in starch gruel.

Protrusion of the Rectum

Where this occurs in horses it is usually due to hard pulling, constipation, diarrhea, or weakness of the wall of the intestine. In bad cases the bowel may protrude to a length of a foot or more, and unless returned to its place will soon become strangulated, cold, dark colored and swollen. Give a pint of raw linseed oil with an astringent power in it. Bathe the part for twenty minutes with hot water to which a little disinfectant has been added, about a teaspoonful to the gallon, then apply a lotion made by dissolving one ounce of acetate of lead in a quart of water, then adding one ounce of tincture of catechu and two ounces of laudanum. After using the lotion return the bowel gently, and if possible, stand the horse with his head down hill. In some cases it is necessary to apply a truss for twelve to twenty-four hours, and watch the animal continuously.

Superpurgation

This name is applied when a dose of physic acts too violently, producing more or less constitutional distrubance in connection with the excessive purging. It is not always due to an overdose, but may under some conditions result from a very moderate dose, especially if the animal is in a weakened or fevered state. Aloes, being a more drastic purgative, is more apt to produce Superpugation than raw linseed oil. Even though the purging is quite severe, treatment is not necessary if the pulse continues at or near the normal, and the horse retains his appetite. If, however, he refuses food, breathes rapidly, shows evidence of colicky pains, the legs become cold, and the pulse becomes fast and weak, there is cause for alarm.

Give one ounce chloral hydrate dissolved in half pint of water and added to a pint of thick, cold gruel. Blanket the animal and bandage the legs. Give half a pint of good whisky diluted with water. When the horse will eat, give a little boiled flaxseed mixed with ground oats. Allow but very little hay for a few days.

Bots

Bots are the larva of several species of gadfly that paste their little white eggs on the long hairs beneath the chin, and on the shoulders, breast and forelegs of horses. These eggs soon hatch, and the young larva craws down to the skin, irritating the part and causing the horse to nibble or lick himself. In this way they are taken into the mouth and pass down to the stomach, attaching themselves to the left half of this organ, the lining of which is a tough membrane like the lining of the gullet, and does not secrete gastric juice. There they remain during the winter, absorbing nourishment from the contents of the stomach, and in the spring loosening their hold, passing out and burrowing into the soil, where in due course they are transformed into a fly.

The accompanying illustration shows the bot fly at the left, and bots clinging to the lining of the stomach at the right. On the head of the larger bot in the middle may be seen the hooks, by means of which he attaches himself to the membrane.

Veterinarians quite generally agree that bots are harmless, unless so numerous and over-crowded that they attach themselves to the more sensitive right side of the stomach, or accumulate in the intestines. They are tough-skinned creatures, and there is no remedy that will destory or remove them that is safe to give a horse in the feed.

Trim off the long hairs from the parts where the eggs are desposited, and apply a little oil daily. This will prevent the eggs from sticking so readily. Another plan is to wash the eggs off each day with soapsuds before they have had time to hatch.

Worms

There are numerous species of parasites that inhabit the stomach and intestines of horses and mules. Most common of all is what is known as the round worm, which sometimes attains a length of twelve to fifteen inches. The presence of worms is indicated by a tendency of the horse to elevate the upper lip and rub it against the manger, rough coat, poor condition, revenous appetite, pot-belly, and the presence of mucus or an occasional worm in the feces passed.

It is doubtful if worms will exist as extensively where the digestive processes are in proper tone and a normal quantity and quality of gastric juice is secreted. At any rate, good feed and keeping the animal thrifty is always important and it also has a tendency to prevent worms. Horses may be put on low level feedings of phenothiazine several days each month or treated with larger single doses of worm medicine. This should be repeated in ten days to get those that hatch out as most worm medicines do not kill eggs. Repeat 3 or 4 times a year.

Another treatment used before modern medicines were available, was as follows: Give two pints of raw linseed oil, then feed the horse sparingly for four days, giving very little hay, if any. Then give a pint and a half of raw linseed oil to which is added two ounces of turpentine, repeating the dose on the following day. Should it seem necessary, the whole course of treatment may be repeated after two weeks.

Remember that these doses are for grown horses, and that colts should receive less according to age.

Pin Worms

These are small white worms, half an inch to two inches in length. They usually inhabit the rectum, and the animal manifests an itching sensation in the part by rubbing against the stall. Another indication of pin worms is the formation of a yellowish white crust at the verge of the rectum.

These worms are best removed by phenothiazine, piperazine, or any other good worm medicine. The same drugs used for round worms will usually get the pin worms. The treatment should be repeated in ten days to break the cycle (worms have a three weeks life cycle). The drug kills the adult worms, but not the eggs present in the gut. A few days must be allowed to let these eggs hatch. Then by a second treatment the worms should be completely eliminated until the horse in reinfected.

Eczema

The use of this name is not confined to any single skin disease of animals, but may be applied to any one of several ailments that are similar in character. Usually it refers to some minor disease in which there is redness of the skin, or minute, blister-like eruptions are present. In some cases of the more severe type, the hair becomes stiff or matted by the drying of a watery exudation, or else it comes out, leaving the skin bare, raw and scabby.

For a horse, dissolve one ounce each of aloes, baking soda and ground ginger in half a pint of boiling water, add half a pint of cold water and give as a drench. Bathe the affected parts well with one ounce of carbonate of potash dissolved in a quart of water, then rinse it off with warm water, and apply the following lotion: One ounce each of salicylic and tannic acid in one quart of alcohol. Mix well and apply to affected parts.

Surfeit

This ailment is marked by the formation of lumps in the skin, usually small, and sometimes appearing over the greater part of the body. They may pass off in a few days, or may remain, and sometimes a slight discharge of a thin, sticky fluid will occur. It is most common in overfed horses that have little exercise, but is not confined to this class, and its presence indicates blood disorder. Give a mild physic if it seems required. Use a tonic to tone up the system. Feed easily digested foods, and an occasional bran mash with a little boiled flaxseed in it. If the animal shows signs of much itching, apply the lotion recommended for Eczema.

Mange

Mange is a contagious skin disease, due to a mite or small parasite, which is usually too small to be seen with the naked eye. It is apt to appear first upon the neck, withers, or at the root of the tail, gradually spreading to other parts. A watery fluid oozes out and dries, and the itching is so intense that the animal will bite or rub the part until it is raw.

To effect a cure the parasites as well as their eggs must be destroyed. First, wash the affected parts with warm water and soap, using a brush to break up the scabs. Dissolve 1 part rotenone in 20 parts acetone then add 50 parts alcohol (rubbing alcohol). Apply to all affected parts.

An old treatment, usually very effective, is to mix two ounces of sulphur and two ounces of oil of tar in one pint of linseed oil, rubbing this well into the affected parts two or three days in succession.

Most mangy horses are in bad general condition, and a few weeks' treatment with some other good tonic is to be recommended.

Lousiness

For lice on horses and cattle, insect powder is probably the best thing to use if the weather is cold. Dust it into the hair thoroughly over the parts affected, which are usually the neck, back and rump. No matter what is used, the applications must be repeated several times at intervals of a week or ten days.

The following is a good treatment to use in warmer weather: Dissolve two ounces of soft soap in a quart of boiling water, then add slowly two quarts of kerosene. The water should be kept at the boiling point while the kerosene is being added. Then stir or churn it vigorously for ten minutes or more, so that the kerosene is well emulsified. Before using, dilute with eight times as much water. This may be sopped into the hair with a sponge or rag, then wipe off as much of it as you can. If used in cold weather, put the animal in a comfortable stable, and blanket until dry.

Sitfast

This name usually has reference to hard, callous formations on the backs of riding horses, due to irritation and pressure from the saddle. Sometimes the part becomes so hardened as to have almost a horny consistency, and the surrounding skin is inflamed and raw.

In cases where there is but a moderately hard callous and little or no soreness, a strong blister applied upon small surfaces at intervals of ten days or so, will be effective. If the part is very hard and there is soreness, mix one ounce each of vaseline, lanoline and glycerine with one-fourth ounce of Fuller's earth, and apply a thick coating of this ointment all over the callous and sore. Repeat the applications as necessary, until the hard formation is softened and loosened so that it may be removed. After that, use Veterinary Healing Oil lightly about once daily until the part is healed.

Ringworm

This is due to a parasite in the skin, and is contagious. It appears as a white grayish scurf usually causing the hair to drop off, and is most often found upon the head and legs of young cattle. Winter and Spring are the seasons in which it is most apt to occur.

First wash the affected parts with castile soap and warm water to remove the scales, then apply tincture of iodine about every third day until three or four applications have been made.

Warts

The large warty growths that tend to bleed when injured, commonly called blood wart or cancerous wart will often yield to treatment with the following ointment: Yellow sulphide of arsenic, one dram: glycerine, two drams; lanoline, five drams. Apply to the surface of the wart once or twice daily until the entire growth seems to have been destroyed, then discontinue and allow the part to heal. If, instead of healing smooth, the growth should start again, repeat the process.

There is no one treatment that seems to work best in all cases. If you should fail to succeed with the above, try terchloride of antimony, commonly called butter of antimony. Apply over the surface of the wart every third day, removing the crust each time. When the wart is reduced a little lower than the surrounding skin, discontinue and heal the sore with oxide of zinc ointment. Neither of the above treatments would be suitable if the wart is located upon the eye or any other sensitive part, or if it is situated that the remedy applied to the wart would get upon the healthy skin of other parts.

Flat warts that do not bleed may be treated the same [as] cancerous warts, first softening them with warm soap sud[s] then allowing them to dry before applying the remedy.

Warts that have a stem or neck may be removed by tyin[g] a stout cord around them tightly until they slough off, the[n] apply a little terchloride of antimony to the root, repeatin[g] on the third day. If the wart does not slough off within [a] week, tie it again.

For warts on the eyelids, tie a string around them if the[y] have a neck, and after they slough off touch the root onc[e] or twice a day with nitrate of silver for a day or two. Fo[r] flat warts about the eyes, scrape off some of the crust an[d] then use acid if it can be done without getting any into th[e] eye. Daily applications of castor oil is effective on most warts[.]

For warts on the teats of milk cows, use the string and ni[-] trate of silver, the same as for warts on the eyelids. Draw th[e] milk with a milking tube while there is soreness.

Some horses become very warty, large growths forming o[n] different parts of the body, and if removed, others will ap- pear in the same places or elsewhere. Usually it is necessary to use local treatment to remove the warts that have already formed, but there are wart vaccines that will help many cases[.]

Scratches or Cracked Heels

This is a diseased condition of the skin in the hollow of the heel. There is more or less inflammation, the skin cracks, forming deep creases, there may be a slight, greasy seepage, and usually the legs are stocked or swollen.

A lymphatic constitution, weak circulation, blood disorder, etc., may be predisposing causes. Among the external or more immediate causes are the following: Leaving the feet wet and muddy; cold air coming through cracks in the stable floor and striking the heels; filthy stables; standing in putrid pools in the straw yards; standing in snow or slush, etc.

Begin treatment by washing the heels with hot water and pure castile soap. If there is considerable inflammation or swelling, it is well to apply poultices for a few days. Apply oxide of zinc ointment, or use Veterinary Healing Oil lightly, about once a day. Feed oats rather than corn. Use a good tonic in the bad cases, or if there is much stocking of the legs. Keep the horse out of the mud, keep the stable clean, and stop any cracks in the floor that admit drafts.

Grease Heel

This disease is similar to Scratches, but in a more aggravated and chronic form. Usually there is more or less general disorder, and use of a good tonic for several weeks will be of assistance. Feed oats and bran principally, and corn only in moderation. Keep the horse out of the mud, and keep his stable clean. If the case is a bad one, poultice the foot for several days, then use the following lotion once or twice daily: Alum, sugar of lead and sulphate of copper, half an ounce of each; acetic acid, one ounce; water, one pint. There is no one treatment that will suit all cases. In some instances our Veterinary Healing Oil is very successful; also oxide of zinc ointment with one dram of iodoform added to the ounce.

Blood Poisoning

Pyemia is the form of blood poisoning most frequently encountered in veterinary practice, and is likely to occur in connection with abscesses or any disease in which there is an accumulation of pus, and especially if any cutting is done about the part. It is due to come of the poisonous pus getting into the circulation, and is indicated by fever and rapid swelling, which sometimes extends to parts quite remote from the point of suppuration, and, if the animal does not die, secondary abscesses may form.

Death is apt to follow within a day or two after the swelling occurs, though a fair percentage of apparently bad cases recover, owing, perhaps, to a naturally strong constitution and greater ability to combat the invading poison. Give tincture of iron, tincture of gentian, and tincture of ginger, one ounces of each, in a pint of water, three times a day until the swelling subsides. Use of antibiotics early will prevent this problem from developing in most cases.

Stocking

This name is applied to swelling of the lower part of the legs, particularly the hind legs. It comes on when the animal stands in the stable, and usually subsides with exercise. In itself it is not a disease, and may be due to a variety of causes, suce as indigestion, blood disorder, etc. It also accompanies most cases of Scratches or Grease Heel. Examine the heels to see whether there is any unhealthy condition of the skin there. Regulate the diet, feeding corn only moderately. Oats, roots, green pasture, etc., should be suitable foods. Give a dose of physic if it seems required. Use a tonic, if this seem desirable to give tone to the system. Let the animal have daily exercise.

Glanders*

This disease is produced by a specific germ, the Bacillus Mallei, and manifests itself in different forms, which are designated as Glanders or Farcy, according to the parts affected, and acute or chronic types of each, according to the rapidity of development and severity of the symptoms. The most prominent characteristics of there four types of Glanders are given farther on, each under its own heading.

No matter in what form the disease appears, it is so dangerous and malignant that the affected animal should be destroyed, and in most states this is compelled by law. While

---

*Editors note: While Glanders has been eliminated in most parts of the world it has been a very serious disease and is included for academic reasons.

in some of the milder cases of the chronic type, the horse may be able to perform his work for a considerable time to come, his services can hardly justify the grave risk incurred by keeping him upon the premises.

Glanders is contagious among horses, though not all the animals coming in contact with the disease take it. The infection does not float about in the air, but is distributed in the discharge that comes from the nose, or from the ulcers upon the legs or body. Many may contract the disease by inoculation, the infection finding access into some cut or abrasion of the skin.

After removing a glandered horse, disinfect the surroundings thoroughly before putting another horse in his place. Remove and burn all litter from the manger and stall. Use some good disinfecting solution freely, thoroughly washing all places where the horse could reach with his nose. If he had been worked, do not forget his harness, the neckyoke, etc. It is better to overdo than to slight a job of this kind.

Mallein Test for Glanders

In a great many cases the symptoms of Glanders or Farcy are not sufficiently marked to determine the nature of the case positively. No doubt many horses having some catarrhal affection have been destroyed upon the mistaken supposition that it was Glanders, while, on the other hand, Glanders in a mild form may fail to present symptoms that will be alarming to one not familiar with the disease.

While Glanders or Farcy are suspected, have the animal examined by a good veterinarian. If after noting the symptoms any doubt as to the nature of the case remains, he will likely apply the mallein test, which is regarded as a reliable means of diagnosis. Mallein is a product derived from a culture of the Bacillus Mallei, and may be obtained from dealers in veterinary supplies, or from the Bureau of Animals Industry, Washington, D.C. The dose required will be given upon the vial containing the mallein and varies according to the strength of the product.

The temperature of the animal is taken three or four times, at different hours during the day preceding the test; for instance, at 10 a.m., 2 p.m., 4 p.m., and 6 p.m. The mallein is then administered by hypodermic injection at about the middle of one side of the neck. Beginning at 6 a.m. the following day, the temperature is again carefully noted every two hours until 6 p.m., and if it ranges two or more degrees higher than the day previous, the presence of Glanders is considered a certainty, and especially if a painful swelling four to eight inches across rises at the point where the injection was made, and remains for several days. Some inject the mallein at about six o'clock on the morning following the day on which the preliminary temperatures are taken, in which case the maximum temperature will likely be reached between six and ten o'clock the same evening.

Chronic Glanders

Chronic Glanders develops slowly, and without the violent symptoms that mark the acute attack. The first suspicious symptoms may be a thin, sticky discharge from one nostril, usually moderate in quantity, drying upon the skin at the edge of the orifice. Sometimes it is tinged with blood. There may be such a discharge from both nostrils, but most frequently only one, and examining the membrane of the nose, small ulcers will be found, and possibly little scars showing where ulcers have healed. In the beginning, however, it may be that neither ulcers nor scars can be seen, as they may be too far up the nose to be easily detected. These ulcers or sores are a dirty gray in the center, surrounded by a deep red or purple edge, and vary from mere specks to the size of a dime. Another indication is swelling of the lymphatic glands inside the lower jaw at about the point where the pulse is felt. These are apt to be enlarged and hard, feeling not unlike a mass of peas or beans stuck fast to the bone, and usually there is no evidence of pain from light pressure upon them. If the discharge is from one nostril, the enlargement of the glands may be upon that side only.

In some mild cases of Chronic Glanders the horse may remain in apparent health for years, no symptoms being sufficiently marked to cause suspicion, yet capable of spreading the disease.

Acute Glanders

Glanders is the name applied where the disease affects the membranes of the nose and respiratory organs. The acute form develops quickly, with shivering spells, high fever, rapid pulse and respiration. The membrane of the nose is red and swollen, and small nodules develop over its surface, which soon take on the form of ulcers. These ulcers have a yellowish gray center and are usually surrounded by a red edge, and as they become developed they seem to eat into the tissue, forming a pit. The membranes may become so swollen that the animal breathes with difficulty, producing a snoring sound. The discharge from the nose is slight at first, but becomes profuse within a few days, and is apt to be tinged with blood. The lymphatic glands inside the lower jaws are usually swollen, and sometimes those of the legs are also affected. In most cases the animal dies within a couple of weeks, but sometimes the acute symptoms subside and the case takes on the chronic form.

Acute Farcy

Farcy is the name applied where the skin and lymphatic glands of the legs, or other external parts of the body, are affected. In acute cases the constitutional symptoms, temperature, pulse, etc., are much the same as in Acute Glanders. In addition, one or both hind legs become swollen, and sometimes the under part of the body as well. There may be some lameness, and the swollen parts are sensitive. The lymphatic glands inside the thigh are also enlarged and tender. The swelling gradually subsides, and small knots or lumps, commonly called farcy-buds, appear over the same surface. In a few days these buds break, and a deep sore or ulcer forms, discharging a foul, sticky substance in which there may be a little blood. The animal rapidly becomes exhausted and dies, or the case develops into some other form of the disease.

Chronic Farcy

In this form of Glanders, the violent symptoms attending the acute attacks are absent. There is more or less swelling in one or both hind legs, and the characteristic farcy-buds form, which burst and develop into deep ulcers with ragged edges and a grayish center, discharging a yellowish, sticky matter. Gradually new ulcers break out, and sometimes the old ones will show a tendency to heal. These buds and ulcers may also appear about the head, upon the withers, or underneath the body. In some instances the disease manifests itself very mildly, and the general health of the animal appears unaffected. For this reason one is apt to be reluctant about destroying the horse, yet it is unsafe to keep him about the premises, as Glanders in any of its forms may be contracted, even from a case of this type.

Big Head

This is a disease of young horses, seldom occurring after the animal has attained the age of six or seven years, and is most prevalent in several of the southern states. In appearance the disease somewhat resembles Lump Jaw in cattle, but is different in character, and is apparently due to defective nutrition, there being a lack of phosphates, so essential to the growth and health of the bones. An enlargement of the bone occurs on one or both sides of the head, and later a discharge may appear. All the bones of the body are to some extent affected, and the trouble may end in complete degeneration of the bony structure.

Treatment is probably never successful except in recent

cases. See that the animal has the best possible nourishment. Let the food be clean and wholesome, and in some variety. The use of tonics is recommended to improve the processes of digestion and assimilation. Lime water is often given with a view to supplying the system with lime, which, of course, is an important element in the composition of bone. It may be prepared as follows: Put a quantity of fresh lime in a suitable vessel and add what water it will absorb. Allow it to slack thoroughly, then fill up the vessel with water and let stand a few days before using. Give a pint of this in drinking water or food two or three times a day. Some report benefit from blistering small surfaces here and there over the enlargement, which might reasonably benefit early in the disease, but we cannot give any definite assurance as to its merit.

Thumps in Horses

This is an abrupt and violent beating of the heart, causing a visible jerking motion in the flank, and often accompanied by a thumping sound that may be heard some little distance. It may be present in connection with organic disease of the heart, or may be brought on by digestive derangement, impure blood, overexertion, excitement, etc.

Put the horse in a quiet and comfortable place away from anything that may tend to excite him. Feed bran mashes and other easily digested foods. Give twenty grains of powdered digitalis three times a day until the thumping is subdued, which will likely be within a couple of days. Follow with a dose of tonic each evening for a week, then one every other day for two or three weeks. When the horse is put to work, avoid heavy exertion for a time.

Kidney Disorders

Organic disease of the kidneys is comparatively rare in animals. It may be observed in horses that the urine is off color or varies in quantity occasionally, but ordinarily this need cause no alarm. The food, work, weather, or any slight constitutional disorder, may have this effect. If it seems advisable to stimulate the action of the kidneys somewhat, this may be done by use of one of the following diuretics: Nitrate of potash, one-fourth to one-half ounce once or twice a day in drinking water; powdered rosin, half an ounce once or twice a day; buchu, half an ounce once or twice a day. Inflammation or any diseased condition of the kidneys is suspected, it is advisable to place the case in the hands of an experienced veterinarian, who can make a careful examination and treat accordingly to the conditions found.

In some urinary disorders the kidneys may not be involved, and the whole trouble may be in the bladder or some of the passages, and may be in the nature of inflammation, paralysis, nervous contractions or spasms, tumorous growths, calculi or limy bodies acting as obstructions, etc. From this it may be seen that expert attention is often necessary in order to determine such conditions. Immediately following, we mention briefly several urinary disorders that we have occasionally been asked about.

Polyuria

This disease is supposed to arise, in most instances, from eating musty foods. It occurs mostly in horses, but may affect other animals. The characteristic symptom is frequent and excessive discharge of urine, very slightly colored if at all. There is also unnatural thirst, and often the animal will eat dirt, or in other ways show a depraved appetite. Loss of flesh and general emaciation follows, and the horse will usually die unless the disease is checked.

Put the animal upon a wholesome diet, but avoid timothy hay for a time. Give dram doses of iodine night and morning until the discharge of urine approaches normal. Two to four doses will usually be sufficient. Dissolve the iodine in a little alcohol, then give as a drench in half a pint or so of water. Mix three ounces of sulphate of iron with six ounces of powdered gentian, divide into twenty-four doses, and follow the above treatment by giving one dose night and morning in bran mash.

Suppression of Urine

Where the passage of urine is very scanty or practically ceases, it is necessary to discover the nature of the trouble. It may be that the kidneys are not acting and very little urine is being secreted, in which case the use of a diuretic remedy would ordinarily be indicated. If, however, the kidneys are not at fault and there is some stoppage of the passages instead, such a treatment would only aggravate the condition. This matter may be determined in the following manner: Use an injection of warm water to clean out the rectum, then oil the hand and pass it into the rectum. If the bladder is full it may be felt below the bowel at a distance of eight or ten inches from the opening, and will indicate that the trouble is not in the kidneys. If it is empty it cannot be felt, and the kidneys are not acting. The latter condition is sometimes brought about by fevers, and in such cases half-ounce doses of nitarate of potash twice a day for a few days will usually correct the trouble. Old and rundown horses are sometimes troubled with a tendency of this kind, and in such cases the following is a good treatment: Two ounces each of sulphate of iron and nitrate of potash, half an ounce powdered digitalis, mixed and divided into twelve doses, a dose to be given night and morning in bran mash.

In cases where the bladder is found to be full, it will be evident that there is something wrong in the passages, and as any one of half a dozen or more conditions may be responsible, a veterinarian should be called.

Bloody Urine

This may be due to strain or injury, or to some ulcerated or diseased condition of the urinary passages. There is also a disease called Idiopathic Hematuria that presents this symptom, and may affect either horses or cattle. It sometimes becomes quite prevalent in a locality, and animals affected show loss of appetite, rapid pulse, stiffness and general weakness, and the urine has a dark reddish color. In a case of this kind blood-clots do not form in the urine, as they do where the trouble is a result of injury.

Allow plenty of cold water and wholesome food. For a horse, dissolve one ounce each of aloes and powdered ginger in half a pint of boiling water, add half a pint or so of cold water and give as a drench. Give cattle a pound and a half of Epsom salts dissolved in half a gallon of water. For both horses and cattle, follow the physic with one ounce each of tincture of iron, tincture of gentian and tincture of ginger, two or three times a day in a pint of water.

In cases that are due to strain or injury, the horse shows stiffness in the hind parts, with soreness in the region of the kidneys, and there may also be more or less fever. When urine is passed and stands for a time upon the stable floor, the blood that is in it gathers in clots.

Keep the animal quiet and give him plenty of cold water. Give twenty grains each of acetate of lead and acetate of zinc, mixed with two drams of catechu. This may be given in a ball or thin gruel. Repeat the dose three times a day until the passing of blood is checked. Three or four doses will be sufficient in most cases. Give the horse a rest and when working him again, avoid overexertion. Your veterinarian has blood clotting agents that are very effective. Feeding sweet clover causes this condition in many cases.

Leucorrhea or Whites

This ailment is of rather frequent occurrence among mares, and is a morbid condition of the membranes of the vagina, accompanied by a whitish or bluish discharge that varies both in quantity and consistency. In some cases the membrane becomes ulcerated, and the discharge may be streaked with blood. It is most common among animals that are dehabilitated or advanced in age where the muscles have lost tone.

Cleanse the vagina daily with warm water injections, and after each cleansing inject an ounce or so of a solution made by dissolving half an ounce each of sulphate of zinc and carbolic acid in a quart of water. Feeding a tonic is a good constitutional treatment in such cases, and has a tendency both to overcome the condition and prevent its return. Continue it three or four weeks, giving a dose each evening for the first week or ten days, then one every other day. Antibiotics will hasten recovery and prevent secondary infections.

Abortion

Where abortion or premature birth of the young occurs, it is apt to be due to a kick, blow, slip, fall, or injury of some sort. Fright may also produce abortion, or it may result from disease of the foetus itself. It is well, also, to avoid smutty grain, overfeeding, close, hot and foul-smelling stables, stalls sloping too much backward, too severe exertion after continued idleness, large drafts of cold water when very thirsty, etc. Do not overwork mares in foal, especially near the end of their term. Remove any exciting causes they might come into contact with during late pregnancy.

Abortion usually occurs during the first half of the period of gestation, but may occur later. If very early in the period, it affects the general health of the animal very slightly, as a rule. If late in the period, there is restlessness, filling of the udder, symptoms of pain, and the usual signs of approaching parturition. If the trouble is discovered early enough, abortion can sometimes be prevented by giving hormones by your veterinarian. In most cases where abortion occurs, no treatment is necessary other than keeping the animal quiet a few days and feeding easily digested foods.

Sterility or Barrenness

There are undoubtedly various causes for barrenness. It is

probably due in some instances to heavy feeding and lack of exercise, or, on the other hand, an impoverished condition of the system. Again, there may be some specific derangement of the generative organs, and no general treatment to meet the requirement in all instances can be outlined. The cause may be infection or a hormone imbalance. A good veterinarian can determine the real cause and treat the specific condition. Time is usually the factor limiting treatment.

Phymosis or Swollen Sheath

Swelling and soreness of the sheath may be due to various causes, such as kicks or other injuries, overfeeding with lack of exercise, an impoverished condition of the animal, accumulation of filth in the sheath, etc. Bathe the part with hot water for twenty minutes at a time three times a day. Dissolve half an ounce of acetate of lead in a quart of water, add two ounces of tincture of arnica, and apply this lotion after each bathing. If there is considerable swelling, suspend the sheath by means of a wide strip of cloth passed under it and the ends fastened over the loins. Use a good tonic if the animal is in a rundown condition. If the horse is fat or overfed, give a dose of aloes, then follow with quarter-ounce doses of nitrate of potash two or three times a day in drinking water.

Paraphymosis

In a case of this kind the penis hangs from the sheath continuously. It may be due to injury, or to general weakness and local paralysis. Suspend with the strip of cloth as in Phymosis. If the organ is hot, swollen and sensitive, keep it wet with a lotion made by dissolving half an ounce of acetate of lead in a quart of water, then adding two ounces of laudanum. If swollen but not feverish, bathe with hot water for twenty minutes or so three times a day, and after each bathing apply some of the following lotion: one ounce each of laudanum and fluid extract of belladonna in a pint of water. If the horse is in good condition, give a dose of aloes and follow with quarter ounce doses of nitrate of potash three times a day in drinking water. If he is thin and weak, give two drams of sulphate of iron and half a dram of nux vomica each evening in bran mash, and half an ounce of nitrate of potash each morning in the drinking water, continuing two or three weeks. In some cases, especially in old horses, amputation may be necessary.

EYE DISEASES

Where blindness or partial blindness in animals is due to some affection of the optic nerve, or to a change taking place in some part of the eye structure, restoration of the sight is impossible. Cataract is not successfully treated in animals. An opaque or milky appearance of the eye is usually incurable, unless merely a whitish scum accompanying inflammation.

We must direct our efforts toward preventing blindness rather than curing it, and proper attention to acute inflammations of the eyes is the best possible means of prevention. All swollen, sore, inflamed and watery conditions of the eyes should receive treatment.

Veterinary Eye Lotion

The use of this remedy is indicated wherever there is any inflammation of the eyes, no matter what the cause. If it were kept on hand and properly used at the right time, there would be little blindness among stock. Loss of sight, except where due to accidental laceration of the eye, is nearly always the result of some form of inflammation, and inflammation of the eyes cannot continue where this remedy is used.

Veterinary Eye Lotion should be used for all weak, watery, swollen, sore and inflamed conditions of the eyes of animals. It is non-poisonous, entirely harmless, costs but little and will keep forever. It is prepared in very concentrated form, and is to be added to one quart of water before applying. There are, also, many good eye powders, sprays, and ointments available. Keep some handy for early use in eye problems.

Inflammation of the Eyes

This may result from colds, injuries, bites of insects, foreign substance in the eye, etc. It is always well to make an examination for chaff or dirt, and espectially if but one eye is affected. If there is considerable swelling or feverishness, bathe the eyes with moderately cool water about three times a day. After each bathing apply Veterinary Eye Lotion freely. This can be done by means of a small, soft sponge, sopping the eyes well and squeezing a little of the remedy into them. Keep the horse in a darkened stable until the inflammation subsides.

Periodic Ophthalmia or Moon Blindness

This disease affects horses, and is marked by an inflammation of the eyes that recurs at more or less regular intervals. Owing to this characteristic, these attacks were by some associated with the moon's changes, supposing the moon, in some unaccountable way, to be responsible for them. There is, of course, no truth in such a theory. Though the ailment is not altogether understood, it seems to be of a constitutional character, the eye trouble being merely the conspicuous symptom. It is not a contagious disease, but is more prevalent in some sections than in others, and a susceptible tendency seems in some measure to be hereditary.

The attack may come on very suddenly, even in a single night, and one or both eyes may be affected. The upper eyelid droops, light is painful and the eye waters freely. In some cases the eyeball may take on an amber color. The trouble usually subsides in about ten days, and is apt to appear again in a few weeks or months. The first attack seldom causes blindness, but repeated attacks derange the eye structure, destroy the sight, and the eye takes on a bluish white appearance.

There is no positive cure for this disease. Some cases are apparently cured, though the trouble is apt to return again soon or later. In most cases the best that can be done is to relieve the inflammation at the time of each attack, and thus ward off blindness. Put the animal in a darkened stable and apply Veterinary Eye Lotion three or four times a day until the inflammation subsides. Also use Riboflavin, a vitamin, to keep the system in proper balance. If this is done the attacks are usually milder and less frequent, and sometimes are avoided for years.

Turned-in Eyelashes

Sometimes the eyelashes tend to turn upward, irritating the eyeball and setting up inflammation. The cause of the irritation is easily detected in such cases, and all that is required is to keep the eyelashes trimmed short with a pair of scissors.

Turned-in Eyelids

In a case of this kind the margin of the eyelid is turned in against the eyeball. Such a trouble is rare, but is occasionally seen in young colts. It is usually corrected by taking out a little section of the skin, then bringing the edges together and fastening them. One method of fastening the edges is to place small pins through them, then wind thread around the exposed ends of each pin like the figure eight. Such an operation should be performed by an experienced person.

Lacerated Eyelids

Such injuries are as a rule slight, and usually the torn edges may be held together by bringing them into proper position and applying collodion, layer upon layer as fast as each dries, until the necessary strength is obtained. Tie the animal in such a way that he cannot rub the eye against anything, which would likely tear the wound open again with still more damage.

Punctured Eyeball

Injuries of this kind may be caused by stiff straws, thorns, nails, etc. There is much watering of the eye, and the animal keeps it closed. Usually an examination will reveal the nature of the trouble. If the wound is deep and the vitreous humor escapes, the eye will be ruined. If only the cornea is punctured, the fluid that has escaped will be replaced when the wound is healed.

Put the animal in a darkened place, and bathe the eye with cold water three times daily. After each bathing, apply a light bandage of clean, soft muslin, and wet it frequently with Veterinary Eye Lotion, properly diluted. Where the wound is a moderate one only, it will usually heal and the inflammation will subside within a week or ten days, sooner if antibiotics are employed early.

HEALING WOUNDS

In healing wounds there is nothing more essential than preventing germ infection. As germs are everywhere and cannot be avoided, we must depend not so much on keeping them out of the wound as destroying those that enter. Every fresh cut should have antiseptic or germ-destroying treatment of some sort. If the remedy possesses healing properties in addition to being antiseptic, so much the better. In the absence of anything more suitable, use a carbolic solution for cleansing the wound, two teaspoonfuls carbolic acid to a quart of water. Carbolated oil, one part carbolic acid to eighteen or twenty parts sweet oil, is a good antiseptic dressing. Apply it rather lightly. Strong and irritating liniments should not be used. As a general rule, it is best not to wash wounds any more than is absolutely necessary to remove dirt or stop blood, and this should be done by flowing water over the wound rather than wiping with a sponge. Washing after the healing begins is seldom required, and usually harms more than it helps. Less damage is done and better results are obtained by using Steri-Foam.

Incised Wounds

An incised or clean cut wound lengthwise of a muscle will usually heal quickly by adhesion if the edges are drawn together and stitched. First, examine the wound for any foreign substance that may be there. If any large blood vessels are cut, they should be tied. Moderate bleeding may be checked by cold water applications. If there is little or no bleeding, and no dirt in the wound, washing is not required.

If necessary to wash to remove dirt or blood clots, flow tepid water through the wound.

After washing, wait a few minutes to let the wound dry somewhat, or then carefully apply Steri-Foam to the lacerated surfaces, draw the edges together and stitch with strong silk or linen thread. The needle should be passed through the skin about a quarter of an inch back from the severed edges, and the ends of the thread tied at each stitch. Put in a stitch about every three-quarters of an inch. Apply the Healing Oil along the cut and over the stitches, repeating the applications lightly once or twice a day.

If the wound is across the muscle and an inch or more in depth, stitching will be of little benefit, as the cut in the muscle will spread beneath the skin. In other respects, treat in the same manner, applying the Healing Oil lightly once or twice a day.

Lacerated Wounds

A torn and ragged wound should be cleaned of dirt and the bleeding checked as recommended for cuts. Then apply Veterinary Healing Oil, and continue with light applications once or twice a day. There is no use in stitching the ragged edges of the skin, as these will slough off in time, and closing such a wound is apt to do more harm than good, as the matter that accumulates does not escape so readily.

Punctured Wounds

Punctured wounds are apt to prove troublesome unless carefully treated, and are always more or less dangerous. They are apt to contain dirt, hair, slivers of wood or some foreign substance. Examine the wound and remove anything of the sort that may be found. Take a soft strip of muslin, moisten with Veterinary Healing Oil, and with a probe press it to the bottom of the opening. Let it remain there. Draw out the muslin and put in a fresh one twice a day for several days. This will destroy any germ infection that may be present, and will prevent the wound from closing too quickly on the outside.

If you have none of the Healing Oil, use carbolic solution or carbolated oil in the same manner. Discontinue the muslin after matter forms, but inject a small quantity of the remedy into the opening occasionally if you can do so. Early use of antibiotics is best, if available. All puncture wound cases should have a tetanus shot as soon as possible.

Veterinary Healing Oil

1 part each of carbolic acid, camphor oil, menthol, thymol, evcalyptus oil. Mix in 95 parts vegetable oil. Scarlet red may be added.

Contused Wounds

By contused wound is meant a severe bruise that does not tear the skin but lacerates the tissues beneath. Ordinarily, all that is required is frequent bathing with a lotion made by dissolving an ounce of acetate of lead in a quart of water. Occasionally a fluid will collect and the part will be swollen, and soft to the touch. Where this occurs open it to allow the fluid to escape, then dissolve one dram chloride of zinc in a pint of water, and with this bathe the part twice daily, also injecting a little of the solution into the opening.

Wire Cuts

The number of horses lacerated by barbed wire is astonishing, and in a large percentage of instances the wound does not receive proper treatment. As these cuts are so frequently received below the knees and hock joints, where, instead of muscular tissue, tendons, ligaments, and cartilage are torn, great care is often required to get them to heal promptly and without leaving blemishes.

Put the animal in a stall where he will be quiet. Cleanse the wound with tepid water or Steri Foam if it seems required, then apply Veterinary Healing Oil somewhat freely. After this, repeat the applications rather lightly once or twice daily. The tendency is to use more of the remedy than is required. Wire cuts vary a great deal in character, and you should use your own judgment as to stitching.

If the injury is not discovered at once and the animal wades through weeds, wet grass and dirt until inflammation is set up in the part, bathe every hour or so with the following lotion: Half an ounce acetate of lead, half an ounce sulphate of zinc, two ounces tincture of arnica, in one quart of water. Keep this up until the inflammation is reduced, then use the Healing Oil. If you haven't the Healing Oil, continue with the lotion, applying three times daily until healed.

There is a tendency in wounds upon the legs of horses, especially if neglected or badly treated, for the center of the sore to fill up higher than the surrounding skin. Where this occurs a blemish is likely to remain after the part is healed. Apply a little powered corrosive sub-limate every third day until the protruding part is properly reduced. Do not use this too freely—never more than a quantity the size of a pea, as it might poison the animal through absorption. Apply with a smooth, flat stick. After reducing the part, go on with the healing applications. Tetanus shot is a good precaution.

Old Sores

In the case of an old sore that refuses to heal, there may be a diseased condition requiring something more than a simple healing remedy. Use Veterinary Healing Oil, applying rather freely about once or twice daily for four or five days, then quite lightly thereafter. If it does not take on a more healthy appearance and show an inclination to heal within a week or so, apply tincture of iodine lightly around the edge of the sore once or twice a week, meanwhile continuing to use the Healing Oil— this treatment will seldom fail.

171

Proud Flesh

In raw sores where through some cause or other inflammation has been set up, a soft, flabby, bulging, unhealthy growth is liable to occur, commonly known as Proud Flesh. Touch the part lightly with a stick of lunar caustic until a thin white film is produced, or dust with powdered burnt alum. Do this daily until the part takes on a more healthy appearance, then use Veterinary Healing Oil.

Maggots in Sores

Where a sore or wound becomes infested with maggots, spray or sprinkle it with chloroform or a commercial product made for this purpose. To guard against maggots, mix one ounce of turpentine, two ounces of fish oil, and three ounces of tar, applying this upon the hair around the sore. There are, also, good commercial mixtures available to prevent infestation.

Fly Repellent

As a fly-chasing mixture for general use on animals, the following has been recommended by several state experiment stations: Fish oil, two quarts; crude carbolic acid, one pint; oil of pennroyal, one ounce; oil of tar, ten ounces; kerosene, one quart. Mix thoroughly and apply with a brush or sprayer every two or three days. There are many good commercial sprays, but flys build up a tolerance for most of them.

Burns and Scalds

It is seldom advisable to attempt to treat severe burns covering a considerable portion of an animal's body. For small burns, you can use nothing better than Veterinary Healing Oil. Cover the burn with a thin layer of cotton batting saturated with the Healing Oil. There is nothing else that will take out the fire so quickly, and you will appreciate this if you should happen to burn or scald yourself, and have some of the remedy at hand to use. For a large burn upon a horse, it is just as well to dilute the Healing Oil with two or three parts of sweet oil or linsed oil. Baking soda applied over the burned surface is also good. The main object is to keep out the air and prevent infection.

Galls

For harness galls of every description, sore shoulders, sore neck, sore back, crupper sores, etc., there is nothing better than Veterinary Healing Oil. It is best to give rest until the sores heal. If this cannot be done, see that the harness fits properly, and relieve the sore parts as much as possible. Wash the perspiration from the sores each evening if the horse is worked, and when dry apply the Healing Oil rather lightly.

Tender Shoulders

Some horses have skins so very tender that the shoulders do not toughen to the collar, but gall almost every time the animal is in harness. Wash the perspiration off the shoulders, wipe them dry, then saturate the hair with the following lotion: Tannic acid, one ounce; alcohol, four ounces; water sufficient to make a pint. Use the lotion daily until the skin is toughened. If there are galls, it may be used just the same, and will be healing in addition to toughening the skin.

HANDLING YOUNG COLTS

The best time to begin educating a colt is when he is but a few hours old, or a few days at most. Cultivate his acquaintance and pet him in such a manner that he will have no fear of you at all. Put a little sugar in his mouth, then teach him to take a lump of sugar from your hand. Give him a name and teach him to come when called. Reward his obedience with a lump of sugar, piece of apple or something he likes. Give him a little attention daily, or every few days at most, but let all his lessons be short.

Teach him to submit to control by placing one hand back of the hind quarters and the other under his neck, then say "go on" and move him forward, then say "whoa" and make him stop. In the same manner teach him to back. Continue this until he knows what the words of command mean, and will respond to them. Put a halter on him next, and with one hand draw tightly on the strap, and with the other hand behind him as already described, command him to "go on." Be patient and always kind, and he will soon learn to know you as his friend and master.

Where these early lessons have not been given, and the colt has grown too strong to be handled in this manner, break him to the halter as follows: Take a light rope twenty-five or thirty feet long, bring the ends together and drop the middle part or loop over the colt's rump, down about where the breeching rests. A little back of the withers tie a knot in the double rope, then bring the loose ends forward, one on each side of the neck, through the ring in the halter. Draw on the ropes, commanding the colt to come to you. In this manner you will shortly teach him to lead with very little floundering, and no danger of his hurting himself. When trying him

174

the first time or two, place the ropes through the stall ring and tie back to the halter, so that if he pulls back the loop over the rump will tighten.

Weaning Colts

Give the colt a little ground oats mixed with bran twice a day for some little time before weaning, and let him have access to all the clean drinking water he wants. If this is done he will not fall off in flesh to the extent that he otherwise would after being weaned. Also, keep him sheltered from the cold autumn rains, which are a frequent cause of rheumatism in colts. Colts should be weaned at the age of five or six months, and it is best to get them started thriving on their new diet before the cold weather sets in.

The first year's care and feeding has a lot to do with the making of a horse. Give the colt a comfortable box stall at night and on cold or stormy days, and a run outside when the weather is fine. Oats are the best grain for a colt. Give him about two quarts three times a day, and a little bran besides. Nice, alfalfa or clover hay is better than timothy, but feed it in smaller quantities. Properly fed, it will not give them heaves or make them potbellied. Don't compel the colts, or any of your other stock, to drink freezing cold water if you can avoid it.

Constipation in Colts

This is quite common in newly born foals and is a dangerous condition. At birth there is an accumulation of hard substance in the bowels, which, should it fail to pass off, will produce a colic that is very apt to prove fatal. If the colt is unable to expel the accumulation, give injections of warm water with a little soap in it. Castile soap is best, but if you have none, use the best you have. If injections fail, give two ounces of castor oil, or four ounces of raw linseed oil. Usually the injections will do the work, and in so young an animal are preferable to the use of medicine, as the stomach is in no way disturbed.

Bent Ankle

In an occasional instance the ankles of the forelegs of a newly born foal will bend forward, even coming in contact with the ground, the bones being too soft to sustain the animal's weight. It is better not to apply splints or bandages, as he skin will soon become scalded and sores will form. Confine the mare in a small place and use the softest bedding possible. Feed her oats twice a day, and once a day give a bran mash with half an ounce of calcium phosphate in it, continuing this for ten days or so. Dissolve an ounce of tannic acid in a pint of water, add half a pint of alcohol, and with this lotion bathe the foal's ankles twice daily. If the ankles become sore, apply a little oxide of zinc ointment. In bad cases where the ankles bend over against the ground, the condition is a difficult one to deal with.

Rupture or Hernia

Upon this subject we shall speak only briefly and in a general way, because there are different kinds of Hernia, some easily detected, while in other cases the nature of the trouble is obscure. Anatomical knowledge is of much importance in the treatment of Hernia, and in some cases surgery is required. Therefore, wherever possible, treatment should be conducted by a veterinarian.

By Hernia is meant a protrusion of the bowel through some natural or unnatural opening in the walls of the abdomen, or even through the diaphragm into the chest. A slight case of the latter kind may produce symptoms similar to Heaves, while a bad case may be suddenly fatal. Ordinarily Hernia is not dangerous unless the bowel becomes strangulated, in which case inflammation, mortification and death follow unless the condition is relieved. Such a case is very painful, and

176

may sometimes be mistaken for Colic, the symptoms being similar. The treatment is to return the bowel to the abdominal cavity by careful manipulation, and usually this can best be accomplished if the animal is turned on his back.

The most common forms of Hernia are Umbilical Hernia and Scrotal Hernia, and these are seen mostly in young colts. In Umbilical Hernia the protrusion is seen at the navel, sometimes forming quite a large bunch or sack. In Scrotal Hernia, the bowel comes down into the scrotum, which is seen to be enlarged. Ordinarily, cases of either kind are not treated, and as a rule the trouble will have disappeared by the time the animal is a year old.

Diarrhea in Colts

This is very common, and is caused by some food the mother has eaten, something the colt has picked up itself, or from overloading the stomach with milk. For instance, if the mare and foal are separated for a time, the colt becomes very hungry and is apt to take more milk than it can properly digest.

When the trouble appears, put the mother on dry food and give the colt two ounces of castor oil and a teaspoonful of astringent powder. If after the oil operates the diarrhea does not stop, give, in half a pint of starch gruel, two teaspoonsful bismuth subnitrate, one tablespoon tincture of catechu, and one tablespoon chalk. Repeat in three hours if required. If a tendency to constipation follows, give a little boiled flaxseed.

Thrush of the Mouth

The mouths of sucking animals sometimes inflamed, and on examination small whitish patches are found on the lips, cheeks and tongue. This is called thrush, and ordinarily the ailment is not a serious one. Sponge the mouth frequently with a rather weak solution of borax or bisulphite of soda.

AGE OF HORSES AS SHOWN BY THE TEETH

The teeth of a horse indicate his age approximately and not with exactness. The mouth is not an open book in this regard, and does not read like type or figures, even to an expert.

Different mouths may present somewhat different appearances at the same ages. The teeth in different animals may differ as to shape, dimensions, position or inclination, the tooth structure may vary in hardness, with a consequent variation in rapidity of wear, or the teeth may have worn away rapidly or slowly, according to the kinds of food that have been eaten most. Nevertheless, the mouth tells more as to age than any other part of the horse, and those familiar with the changes that time brings to the teeth need not guess far amiss.

The colt teeth are twenty-four in number; twelve incisors or front teeth, and twelve molars or grinders. There are six incisors above and six below, and the molars are arranged three on each side above and below.

As the animal matures, the colt teeth give place to the adult or permanent teeth, of which there are thirty-six to forty, according to the presence or absence of tusks or canine teeth, which usually do not appear in mares, or, if they appear, are but slightly developed. The permanent teeth are arranged as follows: Six incisors in the upper jaw and six in the lower jaw, six molars or grinders on each side above and below, and if all are developed, a tusk on each side above and below at some little distance back of the incisors.

The incisors, both in the upper and lower jaw, are named as follows: The two in the center are called nippers, the two that form the ends of the row and are farthest back toward the tusk are called the corners, and the two that are between the nippers and corners are called dividers.

During the life of the horse, the teeth continue to grow, or are gradually pushed up from their sockets, to compensate for the wear upon them. If this were not so, upon reaching a moderate age horses would have their teeth worn to the gums, and would be unable to masticate their food.

In examining the mouth to determine a horse's age, the most attention is given to the incisors, and especially those of the lower jaw. As these teeth grow out and are worn off, their crown or biting surface is changed in shape and appearance. This may be understood from the accompanying 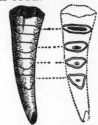 cut, which represents a permanent lower nipper with its face or front side farthest from you. It will be seen that the tooth does not retain the same shape from its crown to its root. If worn to the first dotted line, the crown will be narrower and a little thicker from front to back than at first, presenting an appearance somewhat as shown at the right. If worn to the second dotted line, the crown will be still narrower and thicker from front to back, and the spot in the center will be smaller. If worn to the last dotted line, the crown will have assumed a triangular shape, and when worn still farther the thickness from front to back become considerably greater than the width, which is not shown in the cut.

As the horse advances in age, there is also more or less tendency of the incisors, both upper and lower, to protrude outward against the lips, the jaws present a narrower appearance, and the gums shrink or recede, so that the teeth are longer or more exposed.

The following illustrations of teeth as they are apt to appear at different ages, will, we believe, be of much assistance to those who wish to cultivate to proficiency as judges of age in horses and by noting them carefully the gradual changes that we have mentioned will be observed. With practice one can be very accurate up to approximately twelve years of age. After twelve, more emphasis must be put on the change in shape from square to oval.

One Year

The upper nippers appear first, their forward edges coming through the membrane of the gums when the colt is about one week old, the lower nippers following a few days later. At about five weeks of age the dividers appear, and the corners are first visible at eight to ten months.

The drawing above shows the appearance of the lower incisors at about one year after birth. Observe that the nippers and dividers are slightly worn, and by the cut below, that the corners are not yet in contact when the mouth is closed. The corners will continue to grow and be in contact with opposing teeth at about one and one-half years of age.

Two Years

At about two years of age it will be seen that the nippers are worn smooth all around, the groove through the crown that was visible at the age of one year having disappeared. The dividers are also considerably worn. The corners are well grown, the gums receded slightly from their base, and they have been in contact for three months or more, already showing some little wear along the forward edge. These teeth have served their purpose and will soon begin to be replaced with much larger permanent teeth. Horses usually start training at this age so it is important to keep careful watch of the teeth from 2 years of age.

Three Years

At about two and a half years of age the colt teeth begin to be replaced by the adult or permanent ones. Usually the upper nippers are shed first, and the lower ones a little later.

At three years of age the appearance of the mouth is apt to be about as shown here. The dividers and corners are much worn, and are considerably smaller at the base than at the crown. All the permanent nippers are through the gums, the upper ones more developed than the lower, and may be about as shown below, or even sufficiently grown to meet in contact when the mouth is closed. Examine with the mouth closed.

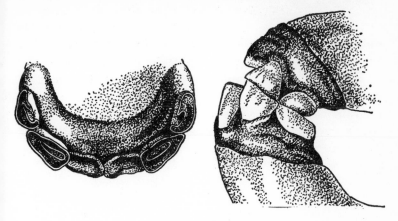

Four Years

At the age of four years the permanent nippers and dividers, above and below, have grown out, and are already considerably worn. All of the old corners are usually remaining at this age, but will soon give way to the permanent ones. They are much worn, and appear small in size compared with the new teeth, somewhat as shown above. At about this age the tusks may begin to appear.

Five Years

By the time the animal is five years of age, the permanent corners will have grown out level with the nippers and dividers, and will likely show some little wear. The nippers are worn almost level, but retain long and narrow cavities or cups, while the dividers present much the same appearance. In male animals, the tusks will likely be well formed by this time.

Six Years

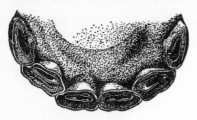

At this age the nippers are apt to be worn entirely level, but may sometimes retain a little of the cup. Usually there are yet shallow cups in the dividers, but these may in some instances be worn level also. The corners are now considerably worn, and the nippers and dividers are slightly more oval in form The front or face of the nippers, as seen by parting the lips, is apt to present a whiter appearance than at five years, due to the wearing away of the yellowish cement.

Seven Years

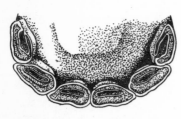

At seven years the nippers and dividers will have worn entirely level, the cups having disappeared, and will have assumed a more oval form, being thicker from front to back. The corners show greater wear, and the cups in them are becoming shallow. In most instances the upper corners are larger than the lower ones, so that at the back part they do not come in contact when the mouth is closed, and consequently are not worn off. This is shown in the drawing below. The yellowish cement is not pretty well worn off the face of all the incisors, showing more of the whiter colored enamel.

Eight Years

At the age of eight years, the corners are usually worn level, and their crown is assuming a more oval appearance. The nippers and dividers are still thicker from front to back, and somewhat diminished in width, so that they have a more rounded form. What is called the dental star is becoming visible, especially in the nippers, and appears as a yellowish line in the crown, about half way between the front edge and the central enamel, which, it will be observed, has become shorter and is nearer to the back edge or border than formerly. As will be seen below, the teeth do not set so squarely as heretofore, but present a more protruding appearance.

Nine Years

At nine years the nippers and dividers are well rounded, being narrower than formerly, and thicker from front to back. The central enamel is shorter, is well toward the back edge or border, and may be assuming a triangular form. The dental star is more distinct, and may appear as elongated spots rather than a line. The appearance of the corners varies in different mouths, as they are often irregular in shape. The notch in the upper corners, spoken of at seven years, has often disappeared by this time.

Ten Years

By the time a horse is ten years of age his nippers have become so much narrower, and so much thicker from front to back, that they appear almost round, somewhat as shown above, and the

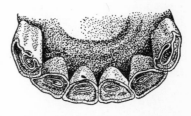

dividers have a similar appearance. The central enamel is smaller, and likely triangular. The dental star is seen well toward the center of the crown. The corners shown above are not characteristic of this age, but merely illustrate irregular forms that are sometimes seen. The tendency of the teeth to protrude against the lips is becoming marked, as seen below.

Eleven Years

At the age of eleven years, the nippers and dividers are still more rounded, the thickness from front to back almost equaling their width. The central enamel has become quite small and is near the back border, while the dental star is now seen at about the center of the crown. The teeth protrude a little more than at ten years, and the lower corners are almost the same size from base to crown, the gum usually fitting more squarely around the base.

Thirteen Years

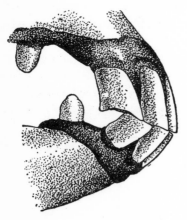

At thirteen years the central enamel has usually disappeared from all of the lower incisors, though sometimes traces of it remain. The dental star is seen as a small yellowish spot at about the center of the crown, and the teeth are not only rounded, but may be assuming a slightly triangular form. In some mouths it will be seen that the upper and lower corners are far from meeting squarely, as shown. This feature varies, however, in different animals, but as a rule a notch will be seen in the upper corner produced by uneven wear.

Fifteen Years

Gradually the jaws have assumed a thinner or narrower appearance, which by this time is quite marked. The nippers and dividers show distinctly their tendency to become triangular. The dental star is seen as a round spot at about the center of the lower incisors. Possibly in a few instances the central enamel will have disappeared from the upper nippers, but as a rule it is still seen in both the upper nippers and dividers. Parting the lips, the lower nippers and dividers are apt to appear shortest, but by elevating the head a little, it will be seen that the upper and lower teeth are about the same in length.

Seventeen Years

By the time this age is reached, the nippers and dividers have a decidedly triangular shape, and the dental star or round spot is seen distinctly in the center of the crown. The jaw is narrow, and the nippers may be separated by a little space. The central enamel will likely have disappeared from the upper nippers, though there may be a considerable trace of it left. The upper and lower teeth come in contact at a decided angle, or, in other words, protrude forward against the lips. Horses usually retain a full set of teeth throughout life, but may lose some through accidents, infections, etc. If a tooth is pulled for any reason the opposite one should also be removed or it will continue to grow and cause trouble.

Nineteen Years

Observing the mouth of a horse at this age, it will usually be seen that the distance across the crown of the nippers from front to back is equal to or even greater than their width. The central enamel will, as a rule, have disappeared from the up-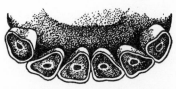per dividers, and the corners show a tendency to draw or point inward. The latter, however, may also be observed is a lesser degree at earlier ages. The upper corners usually retain their notch, produced by uneven wear, as shown below, but this is apt to disappear soon, as the angle of contact will be

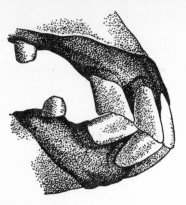

changed as the teeth become more protruded.

Twenty-one Years

The characteristics of an old mouth are now observed in all particulars, though sometimes there is much irregularity, and some of the teeth may be overgrown and unevenly worn. The jaws are thin and narrow, and the teeth are long and protruded forward so that they come in contact at an abrupt angle, and the notch in the upper corner has now disappeared. Owing to this position of the teeth, the corners usually present an elongated worn surface from front to back, as shown below.

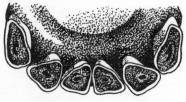

The feed that a horse must eat has a great bearing on the wear of the teeth. A western horse grazing close on sandy soil will wear his teeth very fast and will have a mouth that may show him to be much older than he really is, while the exact opposite is true of a horse fed damp, soft feeds. It is a good plan to have a veterinarian examine the teeth each year on mature animals to determine if they are wearing correctly as many times incorrect wear or bad teeth will cause lack of appetite, poorly chewed food, sore mouths and even death of the animal.

COMMON UNSOUNDNESSES

The horse buyer must be familiar with common unsoundnesses in order to evaluate a horse properly. The following discussions give a definite, description, and the usual causes of the most common unsoundnesses.

The subject of transmissible unsoundnesses is widely debated. Probably no disease is actually inherited, but the fact that individuals may inherit a predisposition to unsoundnesses through faulty conformation cannot be questioned. This predisposition to contact bone diseases is particularly marked; hence, breeding stock should be absolutely free from bone spavin, ringbone, sidebone and similar diseases.

Location of Common Unsoundnesses and Blemishes

I. Head:
   1. Defective eyes
   2. Poll-evil

II. Withers and shoulders:
   1. Fistula of the withers
   2. Sweeney

III. Front Limbs:
   1. Shoe boil or capped elbow
   2. Splint
   3. Wind-gall, wind-puff or road-puff
   4. Ringbone
   5. Contracted tendons, cocked ankle or knuckling.
   6. Sidebone

7. Quittor)
8. Quarter crack or sand crack)
9. Navicular disease) front feet
10. Founder or laminitis)
11. Thrush)
12. Scatches or grease heel)

IV. Rear Limbs:
1. Stifled
2. Stringhalt
3. Wind-gall, wind-puff or road-puff
4. Ringbone
5. Contracted tendons, cocked ankle or knuckling
6. Thoroughpin)
7. Blood Spavin)
8. Bog Spavin)
9. Bone Spavin or Jack) HOCKS
10. Capped hock)
11. Curb)
12. Quittor)
)
13. Quarter crack or sand crack)
14. Founder or laminitis) hind feet
15. Thrush)
16. Scratches or grease heel)

V. General:
1. White horse tumors, black pigment tumors or melanomas
2. Hernia or rupture
3. Thick wind and roaring
4. Heaves, asthma or broken wind.

Defective Eyes

The eyes should always be examined very closely with a flashlight in a darkened stall, or by standing the horse in an open doorway. Cataracts and cloudiness of the cornea usually are easily detected. Other defects are not so easily observed, but the general expression of the head, with unnatural carriage of the ears, may indicate poor eyesight. The horse that is partially blind usually shies at objects, keeps his ears constantly moving, and stumbles frequently.

A pale blue or cloudy, watery eye is characteristic of periodic ophthalmia or "moon blindness." Since the eye may appear quite normal after recovery from the first few attacks, an examination of the interior of the eye by a veterinarian is necessary to determine if the horse is suffering from this disease. Repeated attacks of periodic ophthalmia usually produce permanent blindness in one or both eyes.

Sweeney

Sweeney is an atrophy or decrease in size of a single muscle or a group of muscles. The term is commonly applied to the extreme atrophy of the shoulder muscle. It is usually caused by a blow, ill-fitting collar or severe strain. Sweeney of the hip may follow difficulty in foaling or an attack of Azoturia. Some cases of Sweeney recover after a few months' rest. Blisters and subcutaneous irritants applied under the direction of a veterinarian may hasten recovery.

Splint

A splint is a bony enlargement usually found on the inside of the upper part of the front cannon bone of young horses. It may occasionally occur on the outside of the front cannon bone but is rarely seen on the rear cannon. Splints usually follow kicks, over-exertion or concussions produced by working on hard surfaces. The bony growth may result from irritation between the large cannon bone and small splint bone. Splints are easily seen if one stands directly in front of the horse and observes the outline of the cannon. Splints are very common blemishes of race horses. Aside from the slight lameness which rarely occurs during the first stages of formation, splints are of little importance since horse dealers and judges ignore them almost entirely. Splints can be reduced or removed by one or more applications of a strong blister. If the splint is near enough to the tendons to allow the tendon to rub on the rough surface of the splint, considerable damage may result. The leg will fill and the animal will become very lame. In these cases the splints should be removed and the horse rested until the tissues return to normal.

Shoe Boil or Capped Elbow

Capped elbow or shoe boil is a swelling at the point of the elbow. This condition is usually caused by constant irritation of the heel or shoe upon the point of the elbow when the horse lies with the front leg flexed underneath the body. Recovery usually follows proper treatment. Most important point of treatment is eliminating the cause. This usually means making another shoe slightly shorter to prevent the irritation. If the heel is causing the irritation, it can be bandaged when the horse is in the stall.

Wind-Gall, Road-Gall, Wind-Puff

or Road Puff

Wind-galls are small, puffy swellings which usually occur on each side of the tendons just above the fetlock or knee. Wind-galls are much more common in the young, light-legged breeds of horses than in draft horses. They are formed by an excessive secretion of synovia which distends the sheaths surrounding the tendons. Severe strain, over-exertion or infectious disease may be predisposing factors. Wind-galls are not often considered serious since they usually disappear and cause no lameness unless pathological changes occur within them. Do not attempt to drain them. Bandaging will hasten recovery. Applications of cold water may be beneficial.

Ringbone

Ringbone is a bony growth on either or both of the bones of the pastern which may involve the joints. The ringbone may appear as a hard bony swelling on any part of the pastern. It may be so small that it escapes notice or as large as a walnut or even larger. The outlines of right and left pasterns should always be compared in cases of doubt. Small ringbones may be felt by carefully passing the hand over the pastern. Lameness usually develops gradually but may appear suddenly after severe strain. The lameness produced may not be proportionate to the size of the growth, since a small ringbone may sometimes produce a more serious lameness than a larger one. The location of the swelling is of most importance. Ringbone at the front or rear of the pastern usually produces severe lameness because it interferes with the free movement of the tendons. Ringbone on either side of the pastern is usually less serious. Severe chronic lameness always results if the joints become involved. There is no treatment known which will remove the bony enlargement, but firing or blistering may cause the bones of the diseased joints to grow together, thus relieving the pain. Nerving is occasionally performed as a last resort.

Contracted Tendons,

Cocked Ankle or Knuckling

Contracted tendons, cocked ankle, or knuckling is a partial dislocation of the fetlock or pastern joint produced by the shortening of the tendons at the back part of the cannon. The tendons may contract as a result of over-exertion, founder, or a local inflammation of the tendons. Knuckling must always be regarded as very serious, although some cases may be cured by expert veterinary surgery. Colts usually have a better chance for recovery than mature horses.

Sidebones

Sidebone is an ossification of the lateral cartilage of the foot. The lateral cartilages extend upward above the margin of the hoof so that they may easily be felt under the skin. These cartilages are normally firm and elastic but yield to the pressure of the fingers. Depositions of mineral salts in these cartilages change them to bone so that they become very hard and unyielding to pressure, producing the condition known as sidebones. Sidebones usually occur on the front feet as a result of concussion or injury. They are common in draft horses more than two years old and vary greatly in size and severity. If lameness occurs, it is usually intermittent in character and rarely severe. Although sidebones are considered serious in show and breeding stock, they rarely produce lameness. Sidebones cannot be removed. "Nerving" is sometimes performed if the lameness is severe and persistent.

Quittor

Quittor is a decay of the lateral cartilage of the foot characterized by a discharge of pus through a fistulous tract extending from the cartilage to the coronet or hoof head. Quittor produces severe lameness and shows no tendency to heal. Quittor is more common in the front feet but sometimes occurs in the hind feet. The degree of severity of this unsoundness is dependent upon the structures of the foot which are involved, although all cases must be considered serious. Many cases may be cured by an operation, but several months of rest are required for complete healing.

Quarter Crack or Sand Crack

Quarter crack or sand crack is a vertical split in the wall of the hoof which results from a dry or brittle hoof or improper shoeing. Proper treatment may hasten recovery, but lameness sometimes remains severe until the new hoof has formed. About 12 months are required for the growth of a new toe, while the heels grow in less than half that time. Treatment consists of taking pressure off that part of the hoof to prevent further splitting. Sometimes it becomes necessary to make a V-cut or burn a semicircle into the hoof wall above the split to stop its progress. Recently plastic patches have produced good results in selected cases.

Navicular Disease

Navicular disease is an inflammation of the small navicular bone and bursa inside the hoof just behind the coffin bone and small pastern bone of the front foot. The symptoms of this condition are "pointing" when at rest and a short, stubby, painful stride which may give the impression that the horse is lame in the shoulders. Navicular disease is incurable. In selected cases, veterinarians sometimes perform a nerving operation that will relieve the lameness and increase the usefulness of the horse for a time.

Founder or Laminitis

Founder or laminitis is an inflammation of the sensitive leaves which attach the hoof to the fleshy portion of the foot. It is usually the result of over-feeding, infectious disease, long shipment or standing in a stall for long periods because of some other lameness. Founder may also follow foaling, as a result of infection and inflammation of the uterus. All the feet may be affected, but the front feet are more susceptible. If laminitis is properly treated as soon as it occurs, most cases will completely recover in a few days. If the disease is neglected, however, it will often become chronic, resulting in a dropping of the hoof soles and a turning-up of the toe walls (chronic deformities of the hoof that are incurable). A veterinarian should always be called immediately when founder or laminitis occurs.

Thrush

Thrush is a disease caused by decomposition of stable manure and other filth that is allowed to collect in the cleft of the horn frog, betwen the frog and the bars. Old, severe cases of thrush occasionally produce lameness, but most cases respond to cleanliness and proper treatment.

Stifled

A horse is said to be stifled when the patella of the stifle joint is displaced. If the patella is displaced toward the outside of the leg the condition is serious and usually incurable. If the displacement is in an upward direction, the reaction to a sudden fright that causes the horse to jump may throw the patella back to its normal position. Backing a horse uphill may accomplish the return to normal. However, this condition is likely to recur quite frequently. The stifles may be injected by the veterinarian with a good internal blister to tighten them, thus preventing further trouble.

Stringhalt

Stringhalt is a nervous disorder characterized by a sudden, involuntary flexion of one or both hocks in which the foot is jerked up much higher than normal. The symptoms are usually noticed as the horse is backing from his stall, turning on the affected leg, or when suddenly frightened. The exact cause is unknown, although many horsemen consider the disease hereditary. Stringhalt may be so mild that, the jerking is noticed only occasionally or so severe that the leg is jerked upward at each step. Some cases may be cured by surgery.

Scratches or Grease Heel

Scratches or grease heel is an inflammation of the posterior surfaces of the fetlocks characterized by extensive scab for-

mation. Heavy, highly-fitted show horses seem most susceptible to this condition. Most cases respond to treatment.
Brush and clean the area and apply zinc ointment or a healing powder. Keep the heals clean and dry.

Thoroughpin

Thoroughpin is a soft puffy swelling which occurs on each
side of the gaskin just above the hock in the region known as
the "hollow." Pressure exerted on one side decreases the
swelling on that side but increases the swelling on the opposite side. Lameness does not usually occur, but the condition greatly decreases the sale value of a horse and renders
him worthless as a show animal. Most thoroughpins are incurable.

Bog Spavin

Bog Spavin is a large, soft, fluctuating swelling which usually occurs on the front and inside of the hock. This condition is fairly common in heavy highly-fitted horses with soft,
meaty hocks. It results from an excess secretion of joint fluids
which produces a distention of the joint capsule. A Bog Spavin
is very easily seen and is much larger than a Blood Spavin.
Although a bog spavin does not usually cause lameness, its
presence indicates a lack of wearing qualities and is the object of very unfavorable comment among judges and horsemen. Treatment is usually unsuccessful.

Blood Spavin

Blood Spavin is a swelling over the front and inside of the
hock caused by the dilation of the large vein which crosses
that region. Since lameness never occurs, this condition may
be regarded as a blemish of very little significance. Very mild
blisters with no rubbing may be attempted to reduce the
swelling.

Bone Spavin or Jack

Bone Spavin is a bony growth which may occur on any of the bones which form the hock, although it is usually found on the inside and lower portions. It is caused by an inflammation of the periosteum such as may be produced by strain or over-exertion. Since a predisposition to the disease may be hereditary, affected animals should not be used for breeding purposes. The spavin usually may be seen by one's standing directly behind or in front and a little to one side of the horse. In cases of doubt, lift the foot upward and forward in order to bend the hock as much as possible. After holding for two or three minutes, release the leg and start the horse at a brisk trot. A characteristic lameness will sometimes be noticed if the individual is affected. Bone Spavin is one of the most serious unsoundnesses of the draft horse. Firing tends to make the bones unite and will often relieve lameness if only the flat bones of the hock are affected.

Curb

Curb is a hard, firm swelling on the back surface of the rear cannon, about a hand's breadth below the point of the hock. A large curb is easily seen by observing the hock and cannon directly from the side. A smaller one may help by passing the fingers over the region. Crooked or sickle hocks are most subject to this unsoundness since this faulty conformation throws a greater strain on the hock. A curb usually follows strain or over-exertion but may result from a kick or blow. The initial lameness disappears after the formation of the curb, but the condition must still be considered an unsoundness because an affected hock is thought to be less likely to endure severe strain.

Capped Hock

Capped hock is a firm swelling which occurs on the point of the hock. This blemish may be as large as an apple or so small that it escapes notice. Capped hock usually results from constant irritation, such as might be produced by rubbing or kicking the walls of the stable; hence it may be indicative of the horse's disposition.

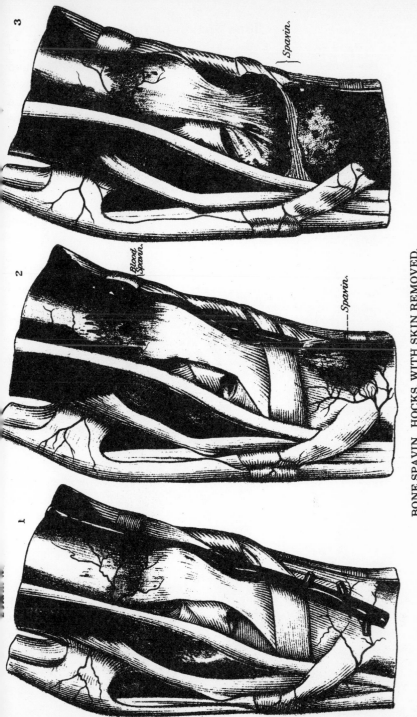

BONE SPAVIN. HOCKS, WITH SKIN REMOVED.

197

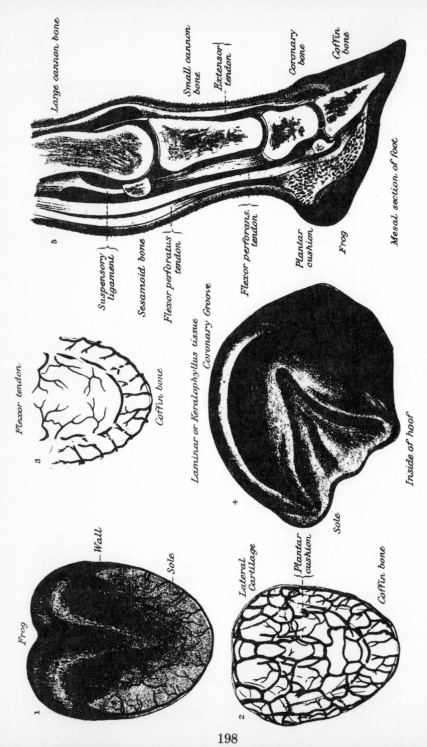

Large cannon bone

Small cannon bone

Extensor tendon

Coronary bone

Coffin bone

5

Suspensory ligament

Sesamoid bone

Flexor perforatus tendon

Flexor perforans tendon

Plantar cushion

Frog

Mesal section of foot

Flexor tendon

3

Coffin bone

Laminar or Keratophyllus tissue
Coronary Groove

4

Sole

Inside of hoof

Frog

1

Wall

Sole

Lateral Cartilage

Plantar cushion

2

Sole

Coffin bone

198

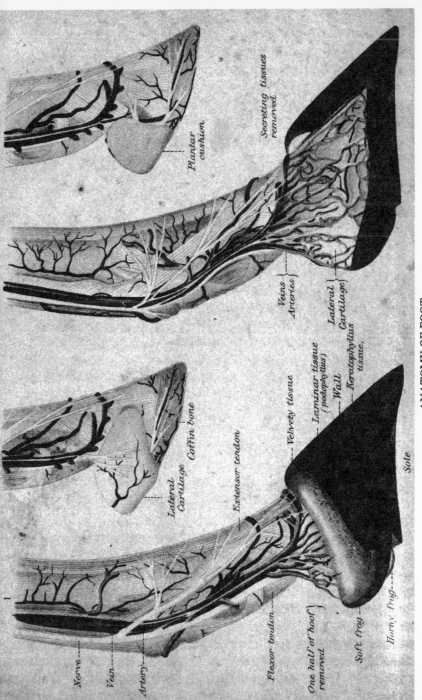

ANATOMY OF FOOT.

Plantar cushion

Secreting tissues removed

Veins
Arteries

Lateral
Cartilage

Laminar tissue (podophyllus)
Wall
Keratophyllus tissue.

Lateral Cartilage
Coffin bone

Extensor tendon

Velvety tissue

Sole

Nerve
Vein
Artery

Flexor tendon

One half of hoof removed

Soft frog

Horny frog

199

SHOEING AND CARE OF THE FEET

A horse's feet need careful attention. Neglected feet may grow long and uneven, so that the weight will be thrown on the foot unnaturally and may lead to tendon strain, unsoundness, or interference.

The important thing is that the hoof wall be kept level and even so that the horse stands squarely upon it. If neglected there is a tendency for the toe of the front foot to grow long, causing the horse to stand forward, with the uneven pressure on hoof wall inviting a quarter crack. The heels of the hind feet may grow too high, the horse then standing too straight behind. From the front the feet should rest true and square on the ground. The horse that stands pigeon-toed will need the inside of the wall trimmed down, while the horse that toes out will need the outside of the foot shortened. Keeping the foot level is especially important with colts and young horses. Some faults in conformation of feet and legs may be remedied or greatly improved by careful trimming and shaping when the colt is young and the bones are immature. The use of light shoes or half plates may be advisable in some cases where wear on one part of the foot is excessive.

With a rasp, hoof knife, and nippers the feet can be given a little shaping upon about every 60 days, or as the foot requires it. Look at the foot first, and determine the points that need correcting. The dead overgrowth and loose flakes of the sole and frog may be removed when the foot is trimmed. The wall is cut down level with the sole with nippers and evened with the rasp. Too much of the frog should not be cut away, as it has a protective function and helps keep the heel wide and open. The bars also act as a sort of brace for the heel and wall and should not be cut much below the level of the hoof wall. A rasp should not be used on the outer surface of the hoof wall as it removes a protective covering.

Many light horses are kept shod, and for some uses shoeing may be practically a necessity. The primary object of the shoe is to prevent breakage and excess wear on the widewall of the foot. Shoeing may also affect the straightness, balance, and length of stride, height of action, etc. A skillful shoer can correct or improve certain faults such as winging, interfering, or going wide behind. The use of such extreme weight as to greatly increase concussion as the feet strike the ground, or shoeing the foot with very long toe and shallow heel may, however, lead to undue strain. Good shoeing is truly an art, and this type of work should be done by a competent, experienced farrier who knows his job.

Shoes are usually reset every four or five weeks. If new shoes are not then needed, the old ones may be used again after the foot has been trimmed where necessary. Pads are usually not used for cinder, gravel, or dirt roads. A plain smooth steel shoe, or one with very little heel calk is preferred by most horsemen. Calks are sometimes used when ice is a factor.

In dry weather, especially with horses stabled off the ground the foot may become dry, the frog loses some of its springiness, and the heels narrow. A wet mud pack on the bottom of each foot after riding will help prevent any drying out of the foot and will help remedy this trouble.

SHIPPING THE HORSE

The truck offers the most convenient method of shipping a few horses a short distance. Automobile trailers are becoming popular for hauling one or two horses. Railroad cars are suitable for shipping several horses for long distance. Airplane shipping is better for long distances.

Horses should not be fed within four hours before loading, since the excitement of shipping has a tendency to produce indigestion. Hay and water may be given enroute on long trips. The horse should be provided with a heavy leather halter, and two heavy rope reins for cross ties. A good heavy rope may be tied around the neck with a bowline knot as additional security. The tail should be braided tightly for a distance of six or eight inches from the base, and a piece of burlap wrapped around the tail and firmly sewed to the line of braiding. This prevents rubbing out the tail hair. If the weather is adverse, the horse should always be blanketed. Always examine a horse carefully for cuts or bruises before loading, and after unloading.

Horses may be loaded into a truck after backing the vehicle against a bank or regular horse loading chute. If several horses are to be shipped, they should be loaded crossways, alternating head to tail, and separated by three or four horizontal poles wired securely to the uprights of the truck rack. A little gravel sprinkled on the floor makes better footing than straw or other bedding.

FEEDING LIGHT HORSES

There are no hard and fast rules to follow in the feeding of horses and there is no one best ration for all horses under all conditions. Fortunately horses can be fed, and will do well, on a wide variety of feeds. It's true that some horses are more difficult to feed than others because they respond differently to certain rations. Extremely nervous, high strung animals require more feed and are usually harder to keep in good condition.

Horsemen generally recognize a number of factors that are essential to the successful management of horses. If a few common rules are followed a lot of trouble can be avoided.

1. Feed regularly. Horses soon become accustomed to a certain schedule of feeding and if this routine is not followed they fret and get nervous. In well-managed stables the feeding periods seldom vary more than a few minutes from day to day.

2. Rations should be adjusted to the needs of the horses. When horses are worked severely they require more grain and should be fed less hay. When horses are idle they should have their grain ration reduced ⅓ to ½ and the hay increased. A practice of this kind reduces the dangers of sickness because of too much concentrated feed.

3. Horses should be watered frequently and liberally unless they are too hot. Then judgment must be used regarding the amount of water that can safely be allowed. A few swallows of water that is not too cold may not injure any horse.

4. All changes in rations should be gradual rather than too abrupt. This is especially true in feeding new grain or hay

after the new crops are harvested. Colic often follows a change of this kind.

5. For best results use only clean, bright feeds. Musty, moldy or dusty feeds frequently cause trouble. Dusty hay may be sprinkled before feeding and the grain can be dampened but this requires considerable time and trouble.

6. Salt is essential and should be kept before horses constantly. Some feeders add salt to the grain ration but if salt is always available horses will eat what they need when they want it rather than depend upon judgement of the feeder.

7. Pasture provides the best "protective feed" available and it simplifies some of the problems connected with good horse management. If horses cannot be worked daily they can be turned on pasture for a time where they will get some good feed and much needed exercise.

8. Horses should have their teeth examined at least once each year by a competent veterinarian.

9. There are numerous parasites which use horses for hosts. Parasites impair the health of horses and require additional feed to keep them in condition.

Properties of a Good Ration

A suitable ration for light horses should possess the following properties:

1. Ration should be made up of a variety of feeds, each one supplying some necessary nutrient. Horses can get along on a ration made up from a single grain and one kind of roughage but such a ration will not be as efficient as one composed of several different feeds. Variety in a ration does not mean that the ration should be changed from day to day but rather that the ration is made up of several different feeds.

2. Feeds should be palatable and adapted to the needs of horses for growth, work or reproduction.

3. Bulk is needed in rations to insure easy and complete digestion. Too much bulk however is not desirable in the ration of a light horse.

4. Rations should have approximately the correct proportions of proteins, carbohydrates, fats, minerals and vitamins to be most efficient.

The successful feeding of pleasure horses requires some knowledge of the common feeds and an understanding of the requirements of horses doing various kinds of work. The horseman must adapt the ration to the need of each animal. Most persons like to keep their horses in good condition but overfeeding so as to produce excessive fat or throw the animal off in the legs is in no sense a favor or kindness to the horse. If horses were worked exactly the same each day their feeding should be comparatively simple but trouble often comes with the horses that are used at irregular intervals and the ration has not been adjusted accordingly.

CONCENTRATES — Oats

Oats is the most widely used grain for pleasure horses and it is probably the safest concentrate available. Oats can be fed whole, rolled or coarsely ground, as the sole grain ration or can be mixed with other grains or commercial feeds. The amount to feed depends upon the size of the horse, age, nature of work and other feeds being used but usually ½ to 1 pound of oats for each 100 pounds of live weight of the horse is sufficient. In most cases 5 to 10 pounds of grain is enough for a thousand pound pleasure horse. Oats furnish considerable protein and total digestible nutrients but is not a good source of the important mineral, calcium. Additional calcium should be furnished through a legume feed or a mineral mixture. Oats is best single feed for light horses in maintaining fettle or spirit.

Corn

A feed very high in energy value but usually considered too heating and fattening to feed in very large amounts to pleasure horses—a little corn, probably up to 25 percent of the ration could be fed to a hard working horse or one that is very thin but it is more difficult to feed a horse even a small amount of corn than oats. Corn is not a good source of protein, minerals or some vitamins but it does contain a lot of energy.

Barley

Barley is a carbonaceous concentrate that is used in many sections of the country as a part or all of the grain ration for horses. Barley is too hard for horses to masticate easily and for best results it should be rolled, crushed or coarsely ground.

Barley can be fed with oats or bran, but in the Cornbelt its use is rather limited because other grains are usually more plentiful and cheaper. "Scabby" barley should never be offered to horses.

Wheat

Wheat is usually too expensive to be fed and it is not a safe feed in the hands of inexperienced feeders. It should be rolled or ground and fed with oats or bran, or mixed with chopped hay. If wheat is fed at all, not more than 15 to 20 percent of the grain ration should be wheat. Because wheat has a high Vitamin E content, it is sometimes recommended for stallions and brood mares.

Wheat Bran

Wheat bran, a bulky, protein-rich concentrate, is valuable in the feeding of all kinds of horses. Bran is a cooling, laxative feed which can be mixed with the regular grain ration or fed in the form of a mash. It is too bulky to feed in large amounts, but for limited feeding and to keep a horse's digestive system in good condition, bran is excelled by few, if any feeds. The substitution of bran for a large part of the regular grain ration on workless days is a practice followed by many successful horsemen.

Bran is a valuable feed to use for mares before and after foaling and for stallions during the entire year, unless they are allowed the use of a pasture during the summer.

Bran mashes are frequently substituted for the regular grain ration when horses are to be idle the following day. A mash is made of about 2 quarts of bran with enough water added to make the mixture the consistency of a thick gruel.

Linseed Meal

Linseed Oil Meal is a nitrogenous concentrate that serves a very useful purpose in horse feeding. Having a high protein content is can be fed with carbonaceous grains or roughages. It is somewhat laxative and therefore can be fed with feeds that are constipating. Oilmeal is used in getting horses in shape for work, especially those that have been running out in cornfields and are in poor condition. It seems to act as a tonic and causes early shedding of long hair, gives life to the skin and improves the general appearance.

Usually not more than 1 to 1½ pounds, mixed with the grain, are given daily. Some feeders do not bother to weigh the meal but just add a small handful to each feed. It is valuable feed for fitting horses for show, sale or market, because it produces a glossy hair coat so much desired in exhibition and sale animals.

Soybean Meal

Soybean meal is similar to linseed oil meal but has not been extensively used for horses. It can be fed up to 1½ pounds daily, but if oats and a legume hay are fed only a small amount of soybean meal should be used. When feeding any protein supplements it is a better practice to feed a small amount with each feed rather than to give all of this feed at one time.

ROUGHAGES — Timothy

Timothy hay, one of the most commonly used roughages in horse feeding, is the standard by which other roughages are compared. It is probably the safest hay that can be fed horses. Timothy is a carbonaceous feed, fairly rich in carbohydrates and fats but lacking in digestible protein and minerals. Whenever the hay is fed, special care should be taken to add protein and minerals to the ration. Oats, bran, soybeans, or linseed meal are valuable protein feeds to use with timothy, while alfalfa, clover or soybean hay are roughages that will help balance timothy. Timothy and clover hay are extensively fed to light horses with very good results.

Timothy has long been a favorite of horsemen, especially city users, because it is usually free from dust and mold. It is not a "washy" feed, which is regarded as an advantage for saddle, show or race horses; in fact, timothy is considered the most valuable roughage obtainable for light horses.

Prairie Hay

Prairie hay is another carbonaceous roughage that is widely used as horse feed. Like timothy, prairie hay is not high in digestible crude protein and must be supplemented with nitrogenous feeds. It can be used for all classes of horses with safety but is not effective for colts, brood mares and stallions unless fed with either a protein-right hay or concentrates.

Alfalfa

Alfalfa is probably the most palatable of all hays for horses. It is high in digestible protein and some minerals and is especially useful to feed with carbonaceous feeds.

In feeding alfalfa, care must be taken not to overfeed as horses will eat more than they should if given an opportunity. A good rule to follow is to feed daily ½ to ¾ pound of this hay for each 100 pounds of live weight. If more roughage is needed, straw, prairie hay, timothy or any other non-leguminous hay may be added.

Alfalfa may become dusty when cured and should then be sprinkled before feeding.

Alfalfa cut when fairly mature seems to be best suited for horses; it is less laxative than when cut earlier.

In feeding alfalfa hay to horses there are three precautions:

1. Limit the amount fed to about ½ to ¾ pound per day for each 100 pounds of live weight.

2. Use hay that is as free from dust as possible.

3. For horses it should be cut when it is fairly mature.

Clover Hay

Clover hay ranks next to alfalfa in value for horses. It is palatable, slightly laxative and has a fairly high protein conten. It is well suited to the feeding of horses of all ages that receive considerable carbonaceous grains as part of the ration. Clover is sometimes rather dusty but can be safely used if sprinkled before it is fed.

Medium red clover is the most commonly used. Other varieties such as mammoth or sweet, are usually coarse and a considerable quantity is wasted. In feeding clover, about the same precautions should be followed as with alfalfa; that is, feed a limited amount and have the hay as bright and clean as possible. A mixture of clover and timothy hay is very desirable roughage for horses and many feeders prefer this combination to straight timothy.

Soybeans

Soybeans are not extensively used as a feed for light horses. Soybean hay (which includes the beans) seems to be the most desirable way to use this feed. Because soybean hay is high in protein it should not make up more than 25 percent of the roughage ration and should always be fed with timothy, prairie or some other carbonaceous hay. Unless fed with the utmost care, soybeans better be left out of the light horse's ration.

Oat Hay, Barley Hay

If the regular hay crop winter kills, oats or barley can be grown and used for horses with good results. The grain should be sown at a trifle heavier rate per acre and cut after it has headed out but before the grain is ripe, usually in the milk stage.

These hays are palatable and their feeding value is similar to timothy but horses may not consume the entire stalk; the remainder, however, can be used for bedding. If fed with corn, some protein should be added.

Oat, Barley and Wheat Straw

The principle use made of straw is for bedding, but some of it can be used for wintering horses. Oat straw is regarded as the most valuable because of a somewhat higher nutritive content and is more palatable, but any straw of good quality can be fed.

Under no conditions, however, should straw be used as the sole winter ration because of its low protein and mineral content. It can be used as a part of the roughage ration with alfalfa or clover hay.

Corn Fodder and Corn Stover

Corn fodder and corn stover are commonly used for wintering idle horses but are not so well suited for working horses. These roughages are low in protein and should be fed with other feeds. Fodder and stover are difficult to feed in the barn because of their bulky nature. Leaves and the top portion of the stalk may be eaten, but the larger, coarser portion is usually refused and must be removed from the mangers.

Fodders when carelessly handled become moldy, partially spoiled, unpalatable and sometimes unsafe to feed.

Bright, clean fodder is usually most economically fed if it is cut or shredded; more will be consumed, and what is rejected can be used for bedding. If the shredded fodder is dusty, it is a good practice to sprinkle it before feeding.

Salt

Salt is needed by horses of all ages. The sodium and chlorine which make up salt are necessary for the proper digestion of the ration. Salt may be fed free-choice, given at regular intervals or fed with the grain. The first method is preferred, since not all horses consume the same amount of salt, and it is difficult for the feeder to know exactly how much is required. As a rule, horses will eat from ½ to 2 ounces per day, depending upon their size and age, the work performed, humidity, temperature, the nature of feed and the character of the soil on which the horses are kept.

Where goiters frequently occur it is a good practice to feed iodized salt, especially to brood mares, stallions and colts. Iodized salt should be kept in covered containers, as it is thought that some of the iodine is lost when kept in ordinary sacks or open bins.

Minerals

Calcium and phosphorus are two of the most important minerals that are lacking in common feeds but can easily and cheaply be supplied. Using a variety of feeds lessens the necessity of feeding a mineral mixture.

The following mixture, a simple combination that adds most of the minerals needed to improve the common rations.

Iodized salt, 20 pounds; finely ground limestone, 40 pounds; spent bone black, 35 pounds; commercial iron oxide, 3 pounds; sulfur, 2 pounds; total, 100 pounds.

The amount horses will consume depends upon their ages and the character of the feed. Some horses will eat as much as 1 ounce daily. Horses are particular about eating anything that has a strong ordor, and that is why spent bone black is suggested in place of bone meal.

Water

Water is an essential nutrient in the ration of horses and yet its functions are often overlooked. Water aids in digestion, carries off waste products from the body, flushes out the system and cools the animal.

It makes very little difference whether horses are watered before, after or during a meal. The main thing is to adopt a definite plan of watering and then stick religiously to it. It is seldom that horses will drink too much water under normal conditions. If horses are too hot, or if water has been withheld from them for a long time it is not advisable to allow them to drink all they want, but if they have been handled carefully, they should be allowed to satisfy their thirst.

Rations for Light Horses

There are numerous rations or combinations of feeds that can be used for light horses with good results. A feeder should watch his horses carefully and adjust the ration according to the way the horses respond to the feeds.

The following rations are merely suggestions and can easily be changed to suit the needs of light horses for the kind of work they are doing.

Suggested daily rations for Light Horses weighing approximately 1,000 pounds:

Oats, 7 pounds
Wheat bran, 2 pounds
Timothy hay, 8 pounds
Alfalfa or clover hay, 4 pounds

Oats, 7 pounds
Yellow corn, 1 pound
Linseed Oil Meal   )
       or   )   ½ pound
Soybean Meal   )
Timothy, 10 pounds
Alfalfa or clover hay, 2 pounds

Oats, 6 pounds
Timothy hay, 8 pounds
Pasture

Rolled oats, 4 pounds
Rolled barley, 4 pounds
Prairie hay, 5 pounds
Alfalfa or clover hay, 5 pounds

Fattening Ration

Oats, 4 pounds
Yellow corn, 4 pounds
Wheat bran, 1 pound
Linseed meal, ½ pound
Timothy and clover   )
     or   ) 12
Timothy and alfalfa hay)

This grain mixture
moisten with
½ pint molasses
and 1 quart of water

Rations for Stallions in Service

Oats, 5 pounds
Yellow corn, 2 pounds
Ground wheat, 1 pound
Bran, 2 pounds
Alfalfa, 6 pounds
Timothy or
Prairie hay, 6 pounds

GLOSSARY OF TERMS USED IN STABLE

1. *The Aids.* The aids are signals by means of which the rider indicates his intentions to the horse. These signals are given through the medium of the hands which direct and control the horse's forehand with the reins, and the legs, which, when applied behind the girth, control and collect the horse's hindquarters. The aids are used simultaneously and in harmony with one another, whilst the rider's body, by leaning backwards or forwards, or to either side, assists to emphasize these indications.

The voice is the fourth aid and may be used in conjunction, and will assist in steadying a frightened horse if used in a soothing tone. Whips, martingales, nose-bands, and spurs are known as the artificial aids.

2. *Balance.* A horse is said to be "balanced" when he carries his own weight and the weight of his rider in such a way that he can use himself to the best advantage in any circumstances.

3. *Behind the Bridle.* This term means that the horse is not going up in his bridle, but is hanging back. A fault to be found with sluggish horses. Horses get into this habit of being "behind the bridle" from being ridden by slovenly riders who do not endeavor, or know how, to ride a horse in a collected manner by the correct application of the aids.

4. *Bishoping.* Tampering with the incisor teeth in order to falsify or camouflage a horse's actual age. This trick can be easily detected by the absence of enamel which has been removed by the file in the process.

5. *Body Brush.* For removing scurf from the horse's coat.

6. *Boring.* When a horse leans the weight of his head and neck constantly on the bit is called "boring."

7. *Breast-plate.* An article of saddlery which goes around the horse's neck, and is secured to the girths between his forelegs, and is also attached to the "D's" in the front arch of the saddle. Its object is to prevent the saddle from slipping back, and it is used with horses which run up light like greyhounds or are "herring-butted."

8. *Broken Wind.* An infection of the lungs. Broken-winded horses have considerable difficulty in expiration. Broken wind can be detected by watching the flanks, particularly after the animal has moved at a fast pace.

9. *Brushing.* A term used to describe a faulty action when the horse strikes either fore-or hind leg with the adjoining one, when in motion, on the inside of the fetlock joints. Brushing is usually due to faulty action, fatigue, want of condition, or bad shoeing, e. g.,a shoe projecting and nails not properly clinched. Consistent brushing will cause a permanent enlargement on the inside of the fetlock joint.

Brushing boots should worn on the least indication of this bad habit. The simplest form of brushing boot is that known as the Yorkshire boot. This devise is best made out of a piece of Jersey horse clothing, which should be cut to the size of 12 inches by 9 inches. This piece of cloth should be applied around the fetlock with the junction at the front, and a piece of tape should be tied around the center just above the fetlock joint. When the tape is tied, the top portion of the cloth would be turned down so that is will form a double fold around the fetlock.

10. *Burnisher.* A saddle-room requisite for cleaning bits and stirrup-irons and all steel devices. It consists of a closely interlaced square of chain on a chamois leather.

11. *Calf-legs.* A horse whose legs are too short in proportion to his body is described as having calf-legs, and having calf-knees when viewed from the side of the line down the front of the knee is inclined to concavity.

12. *Calkins or Caulks.* Projections turned down at the extremity of a horseshoe for the purpose of lifting the heels off the ground or for giving foothold to draught animals.

13. *Cantering Disunited.* When a horse canters or gallops disunited, it means that his leading hind leg is on the side opposite to the leading foreleg. See definition of terms cantering or galloping "true."

14. *Cantering False.* A horse is said to be cantering or galloping "false" when, at either of these paces, he moves in a circle to the right with the near fore—and near hind leg leading, or to the left with the off fore—and off hind leading.

15. *Cantering True.* When a horse is cantering or galloping "true," the legs should move in such a manner that whichever foreleg leads, the hind leg on the same side must also lead.

16. *Cavesson.* A head-piece used in horse training which has a weighted nose-band with three rings to either of which the lunging-rein can be attached.

17. *Collected.* A horse is said to be "collected" when he is being ridden well up in his bit with his head flexed, jaw relaxed, and his hocks well under him, ensuring that he has a full control over his limbs and ready to respond to the signals or aids of his rider.

18. *Cow-hocks.* A horse whose hocks are turned inwards at the points, like a cow, is said to have cow-hocks.

19. *Cradle.* A stable appliance which is strapped round a horse's neck to prevent his biting at a bandage, or licking a sore.

20. *Crupper.* A leather loop which is passed under the tail and attached to a "D" in the cantle of the saddle to keep it in position and from slipping forward. It is rarely used except with extremely narrow-shouldered or low-withered horses and mules.

21. *Curry-comb.* An implement used in grooming which has a series of toothed metal edges parallel to each other. It is not applied to the horse's coat; its purpose is solely to remove the scurf from the body brush. The Army curry-comb with the webbing back is preferable to the civilian pattern with a handle, as it enables the groom to lean the back of his hand against the horse if necessary.

22. *Dandy Brush.* A stiff brush of fibre for removing dry mud from the horse's legs, or for brushing out the horse's

mane or tail. It is too hard to use as a body brush except on a thick-coated horse just up from grass.

23. *Dishing.* A fault in the horse's action in that he throws one or both of the forelegs from the knee outwards as he raises them off the ground when trotting.

24. *Docked.* The term for a tail cut short; it means the actual amputation of the tail bone. It is an objectionable form of multilation which is now practically an obsolete custom. Once a horse's tail is docked his purchase value depreciates by at least 25 percent.

25. *Ewe-neck.* A horse is said to be ewe-necked when his neck at the crest (between poll and withers) is concave instead of convex.

26. *Feather.* The abundant growth of hair to be found on the fetlocks of Clydesdale and Shire horses.

27. *Fiddle-heads.* A term to describe a horse with an ugly-shaped head.

28. *Flexions, The.* A term connected with the horse's head carriage in conjunction with neck movement from the poll. There are direct and lateral flexions.

29. *Forehand, The.* All the parts of a horse before the saddle, i. e., the head, neck shoulders, withers and forelegs.

30. *Forging.* A noise made by the striking of the hind-shoe against the fore as the horse is trotting. Horses "forge" when young and green, when out of condition, or fatigued, and when they are ridden in a slovenly manner.

31. *Forelock, The.* The part of the mane which hangs down over the forehead between the ears of a horse which has not been hogged.

32. *Frog.* The frog is a triangular-shaped formation in the sole of a horse's hoof. The frog has an elastic action and expands laterally when pressed upon.

33. *Galvayne Groove.* A brownish-colored groove on the corner incisor teeth which appears when the horse is ten years old, and can be used to denote approximately his age between ten and twenty.

34. *Goose-rumped.* When a horse's hind-quarters slant down from the croup to the dock in a very pronounced manner, he is said to be goose-rumped.

35. *Hand.* A term used in measuring a horse. A hand represents four inches. A horse's height is taken from the highest point of the withers to the ground. A horse standing 15 hands, 3 inches would be therefore 63 inches high.

36. *Haute Ecole.* A term used to describe horsemanship exploited in most scientific methods for show ring and show jumping. Studied greatly in Continental riding-schools. The Spanish schools in Vienna were the greatest exponents of haute ecole in modern times.

37. *Herring-gutted.* A term used to describe a horse which runs up light like a greyhound and is deficient of sufficient room for heart and lungs. It is an indication of inability to stay.

38. *"Hobdayed."* A horse is said to be "hobdayed" when he has had the Hobday operation performed on his larnyx as a cure for "roaring." This operation was made popular by Prof. Sir Frederick Hobday, C.M.G., F.R.C.V.S., Principal and Dean of the Royal Veterinary College, London.

39. *Hoofpick.* An implement for picking dirt out of the horse's hooves or for removing any stone which has become lodged between the frog and the shoe. The point of the pick should be blunt. As a hoofpick invariably gets lost in straw bedding, it is advisable to tie a piece of red cord to the handle to facilitate its being found.

40. *Horse Length.* A term of measurement equivalent to eight feet. This represents the length of ground a horse stands over.

41. *"Independent Seat."* The definition of a seat which has reached that degree of firmness from balance and grip which ensures that the rider is entirely independent of the reins or stirrups.

42. *Indirect Rein.* A term for neck-reining; e. g., when the off rein is carried over the horse's neck to the near side and is pressed against it without any tightening of the near rein, the horse if properly trained will turn to the left. The indirect rein is always employed when all the reins are in one hand, particularly in polo. The direct rein is the term for tension on the side of the horse's mouth, with the rein on the side to which it is intended to turn.

43. *Lane*. A long, narrow, fenced-in enclosure used in teaching the horse to jump. Various kinds of obstacles are placed at equal distances apart. The lane ensures that the horse cannot run out at his fences. The jumps are raised gradually during this progressive system of teaching horse and rider the correct way of jumping.

44. *Lunging.* A term used in the initial stage in training the horse. Lunging means to lead or ring the horse by means of a long lunging-rein attached to the Cavesson.

45. *Manege*. Another term for a riding-school, which is usually understood to be a fenced-in enclosure of riding-school dimentions for the purpose of teaching equitation.

46. *Martingale*. Standing martingale.—An appliance which is used as a check to prevent the horse from throwing up his head too high—it gives the rider more control over his horse. It is attached from the noseband and passing between the horse's forelegs is fastened to the girth. It is kept in position by a neck-strap.

Running Martingale. This pattern martingale is attached to the reins by means of rings which the reins pass through—it is then similarly adjusted as a standing martingale to the girth. Its object is to keep a horse's head in the right position and keep him straight and steady when riding at a fence. If used with a double-bridle the running martingale should be attached to the bit or crub-rein.

Irish Martingale. Two reins connected together by four inches of leather through which the reins pass.

47. *"Nagging."* The process of training or schooling a horse for riding and hunting, and teaching him manners and behavious with hounds. A "nagsman" is the term for a horseman skilled in riding young horses and horses with vice and bad habits.

48. *"Nappy."* Horses which "refuse" from temper and are difficult to ride are generally called "nappy" horses.

49. *Near Side*. The left side of a horse is called the near side, and the right is called the off side.

50. *"Niggle" or "Jiggle."* A short-stepping action which is very tiresome for the rider.

51. *Numnah*. A felt pad shaped like a saddle which is used

between the saddle and the horse's back in order to prevent pressure or friction from the hardness of the saddle.

52. *Overbent.* When a horse's action is such that he moves in an exaggerated collected manner with his head too bent at the poll, he is described as being overbent.

53. *Overreach.* Striking the inside of the heel of the fore-leg with the inner rim of the toe of the hind-shoe; it is rarely caused by the toe of the hind-shoe. Overreaching may cause a severe wound or bruise.

It is caused by galloping suddenly into heavy "going" or by pulling up suddenly.

A horse which is liable to overreach should wear an india-rubber overreach boot which fits round the pastern joint, and care should be taken to "bevel off" the inner rims of the hind shoes.

54. *Passage, The.* A lateral movement by which the horse moves to a flank, keeping his neck and body parallel with the object he is moving away from or towards.

55. *Pointing.* When a horse rests a forefoot it is known as pointing. It is an indication of lameness or navicular trouble.

56. *Port.* The curved portion on the mouthpiece of a bit.

57. *"Rising" and "Off."* Terms used in connection with the age of a horse. A horse nearly four years old would be said to be "rising four" whereas is just over four years it is said to be "four off."

58. *Roach-backed.* A horse with a prominent spinal column is said to have a roach-back. A roach-back is the converse of a hollow back.

59. *Roarer, A.* A horse which makes a noise when breathing quickly—as in galloping. It is affection of the larynx. A lesser degree of "roaring" is known as "whistling."

60. *Roller.* A broad girth of webbing which goes right round the horse's body to keep the rugs in position in the stable.

61. *"Roughed Up."* A term for describing the gradual stages in the change of conditions through which a hunter passes when the hunting season is over and before she is put out on grass. This preparation usually lasts from two to three weeks.

62. *Short-coupled.* A horse is said to be short-coupled when he is short in the middle piece or back. Arabins have one less vertebrae.

63. *Sickle-hocks.* Hocks which are shaped like a sickle, i. e. bent at too much of an angle like a greyhound's. Hocks of this description can never be properly under the horse, and are a sign of weakness.

64. *A Skip.* A wicker basket for collecting the "droppings" in a stable.

65. *Sold with a Warranty.* Horses sold at Messrs. Tattersall's as good hunters, "must be sound in wind and eyes, quiet to ride, have been hunted, and be capable of being hunted." Good hacks must be sound in wind and eyes, quiet to ride, and not lame. These are called warranties.

66. *Star-gazer.* A term for a horse which has the habit of holding his head in an awkward position; it is a common fault with ewe-necked horses. A standing martingale is the most effective method of checking this bad habit.

67. *Strapper.* Another term for a groom; strapping is stable parlance for grooming.

68. *String Halt.* This is a fault which causes the horse to lift one or both hind legs abnormally high when moving. It is sometimes curable with surgery. It gets worse with age. String halt is an unsoundness and may give rise to lameness.

69. *Surcingle.* An all-round girth which goes right around the horse's body, passing over the saddle. It keeps the saddle firmer in position when used, and prevents any movement of the saddle-flaps.

70. *"Tack."* A stable work for saddlery. "Tack" is an abbreviation for the word tackle, meaning harness.

71. *Tied in Below the Knee.* A fault in conformation when the measurement immediately below the knee is smaller than lower down the cannonbone.

72. *Tubed.* A horse said to be "tubed" is one with an artificial tubelet into his windpipe. The operation is termed tracheotomy. Also refers to passing a stomach tube to worm or give other medicine.

73. *Tushes.* Small pointed teeth which are to be found in the gums a short distance behind the corner incisors and in

front of the back or molar teeth. Only horses are provided with tushes, these teeth being absent in mares: there are, however, exception cases where they are found in a rudimentary stage in a mare's mouth, but such an occurrence is very rare. As a horse ages the tushes become blunter gradually. Tushes make their first appearance when the horse is between four and five years old.

74. *Twitch, A.* A stable appliance used in giving medicine, or when clipping restive horses; it is adjusted to the upper lip by means of a loop of rope which passes through the end of a stick and which is kept secure by twisting like a tourniquet.

75. *Unnerved.* A term describing a horse's foot which has had the nerves removed in order to ameliorate navicular disease. A horse which has been unnerved is unsound. May be detected by picking the skin just above the coronet band with a sharp object. The horse will not feel the pick if the nerves have been cut.

76. *Well-ribbed Up.* An expression for describing a horse's conformation when he has well-rounded or well-hooped ribs with a minimum of space between the last rib and hip.

77. *Whistler. A* See definition 59 for a "Roarer."

78. *Wind-sucking and Crib-biting.* A term for a stable vice. A horse subject to "wind-sucking" draws in air and swallows it. It is simple to detect as the horse can be watched going through the motions of this bad habit in arching his neck and gulping.

Crib-biting is an aggravated form of wind-sucking. With this vice the animal goes through the same motions of wind-sucking, but catches hold of the manger or half-door of his box in order to do so. When swallowing the air the horse emits a "grunt." Once a horse has started crib-biting he will always endeavor to do so, but much can be done to prevent him by removing the manger and all wooden devices which he can grasp in his teeth, and by feeding him off the ground level.

79. *Wings.* Hurdles interlaced with furze or wattles which are placed on the flanks of artificial jumps to keep the horse from running out.

80. *"Wisp."* An essential adjunct for grooming. A wisp is made of rope of hay or straw. Commencing with the figure of eight, it is interlaced in such a mannor as to form a pad. Wisping is really a form of massage. It is a most valuable method of improving the condition of the skin and coat and for making muscle. It stimulates the skin and improves circulation.

81. *"Yawning."* When a horse reaches out and down with his mouth it is called "yawning."

A horse that yawns and bores at his bridle should be ridden in a Cavesson nose-band.

CONFORMATION OF FEET AND LEGS

A perpendicular line drawn downward from the point of shoulder should fall upon the center of the knee, cannon, pastern, and foot No. 1 represents the correct conformation. Nos. 2 to 7 inclusive, represent common defects. No. 2, slightly bow-legged. No. 3, close at knees and toes out. No. 4, toes in. No. 5, knock-kneed. No. 6, base narrow. No. 7, base wide.

A perpendicular line drawn downward from the center of the elbow joint should fall upon the center of the knee and pastern, and back of the foot, and a perpendicular line drawn downward from the middle of the arm should fall upon the center of the foot. No 8 represents the right conformation. No. 9, leg too far forward. No. 10, knee sprung. No. 11, calf kneed. No. 12, foot and leg placed too far back.

A perpendicular line drawn downward from the hip point should fall upon the center of the foot and divide the gaskin in the middle; and a perpendicular line drawn from the point of the buttock should just touch the upper rear point of the back and fall barely behind the rear line of the cannon and fetlock. Correct position of the leg from this view is most important in a horse.

No. 13 represents the correct conformation. No. 14, leg too far forward and hock crooked. No. 15, entire leg too far under and weak below hock. No. 16, entire leg placed too far backward.

A perpendicular line drawn downward from the point of the buttocks should fall in line with the center of the hock, cannon, pastern and foot.

No. 17 represents the correct conformation. No. 18, bow-legged. No. 19, base narrow. No. 20, base wide. No. 21, cow-hocked and toes out. Very serious fault.

CONFORMATION OF FEET AND LEGS

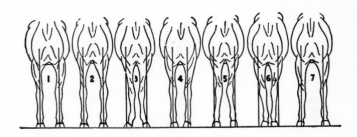

Front view of fore limbs.

A perpendicular line drawn downward from the point of shoulder should fall upon the center of the knee, cannon, pastern, and foot.

No. 1 represents the correct conformation. Nos. 2 to 7, inclusive, represent common defects. No. 2, slightly bow-legged. No. 3, close at knees and toes out. No. 4, toes in. No. 5, knock-kneed. No. 6, base narrow. No. 7, base wide.

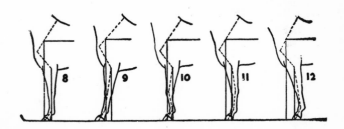

Side view of fore limbs.

A perpendicular line drawn downward from the center of the elbow joint should fall upon the center of the knee and pastern, and back of the foot, and a perpendicular line drawn downward from the middle of the arm should fall upon the center of the foot.

No. 8 represents the right conformation. No. 9, leg too far forward. No. 10, knee sprung. No. 11, calf kneed. No. 12, foot and leg placed too far back.

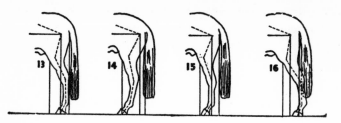

Side view of hind limbs.

A perpendicular line drawn downward form the hip point should fall upon the center of the foot and divide the gaskin in the middle; and a perpendicular line drawn from the point of the buttock should just touch the upper rear point of the back and fall barely behind the rear line of the cannon and fetlock. Correct position of the leg from this view is most important in a horse.

No. 13 represents the correct conformation. No. 14, leg too far forward and hock crooked. No. 15, entire leg too far under and weak below hock. No. 16, entire leg placed too far backward.

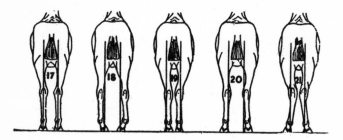

Rear view of hind limbs.

A perpendicular line drawn downward from the point of the buttocks should fall in line with the center of the hock, cannon, pastern and foot.

No. 17 represents the correct conformation. No. 18, bow-legged. No. 19, base narrow. No. 20, base wide. No. 21, cow-hocked and toes out. Very serious fault.

THE HEAD AND NECK

The head should be lean and proportionate to the body in size. Intelligence is indicated by a broad, full forehead with great width between the eyes. A straight face is usually preferable to a concave or to a convex profile (Roman nose). The jaw should be broad and strongly muscled. Thin, firm, even lips indicate quality. Large, open nostrils are desirable. The eye should be large, full, prominent, clear and bright. Small eyes that show a great deal of the white indicate a bad disposition. The ears should be of medium size, pointed, and alertly carried. Horses that lay back their ears when approached are usually vicious.

The neck should be fairly long, slightly arched, lean, muscular and free from meatiness or thickness about the throatlatch. The windpipe or trachea should appear large and perfectly cylindrical. The head should be carried high. Avoid buying horses with short thick necks, long "mule" ears, meaty throatlatches, small "pig" eyes, sagging lips, small nostrils, bad teeth, and sunken, concave foreheads.

The head of the stallion should express boldness and masculinity. The chest should be fairly heavy and well-arched, but an unusually heavy crest may break over to one side as the stallion becomes older.

The brood mare's head should show more refinement and feminity. Thick, heavy, staggy necks are very undesirable in brood mares.

THE FOREQUARTERS

The forequarters include the shoulders, arms, forearms, knees, cannons, fetlocks, pasterns, and feet. The shoulders should be smooth, well-muscled, sloping, and blend smoothly with the withers. The arms should be short, wide and strongly muscled. If the elbows lie too close to the body the horse will toe-out. If they lie out too far, the individual will toe-in. The foreams should be fairly long, broad and strongly-muscled, especially in the uppor portion. The knees should be broad, deep, straight, clean-cut, strongly supported and free from soft fluctuating swellings. If the knees, when viewed from the side are bent forward, the condition is known as "knee-sprung," "buck knees," or "over at the knees." The opposite condition is known as "calf knees" or "back at the knees". The cannons should be short, wide, flat, and clean with large, sharply-defined cord-like tendons, and free from any indication of roughness or coarseness. The fetlocks should be wide, clean, and well-supported. Moderately long, sloping, strong, clean pasterns are desirable. The degree of slope of the pasterns is closely associated with that of the shoulders. Oblique shoulders and pasterns diminish, concussion, lessening the possibility of the development of an unsoundness. The ideal angle of the shoulders and pasterns is about 45 degrees. When viewed from the front, a perpendicular line from the point of the shoulder should fall upon the center of the knees, cannon, pastern, and foot. From the side, a perpendicular line from the center of the elbow joint should fall upon the center of the knee and fetlock and strick the ground just back of the hoof.

Horses which toe-out are very apt to interfere. In growing

colts, the condition may be corrected by keeping the outside of the foot trimmed lower than the inside. Horses very commonly toe-in, giving them a tendency to "wing" or "paddle." This condition may be corrected by frequently trimming the feet as the colt grows, taking off more on the inside than on the outside. Horses close at the knee are likely to travel too close, and to interfere. The same corrective measures should be used as for toeing-out. Since the front feet maintain about 60 percent of the horse's weight and are subject to greater concussion, they should always be observed very carefully. The ideal foot should be large, round, uniform, and shapely, with dense, smooth waxy horn, concave sole, strong bars, wide heels, large, prominent, elastic frog, and clean soft hoofheads. Figure 17 shows how wear of the hoof affects the slope of pastern. If the toe is allowed to grow too long, the pastern is broken back. When the heels grow too long, the pastern becomes broken forward. Both conditions cause undue strain on the bones of the pastern, and may ultimately result in unsoundness.

THE BODY

The withers should be the same height as the hips, muscular, well-defined and extend well into the back. A deep, wide chest and a large, full heart girth indicate a strong constitution and staying qualities. Extreme width, however, may produce a rolling movement at the trot. Long, deep well-sprung ribs give the chest its depth, width and capacity. A horse is said to be "closely-coupled" if the distance between the last rib and the hip is short. The back should be broad, short, heavily-muscled and strongly supported. A distinct arch over the loin is known as "roach back." A sagging condition is "sway back" or "easy in the back." Both of these conditions are very undesirable. The loin or coupling must be short, wide and heavily muscled. A long underline is desirable with low, deep, full flanks. High, shallow flanks make a horse "wasp-waister," "tucked-up," or "cut up in the flank" and always indicate poor feeding qualities.

THE HINDQUARTERS

The hips should be level with each other, broad, smooth and well-muscled. A long, wide, full, heavily-muscled level croup is preferable to a short, narrow, markedly dropping one. The tail should be attached high and carried in a stylish manner. The quarters consist of the upper thighs and lower thighs or gaskins. They should be deep, broad, thick, strong and heavily-muscled with prominent, clean, well-set stifles.

Since the hocks are subject to so many unsoundnesses (bone spavins, bog spavins, curbs, and thoroughpins), good conformation in that region is especially desirable. The hocks should be wide, deep, flat, clean, hard, strong, well-supported, and correctly-set with prominent points. Many horses have large, round, thick, meaty, coarse, soft or puffy hocks which are not only very unsightly, but are subject to many serious unsoundnesses. A common malformation of the hocks is termed "crooked hocks," "sickle hocks," "saber hocks," or "set hocks," a condition in which the angle of the hock is increased so that a line parallel to the back of the cannon would pass to the rear of the point of the buttock if extended upward. The opposite condition, ' straight hocks," or "post-legged," is much less common. A horse that has hind legs that stand base wide, with the points of the hocks too close together is said to be "cow-hocked." The opposite condition is known as "bow-legged hocks." Many horses show an undesirable tendency to become mealy, soft and coarse about the rear cannons as well as the hocks.

The fetlocks and pasterns should be similar to the front ones, although the pastern may be less sloping, presenting an angle of about 50 degrees. The hind feet should be similar to the front ones in quality and texture of hoof but may be somewhat smaller. If the hind legs have the correct conformation and are placed properly, a perpendicular line from the point of the buttock should fall upon the center of the hock, cannon, and foot when viewed from the rear. Viewed from the side, this perpendicular line should touch the point of the hock and run parallel with the back of the cannon.

TEMPERAMENT AND VICES

The disposition of a horse must always be considered in determining his value. The ideal horse should be well-trained, quiet and docile, yet always alert and willing to do his work. Horsemen believe a wide, full forehead, well-carried ear and large prominent eye indicate a good disposition. The buyer should always ask that the horse be tried at the different types of work which he will expect the horse to perform.

Many of the common vices and habits may be detected by a careful examination of the horse and his stall.

Cribbing and Wind Sucking: This condition is indicated by freshly chewed mangers or feed boxes. The incisor teeth of the confirmed cribber are sometimes worn fairly short.

Halter Pulling: Halter pullers usually wear a very heavy halter or are tied with a heavy rope or chain around the neck.

Kicking: A kicker may be detected by examining the stall partitions for hoof or shoe marks. Heavy chains or bags of straw are sometimes suspended from the ceiling in an attempt to discourage this habit. Capped hocks or scarred hind legs indicate that the horse may be a kicker.

ACTION OF THE HORSE

Since action is largely dependent upon body conformation, age, placement of feet, shoeing, training and temperament, one can form a fair estimate of how a horse will move by observing him in the standing position. A horse that toes-in or stands "toe-narrow" or "pigeon-toed" in front may "paddle" or "wing" at the walk or trot. One that stands "toe-wide" or toes out may "interfere," that is, strike the supporting front foot with the moving foot as it passes. Horses that stand with their hocks wide apart may "spraddle" or "go wide at the hocks" when moved. Long, sloping, spring pasterns provide greater ease and freedom of movement, while short upright pasterns and straight shoulders cause the horse to move with a short, stubby stride and stumble frequently. Extreme width through the chest may cause a horse to "roll" when in motion. Very short-bodied horses may "forge," or strike the front supporting foot with the rear moving foot.

After one observes the horse in the standing position, he should be closely watched directly from behind, from in front, and from the side at the walk and trot. Action at the walk is of prime importance. The walk should be free, straight, fast, and easy. Each foot should move straight forward in a long smooth stride with as little deviation from the line of movement as possible. The feet should be lifted fairly high and set squarely each time they return to the ground. The hocks should brush past each other as closely as possible without actually touching. The most common faults of many horse's actions are "paddling" in front and "going wide" behind.

Action at the trot usually accentuates the faults or good points of action at the walk. Slight lameness and diseases of the respiratory organs are also more apparent at this gait.

"Green" colts and untrained horses should never be expected to display as good action as well-trained show horses or racing stock.

Many horses move poorly because they are improperly shod. On the other hand, if a horse is shod in an unusual manner, one should always suspect that an attempt has been made to correct a faulty gait or to relieve lameness. Heavily-shod horses usually show greater flexion of knee and hock than barefooted horses.

GROOMING

Grooming is important in keeping a horse in good, healthy condition. Grooming removes the dust, dirt and other impurities from the skin which might interfere with functioning of oil and sweat glands, keeps skin clean and healthy. It also helps produce a short, glossy coat of hair by removing dirt, increasing secretion of oil glands, and by some polishing of the hair itself. There is an old adage "That a good grooming is as good as a feeding." Your horse's coat will bespeak the grooming that the horse is getting.

Horses shed their hair coats twice a year, Spring and Fall. Grooming hastens removal of the old hair and in addition makes an animal less subject to mange and other external parasite troubles.

Good horsemen will walk their horse at least the first half mile, and whenever possible walk the last 10 or 15 minutes to bring the horse in cool. The horse that comes in from work hot and sweaty must first be dried and cooled out before being returned to the stall. In cooling, scraping off with the scraper is followed by a good rubbing over body and legs with a wool cloth about a yard square until the horse is dry. Or the horse may be covered with a cooler and walked until dry. A wool blanket absorbs moisture better than other materials and should be large enough to come up over the neck, down over the rump well below the belly. Some rubbing may be done at the same time, especially on the legs, or part of the cooler may be turned back to permit rubbing on the body. A heated horse should not stand any longer than necessary before cooling out, nor should he be allowed any water after working until well cooled down. Watering may be done moderately during the course of the ride or drive if the horse is to continue working, but giving hot horses all they want to drink at the close of a workout before cooling down will frequently lead to founder.

After horse is dry he is gone over with a rubber comb, using circular strokes beginning at the head and working back. A stiff dandy brush is used for removing mud, but a body brush and rubber comb are used for the main work. The most necessary requisite for good grooming is "elbow grease." A curry comb should be used only to clean the brush. Never use a metal comb on a horse's legs. Start on the near side of your horse beginning at the head, then proceed down the neck on down to the chest and shoulders, near foreleg, back, flank, belly, loins and croup, then the near hind leg. Loosen all the dirt with the dandy brush and rubber comb, then follow up with a body brush and rub rag. After completing the near side proceed in similar fashion on the off side. In grooming throw the weight of your body against the horse. After rubbing with the rag polish with some hand rubbing. Nothing will exceed this in adding bloom to the coat after it is once cleaned. After the horse is cleaned and polished wash the eyes, nostrils and dock with a moist sponge in the order named. A horse's feet should be picked up and cleaned with a hoofpick after he is groomed. The grooming outlined provides a thorough grooming and cleaning which is more elaborate than ordinarily required daily unless the horse is worked or raced hard and regularly, but it is a good idea once a week for any horse or as extra time permits. In any event, a few minutes may well be spent each day in brushing and cleaning the coat. The results will be gratifying and the horse will appreciate it. It will take an hour to do a proper grooming job. If any treatment is required or the legs are bandaged this will take extra time. Regular grooming also provides the opportunity to check any swellings, abrasions, or other troubles that may develop. A veterinarian should be called for any condition not fully understood by the groom or rider, or trainer.

The mane and tail should be cleaned regularly. Begin at the end of the hair and gradually work up to the roots, separating hair with the fingers. Tails require frequent washing with soft water and castile soap. A good application of olive oil after a thorough washing is very beneficial. The pasterns and ears should be kept trimmed.

In the case of three-gaited horses the mane should be kept close and the tail plucked and clipped. Five-gaited horses and Arabians should have that part of the mane under the head stall kept trimmed. It will add pride of owning a good horse to keep him well groomed and well cared for. When grooming horses it must be remembered that some have very thin skins and are very tender. This is especially true of high-bred horses. Many runners and trotters have been made into vicious biters and strikers by ignorant grooming. A horse enjoys a good grooming if not tortured in the process.

Since the horse is going to be put in the stall after grooming this might be a good place to comment on stalls. They do not have to be elaborate, but there are a few essentials to proper stalling to insure proper health of your horse.

The stable should be clean, dry, light, airy, and free from direct drafts. Box stalls are preferable to slip stalls where the horse has to be tied. These stalls should be no less than 10 feet by 11 feet and 12 feet by 12 feet is more desirable for free movement and prevent the horse from becoming cast in the stall. A dirt or clay floor is best and can be refilled as required. A wooden floor can be used, but never stand a horse on a concrete floor for very long. A hard floor predisposes all kinds of leg problems and even back lameness. Straw is most commonly used as bedding, although shavings, cane pith, ground corn cobs, and peanut hulls are sometimes used. Oat straw is the most absorbent, while wheat and rye straw is more durable. Sawdust and wood shavings sometimes have a fungus that will affect the skin of the horse. If they show any sign of breaking out or redness, this bedding must be discontinued.

Box stalls need daily cleaning with new bedding provided as needed to keep the stall dry and clean. It is a good idea to completely clean out and disinfect any new stall a horse is moving into and his own stall at least twice a year. This will help control parasites, germs, and undesirable odors. A couple of handfuls of ground limestone sprinkled on the floor daily will keep the stable fresh.

Stable equipment most commonly used includes a broom, fork, bushel basket, water and wash pails, combs, brushes, sponge, hoofpick, sweat scraper, disinfectant, feed measuring containers, rubbing cloths, hoof knife, rasp, nippers, feed tub, several large screw eyes, halter, lead shank, cooler, stable sheet, a trunk to keep the equipment available and in order.

In addition to grooming the horse, the leather tack needs frequent cleaning with a good saddle soap and an occasional oiling to prolong its life. It is economy to purchase leather goods of high quality, and then to take care of them. Harness, hopples, cinch straps, reins, or stirrup straps that begin to show wear should be replaced or repaired promptly as a safety measure.

Going over the tack with a damp sponge after using helps remove dirt and grime and improves its appearance. Bits and stirrup irons should be wiped clean after use. Washing thoroughly with a good saddle soap occasionally is desirable. When this is done, the buckles and studs should be unfastened so that you reach the part of the leather that receives the most wear. It is customary to let the leather dry for about 15 minutes after soaping, then rub with a dry cloth. This procedure will keep the leather in excellent condition. A little harness dressing will add a bright, attractive finish. Neatsfoot oil is a good leather oil, and should be used with a small sponge as needed in keeping leather soft, pliable, and free of cracks. A water soluble oil put in the wash water also does a very satisfactory job in that it leaves a residue of oil on the leather.

USEFUL INFORMATION
CONCERNING HORSES

The age of a horse is figured from January 1st. Thus a colt foaled December 1st would be called 1-year-old January 1st in a great majority of our shows when in reality the colt is only 1 month old. Remember this and you may be saved an argument about the age of an autumn colt. All racing stock follow this rule.

Horses are usually measured in hands. A hand is four inches. Thus a horse 60 inches tall is 15 hands and one 62 inches is 15:2 or 15½ hands. In measuring a horse we take the vertical measurement from the ground to highest point of the withers. Many horsemen know the height of their chin, nose or eye from the ground and they measure the horse by what is commonly called "chinning."

Cutting the foretop or roaching the mane detract from the appearance of the colt or horse. Usually roaching a colt will cause it to appear low in the back.

A sluggish leader or showman detracts from the appearance of the colt or horse.

The place to train a colt or horse is at home and not in the show ring.

Tell the judge the truth in all questions he asks you. He may know the answer himself and is only testing your truthfulness.

Careless foot trimming or the entire lack of it loses many a good colt a higher place in the show.

To guard against a colt, horse or even cattle refusing to drink at a show, use a little molasses in drinking water several days to a week prior to going to the fair. Just dip finger in molasses and wash off in colt's pail. Continue this treatment at the fair and then all water has the same taste.

When buying a horse or colt remember feet, legs and action are at least 90 percent of the horse. Remember the old Scot's saying, "Tops will come but bottoms never."

Bore a hole in each end of a two foot 1x2 inch board. Use this on the mare's halter rope to prevent hanging of colt in mother's halter rope.

Halter Puller. Best to use a heavy strap with ring on each front pastern. Securely connect these strap rings with about one and one-half feet of strong rope. Then run the halter rope through the manger and tie to the middle of the hobble rope. Thus, when the horse pulls back, he pulls both front feet from under him. Leave him tied this way for a week, or until after he shows any inclination to pull. Every time you go in the barn go in his stall and try to induce him to "pull"—crawl in the manger, wave your hat, rub his ears, etc. This will cure him. The head and foot tie may also be used successfully. As well as the come along.

Ear Shy and Hard to Bridle. Many horses and mules are ear shy. This is only fear. Tie the animal so it cannot break loose, then slip a blanket over its head (it may be necessary to tie up the hind leg), slowly work your hand up the animal's neck until you can stroke ears. This may take some time, but go slowly, talking to animal and trying to win its confidence. As you reach the ears stroke with the grain of the hair. Soon he will let you stroke his ears and head under the blanket. Remove the blanket and try without covering. As soon as you can handle his ears from side, stand in front of him and try. At each success pet him and encourage him. Kindness and patience will win out.

Kickers. The Scotch hobble, will give good results with animals that are touchy about their legs. The horse that kicks in the harness is another matter. If the horse has this habit or you are suspicious of the colt, tie a strong rope to the inside bridle bit, run from the breeching by a hame strap loop or small piece of rope, this prevents if from falling down over the hocks, run it along the other side of the animal and through the bit ring. Keep this free and handy and as soon as the horse starts to kick, pull up on the rope. He will kick himself in the mouth and will not kick long. Some horses pick up the habit of kicking the stall. Many trainers control this habit by fastening a 6 inch chain to a strap. Then fastening the strap around the ankle or just above the hock. This type of treatment will ordinarily stop stall kicking.

Strikers. Tie them with the Scotch hobble and work around their front legs until they grow quiet. A bad striker is far more dangerous than a kicker.

Biting. This vice is principally practised in self-defense. Get the animal's confidence by petting and firm treatment. If a small block of wood is placed in the mouth so that the horse can not get his teeth together, he will soon stop the biting habit because he thinks that he cannot.

Balking. If a horse should get down and refuse to get up, one of the following methods is very helpful:

1. Stand out in front of the horse so that he can see you and then run toward his head making plenty of noise. The horse will usually get up because he thinks that you are going to run over his head.

2. Hold his nostrils so as to shut off his breath.

3. A hot shot battery applied under the tail is very effective.

4. As a last resort put a drop of ammonia in each nostril.

5. Should the animal insist upon lying down, tie him there for several hours and let him think it over. In tying the horse down, do it so that he can nearly get up and still not make it. (This is easily accomplished by tying halter rope to one hind foot, allowing about two feet of slack.) When you do allow this animal to get on his feet, he is usually very glad to stay there. Never allow a horse to get the best of you by lying down. If you unhitch him, and put him in the barn, he will be sure to try the same tactics the second time.

A pinch of red pepper on a balker's tongue usually causes him to forget his troubles.

A couple of drops of carbon disulphide placed just above the hoof on the heel of each front foot will cause the balker to keep raising his feet and thus not be able to plant his feet and balk.

Looking at Teeth. Place left hand on halter and right hand just behind colt's left ear. Stroke the colt over the poll and slowly down the face, running the hand on down over the nose. You can usually slip up the upper lip. To bring a hand up under the chin or abruptly against the chin usually causes a colt to dodge, especially if he has grown up in a "nose fly" country.

Putting Crupper Under the Tail. This is always a ticklish operation with the amateur but not as dangerous as it seems. First raise the tail, adjust the crupper, then pull the tail to one side and allow it to slowly slide down over the buttock and thigh. The colt will seldom notice the strap under his tail. Should the tail be dropped suddenly on the crupper he may kick.

Horses That Will Not Get Over in the Stall

This is a very perplexing habit and the animal should be broken of it as soon as possible. Use a long rope for a halter rope. Run this rope through the manger and bring it back along side of the colt and tie it to a post or solid timber behind him. When you wish to go in along side of the colt, simply tie this rope tightly in a manner that it holds him over against the stall. This will allow you to pass in and out without danger of being crowded and will also allow you to untie the horse without going into the stall. Many men use this method in harnessing colts.

Care of Colt's Feet

A mature horse is no better than his foundation, therefore it behooves the horsemen to take a great deal of pains with the feet of the growing colt. Probably one of the first lessons that the colt should have is that of foot handling. The first few lessons that the colt receives should convince him that he is powerless to resist the master in the matter of raising and holding up the foot. Too many horses are spoiled by the owner half-heartedly trying to raise the foot, and because of a little struggle with the colt, allowing him to have his own way.

When you start a thing with a horse, finish it. A horse should never get an estimate of his strength in comparsion with that of a man.

Lifting the Front Feet. Throw the rope over the animal's back, catch it again under the belly, wrap the end several times around the colt's left pastern and tie securely. (Use a bowline knot.) Now, slip the loose end of the rope through on of these wraps and you are ready to raise the leg. The average horse will fight the lifting of the fore foot much more than it will the rear. Should the horse insist upon lying down, put a "Rarey" strap and let him lie on the ground until he gets up of his own accord.

The Rarey strap is simply a strap around the pastern and around the forearm in a manner that prevents the animal from unbending his knee.

Lifting the Rear Feet. The Scotch hobble is one of the safest ways of doing this.

Another method which is also very satisfactory in trimming the feet of animals that are fairly gentle but still refuse to allow the foot to be raised.

Buckle a strong strap with ring attached to the rear pastern of the foot that is to be trimmed. Tie a rope to the tail with a couple of half hitches, run the rope down through the ring on the pastern and back to a post or some stationary object. By pulling up on the rope you can raise the foot and put it back in the position that it should be to make the trimming operation convenient. In case the horse has a short tail, the rope may be tied in a large non-slipping loop to the neck of the horse, run it back and put a half hitch over the tail and then down through the ring on the pastern and back to the stationary object.

Foot Trimming on Colts

The trimming of the feet of a young colt may mean a long,

useful life for him while neglected feet sometimes cause permanent injuries. The bones of the colt are more or less soft and the incorrect wearing of a hoof many times causes the leg or pastern to grow in a twisted position. The trimming and correct shoeing of the foot will many times prevent this trouble.

The colt should stand squarely on all his feet. Should he stand too far ahead, you will probably find the toe too long, while if he stands too straight behind, you will probably find the heel too high. Standing in front of the animal, the legs should be straight to the ground. If the colt toes in, in front, you will find that the hoof is wearing too fast on the outside; if he toes out, he will be wearing too fast on the inside. By trimming off the long portion and not touching the wearing portion, the foot may be able to correct itself. Sometimes it is well to tack a light shoe or half plate to the side of the foot that is wearing too fast.

When trimming the foot first get the outline as the horse stands at rest and notice the points that should be corrected, then take up the foot and take off the wall, level with the sole of the foot, unless there is some angle that you wish to correct. Then level up the bars of the foot but do not cut too close, because the bars support the heel and if they are cut away the heel may contract.

Only the dead flakes of the sole or frog should be taken away when the foot is trimmed. The healthy frog acts as a cushion to the foot of the animal. The frog strikes the ground at each stride of the horse and takes up the shock of the impact. This pressure of the frog causes the heel to be wide, open, and healthy. Should the frog be trimmed away or allowed to be reduced by disease, the heel will contract, causing the animal all kinds of foot trouble.

After trimming the foot, notice if the crevices between the frog and the bar are wet and foul smelling. If they are, clean them and swab out the infected places with creosote dip. This foulness of the foot is called thrush and is caused by keeping horses in poorly cleaned barns or wet, mucky yards.

The correctly trimmed forefoot should present a nearly round appearance. The rear hoof should have an inside wall that is nearly straight up and down while the outside hoof wall flanges out. Many horses have the inside wall of the foot too long, causing them to knuckle and travel in a manner that causes interfering or striking the opposite leg.

Hauling the Horse

There are several conditions which should be tended to in handling horses in transit.

1. The horse should be securely fastened so that he cannot move around or jump out of the vehicle. He should not ride with his head toward the front of the vehicle unless it is enclosed so that there is no draft. Many horses catch bad colds from being hauled facing the wind.

2. Blemishes and leg swellings can be prevented by wrapping the legs with ankle wraps. The wraps or bandages will need to be about six to eight feet in length and 2 to 3 inches wide. They should start at the ankle and extend up the leg just below the hock and knee. A protective layer of cotton is often placed under the wrapping. This will keep the horse from being injuried by other horses which may be hauled with it besides keeping the swelling down. As soon as the horse has been unloaded and walked around it is best to take off the wraps unless they are being used for some other purpose.

3. In the winter time the horse should always have a heavy blanket when it is hauled and if a hood is available, it should also be used.

4. The horse should be so tied that it cannot rub its mane or tail.

5. Two types of leads can be used in handling horses that are hard to load. The use of the come-along, of the foot lead, are very helpful.

Hints to Buyers

The following unnatural ways in which a horse is handled may be indications of some vice with which the amateur would not be familiar but which would lower the value of the horse considerably:

When planning to buy a horse, the conditions under which he is kept should be carefully noted. For example, if you walk into the barn and notice that the horse is wearing a wide strap around its neck which is pulled up rather tightly, it is a good indication that the horse is a "cribber" or "wind sucker," a very annoying habit and one which will eventually impair the usefulness of the horse.

If an inspection of the horse's mouth indicates that the teeth are worn crooked, this is also an indication that he is a "cribber. "If the stall is wired with small electrical wires or the wood has been especially treated, it would be an indication of a "cribber."

If the sides of the stall are torn up or the horse is wearing chains which dangle from either the hocks or the pasterns on the rear legs, it is an indication that the horse may be a "kicker," especially in the stall.

If the eye has a blue or cloudy tinge to it, the horse's eyes will bear veterinary inspection.

A horse with a "glass" eye can see alright. In fact glass-eyed horses very seldom go blind.

If the horse is wearing a muzzle or a heavy leather bib which hangs under the lower jaw, he is probably mean about pulling his blanket off.

If the horse is bandaged in the legs, there is probably soreness of some kind unless he is being transported.

If the horse kept tied in a box stall, he may be of an exceptionally nervous type and have a tendency to do a great deal of walking in the stall or perhaps claw the sides of the stall.

If the examination of the feet indicates that a rubber pad is used underneath the shoe, this may be an indication of some soreness in the foot.

If the horse is tied by having a rope around the neck and ran through the halter, he may be a "halter puller."

If the set tail is tied in position with a string when showing on a gaited horse, there is a strong possibility that the tail is crooked.

If a horse is being fed timothy hay and a wet mash, there is a chance that he has heaves.

Points to Consider in Selecting a Horse

Temperament, conformation, action, soundness, age and education are the general characteristics to bear in mind when choosing a serviceable horse.

A systematic examination will minimize the chances of overlooking serious faults. Ample time should be taken to make the examination.

Common faults of conformation, from a utility standpoint, are narrow chest, straight, short shoulders, shallow barrels, long, weak, backs and loins, poorly developed muscles in the hind quarters, and weak, improperly formed feet and legs.

Common unsoundness that impairs a horse's usefulness for most tasks are bone spavin, extreme fistula, roaring, heaves, ringbone, crub sidebones and splints when close to the knees.

Serious faults of temperament or manners are balking, kicking, rearing, backing, halter pulling, and shying.

In the final judgment of a horse's stability, weigh the good qualities against the defects.

Sale Terms and Their Meanings

"Sound"—Horse is free from all unsoundness or blemishes.

"Legs go"—Horse is sold with legs as they are. Such an animal usually has a number of unsoundnesses and blemishes on the legs.

"Blue eye"—*"Smoky eye"*—*"Speck in eye"*—*"One good eye,"* etc. Eye or eyes are faulty.

"Crampy"—*"Stringy"*—*"Raises one leg"*—*"Jerks a leg,"* all refer to a crampy or string-halted horse.

"Gristle on heel" -*"Hard on heel,"* etc., means animal has one or more sidebones.

"Smooth mouth"—Cups are worn away from teeth and animal is usually 10 years old or over.

"Good mouth"—Smooth mouthed but not much over 10 years.

"Round Hock"—Animal has a curb.

"Sell at halter"—Nothing guaranteed except title. Animal is usually faulty in disposition or soundness or both.

"Green broke"—Has been hitched one or two times. Not trustworthy yet.

"Wire"—Has a wire scar.

"Plain ankles"—Puffed or common around ankles.

"Wind and work"—Animal is said to have good wind, and will work.

"Serviceably sound"—Animal is sold to be sound enough to work.

THE FORGER AND CRAB

Forger

This is generally a low-headed, flat-rumped horse, with a low, level gait: is not inclined to break. When going at a moderate speed, his hind feet drop into the tracks of the front foot: some half an inch beyond: some half an inch back. When urged to greater speed the horse straddles more behind, and the tracks of the hind feet go outside and beyond the tracks of the front feet. They usually exhibit some speed.

Crab

Trotting horses do not crab, but all others may. The hind feet follow the near forefoot: the right forefoot wings off to the right, the right hind foot often fits in the track of the near fore foot: the left hind foot a little to the left. The right hind foot is often worn down to the quick just above the toe clip. The crab will also make three foot prints side by side, and does not forge. When the crab has a little speed he will carry the near hind foot beyond the foot prints of the near fore foot and the off hind foot. There may be slight variations of this. Driving horses always hug the near side and pull on one line perhaps leading to a diagnosis of bad teeth. However, correcting the teeth does not correct the gait. You can notice the back strap of the harness does not follow the spinal column. There are many crabs in thoroughbred race horses. The "grabbing" of the near foot with the off hind foot causes many falls in races.

Cause

Ossification of the lumbar vertebrae, and for some unexplained reason this is always on the near side. No one recalls a horse that wore his foot to the quick on the near hind foot, always on the off side.

Index

251